WIT
Speedw

The Library of World Biography

Books by Melveena McKendrick

Ferdinand and Isabella

A Concise History of Spain

Woman and Society in the Spanish Drama
of the Golden Age

Cervantes

Cervantes

by Melveena McKendrick

THE LIBRARY OF WORLD BIOGRAPHY

J. H. PLUMB, GENERAL EDITOR

Little, Brown and Company — Boston — Toronto

FIRST EDITION

Library of Congress Cataloging in Publication Data
McKendrick, Melveena.
    Cervantes.
    (The Library of world biography)
    Bibliography: p. 301
    Includes index.
    1. Cervantes Saavedra, Miguel de, 1547–1616 — Bio-
graphy. 2. Authors, Spanish — 17th century — Biography.
PQ6337.M134   863'.3 [B]   80–17572
ISBN 0–316–56054–5

BP
Published simultaneously in Canada
by Little, Brown & Company (Canada) Limited

PRINTED IN THE UNITED STATES OF AMERICA

To Neil

Acknowledgments

IN THE PREPARATION of this book I have incurred many debts of gratitude: to Girton College, Cambridge, for granting me sabbatical leave to complete it, to the British Academy for the award that permitted me to visit Spain to pursue my research, and to all those scholars whose help and advice I was fortunate enough to profit from at different times and in different ways — Brendan Bradshaw, J. P. Somerville, Anthony Close, Colin Smith, Owen Chadwick, Geoffrey Elton, Toby Bainton, Ruth Morgan, Henry Kamen, Keith Whinnom, Michael Mallett, and Nicholas Davidson. My greatest debt, as usual, is to my husband both for his unfailing interest, encouragement, and support and for his rigorous scrutiny of the text at every stage of its development. No one could have a more helpful critic. I must not end these acknowledgments without mentioning my two small daughters who have been endlessly patient with mother as I wrote my "story" when they would have far preferred me to be doing other things. Needless to say, neither they nor the others I wish to thank are responsible for its shortcomings — these are entirely my own.

Cambridge
May 1979

Contents

	A Note on Currency	viii
	Foreword by J. H. Plumb	ix
	Introduction	3
ONE.	The Early Years	13
TWO.	The Hazards of War	33
THREE.	The Captive's Tale	60
FOUR.	New Beginnings: Of Love and Literature	90
FIVE.	Of Corn and Oil: The King's Commissary	118
SIX.	A Man and His Time: A Period of Crisis	160
SEVEN.	The Flowering of Genius	188
EIGHT.	"The Noblest Novel in the World"	210
NINE.	Hostages to Fortune	231
TEN.	The Last Years	260
	Works by Cervantes	299
	Select Bibliography	301
	Index	305

A Note on Currency

The basic money denomination in Spain in Cervantes's day was the *maravedi*, of which there were 34 to the silver *real*, 400 to the gold *escudo*, and 375 to the ducat. The terms ducat and *escudo* were often used interchangeably, although their monetary value was not exactly the same, because the ducat, unlike the *escudo*, was not a coin but a unit of account. To avoid confusion I have, whenever possible, used the more familiar "ducat" throughout this book.

The difficulties involved in trying to give present-day equivalents for old coins and currencies are enormous, and the rate of inflation in Spain at the time, and our own too, of course, makes it almost impossible to give accurate and meaningful values to prices and wages over a period of time. As far as I can discover, the psychological value of the ducat/*escudo* during these years would for us now be of the order of ten dollars or five pounds.

Foreword

Fortuna — CHANCE, LUCK, the way life lifts or slips like a children's game of snakes and ladders — haunted the creative artists of Renaissance Europe and the centuries that followed. The whirligig of Fate threads Shakespeare's plays, lies at the heart of Goldsmith's immensely popular *Vicar of Wakefield,* and is still a factor of importance in the realistic novels of Balzac and Dickens. In the twentieth century, moments of luck in life, sudden reverses of fortune, are rarely explored by novelist or poet. This reflects a great change in the structure of European societies, and indicates the gradual growth of economic and social stability in individual lives. We are all much more settled and secure than our ancestors. In Cervantes's day, bankruptcy was commonplace, sudden promotion could be overturned by sudden dismissal, affluence followed by destitution. These were not rare experiences but haunted the lives of courtiers, lawyers, priests, clerks, soldiers, and sailors, as good harvests and famines played ducks and drakes with the lives of the peasantry. It was a world, too, in which power was easily abused, far more easily abused than we can often grasp. And it was a world in which crime and violence, great and petty, flourished to a horrifying degree and, more often than not, without any redress. Such conditions created not only fear and anxiety but also a yearning for the good and the noble, a longing for the just to triumph, for relief from the horrors and terrors of the world of experience.

Without an understanding of the social terrors, horrors, and longings of the early modern European world, it is hard to grasp the impact not only of Cervantes's work but also of so much European literature of his time. Without it we cannot fully understand the appeal of *Don Quixote* — one of the great books of the European literary tradition.

Cervantes's own life reflected the vast insecurities in Spanish society of that day. His days as a soldier, his capture and long imprisonment in Algiers, the minor government jobs that came and went, the terrible debts, the moments of affluence were all part of a life in which survival meant everything. Although at times evidence vanishes for years, we know a surprising amount about Cervantes's life — much more than we know of Shakespeare's — and Melveena McKendrick has used every scrap of evidence to create a remarkable portrait of the man Cervantes, who emerges as both complex and deeply human. She uses his works to give added depth and understanding to his character — for he was born a compulsive writer and wrote far, far more than *Don Quixote.* Nor does she miss any of the moments of irony that tend to thread all writers' lives, and realizes, too, how accidental works of genius can be. The abilities of a writer find, almost by chance, the vehicle for their genius. This is particularly true of *Don Quixote,* for what began as a short parody of the romances of chivalry became the first great modern novel, largely because a hack writer wrote a spurious Part Two, which goaded Cervantes into finishing his epic novel. That whirligig of Fate which tossed Cervantes around through so much of his life at the same time gave him penetrative insight into the hopes, the despairs, the wonderful endurance of men and women.

What is so splendid about this biography is that it fulfills admirably two important functions — it re-creates a human life in all its complexity and richness and, as well, explains with great sensitivity the literary achievement of one of Europe's greatest writers.

J. H. Plumb

6 February 1980

Cervantes

Introduction

It has been said — with justification — that Spanish literature travels badly. The reasons for this are not easy to determine, though various hypotheses could be constructed on the basis of Spain's insular view of itself through history and its limited cultural relations with the outside world. What is certain is that the loss is the world's, for Spanish literature can stand comparison with that of any country. It boasts an early epic masterpiece superior in the eyes of many to the *Chanson de Roland,* a medieval balladry arguably the finest in Europe, a seventeenth-century drama of unique richness and often outstanding quality, a nineteenth-century novelist who has rightly been ranked with Dickens, Balzac, and Tolstoy, and a twentieth-century poetry of glittering talent. Yet how many have heard of the *Poema de mio Cid,* of Lope de Vega and Calderón, of Pérez Galdós, or any of the modern Spanish poets other than Lorca, much less read them? Only one Spanish writer has achieved world-wide fame, and this on the strength of only one work. And even Cervantes's genius has been emasculated for the layman by the shortened and watered-down versions with which the Victorians relegated *Don Quixote* to the world of the nursery, and latterly by the truly dreadful distortions of the filmmakers. Fortunately, genius withstands such assaults, for it is a robust and vital thing; and, unlike the archaeologist who has so painstakingly, so delicately, to dig and brush away the accretions of the ages that weigh down the hidden city, the reader can go quickly and directly to a text and discover its glories for himself.

Cervantes, it has to be said, for all his belief in himself, would have been amazed to learn that he would in time come to be considered not only one of the giants of Spanish literature, but also a literary genius on a world scale. His contemporaries would have been astounded. As far as they were concerned, Miguel de Cervantes was a worthy man with a good war record, an unsuccessful playwright, a competent poet, and the author of some excellent short stories and an immensely funny and extremely successful parody of knight errantry. He was not a member of the fashionable literary circles, he was always short of money and in search of employment, and he enjoyed neither the popularity and fame of a Lope de Vega nor the official recognition and approval at court of a Calderón. And there is no doubt at all that his subsequent reputation rests on the one work he wrote that was a large-scale commercial success. But for *Don Quixote,* and perhaps several of his short stories and one-act plays, even the student of literature would scarcely read Cervantes today, and then only out of historical interest.

The fascinating thing is that Cervantes's view of his work was very different from that of posterity, and that his surprise at his subsequent lasting fame would have been compounded by his bewilderment at the identity of the book responsible for it. The one pastoral idyll he wrote, *The Galatea,* seems to have occupied a place nearer his heart than the burlesque *Don Quixote,* and the work on which he believed and hoped his reputation would rest was a farfetched romance of love and adventure called *The Trials of Persiles and Sigismunda*. Few Spaniards have heard of either. Yet while the progress of these two works, along with most of his others, has been one of decline, from moderate popularity and appreciation to incomprehension and neglect, that of *Don Quixote* has been one of almost unbroken ascent. In its own day it attracted a great deal of attention and was widely read; but with time it has achieved a life and a vitality entirely its own, becoming one of those works that are rediscovered afresh by each age and found by successive generations to respond fully to their own perceptions and sensibilities, their own apprehension of reality. Like Don Juan and Faust, Don Quixote has become a myth figure, a shifting symbol of something easy to recognize but difficult to define, that its creator would hardly have recognized in some of its guises.

While Cervantes's surprise at the extent of his own and *Don Quixote*'s success would have been genuine, however, we must not make the mistake of misconstruing his literary judgments or of underestimating his awareness of the complexity and subtlety of his writing. He was a self-conscious, experimental writer, fascinated by the theory and practice of literature and fully conversant with the heated literary controversies of his time. The humanists of the sixteenth century had been galvanized by the rediscovery of Aristotle's *Poetics* (published in Latin translation in Italy in 1498) into excited discussion of the nature of literature and its relation to questions of truthfulness and morality: the development of printing and the growth of a reading public made these problems as relevant then as television does today. The dualism in Cervantes's works — between what has flourished and what has been forgotten — is directly related to this preoccupation. Truthfulness in literature was considered to depend not on realism but on probability, and the highest forms of literature depicted not life's realities, but universal truths. The sort of distinction we make between the idealized and the realistic in literature is, therefore, in the context of Cervantes's time, a meaningless one, since both are merely different manifestations of the truth. In the light of this, the dualism that strikes us so forcibly in Cervantes's works becomes more comprehensible, even if our different attitude to literature means that it can never be entirely acceptable; no Cervantes specialist will ever persuade us that *The Galatea* is superior to *Don Quixote*.

The irony is that it was Cervantes who wrote the work that set European literature on its course toward the "modern" realism of the nineteenth century — hence, the overworked description, "Father of the Modern Novel." There had, of course, already been indications of the way things were to go, but Cervantes was the writer who, in an extended, sustained narrative about a mad knight, firmly established realism and characterization as the twin foundation stones of the novel. In doing this he illustrated a control of both so masterly that not only has it never been surpassed, but it enabled him to play with the idea of literary reality and the concept of character in a way that delights the most demanding of modern readers. And it is quite apparent from *Don Quixote* that the game was both exploratory and deliberate.

But there is no contradiction between Cervantes's literary ideas and the vision of life projected by his masterpiece. The popular view of Don Quixote as a dreamer who ignores base realities in pursuit of an impossible but noble ideal is a gross simplification. Cervantes started his work as a parody of the chivalric romances that gripped the imagination of the Spanish reading public in the sixteenth century, mocking them for their absurdities and their harmful distortions of the laws of probability. Even when Cervantes is carried away by his creative powers into a work far more complex and ambitious than mere parody, the very real transfiguring power of Don Quixote's imagination never diverts Cervantes from the truth — the truth that Don Quixote is a madman whose idealism is folly because it so far exceeds the limits of the possible. For all its sublime differences, therefore, *Don Quixote* fits snugly into the pattern of Cervantes's literary beliefs.

Yet it is the differences, of course, which make Cervantes the literary giant he is. *Don Quixote* is an extraordinarily vital and expansive work. Written at the turn of the seventeenth century, it seems at once the distillation of personal experience, of the life of a nation, and of the human condition in general. It ranges in masterly fashion across society, and penetrates the recesses of human personality. Its perceptions are dazzling, its compassion and humanity unforgettable. It toys with the changing face of truth and reality without losing its grasp on either. Its experience seems complete, its tolerance infinite, yet its values are never in doubt. Its moods are legion and its capacity to nourish and entertain inexhaustible. If we ask how a man like Cervantes came to write such a work, we are grappling with the unknown and unknowable. Chance must have played its part. Had Cervantes not decided to write a short parody of the romances of chivalry, he would probably never have embarked upon the sort of book *Don Quixote* eventually became; had another author not written a spurious continuation of Part I, Cervantes might never have been spurred into completing Part II. The greatest works, of course, are like children: once given birth to they inevitably achieve autonomy, changing and developing as they respond to the times through which they pass. But whereas modern science has given us the key to the secret of human life, it has not yet succeeded in exposing the wellsprings of human genius. The only available point of departure in such a quest is the fact that art is in some way or other a transmutation of experience. And this is where biography comes into its own.

The problem is that Cervantes's life, like that of most men of his age who were not courtiers or statesmen, is only very partially documented, and the man behind the writing is, therefore, an elusive, often shadowy, figure. His military exploits and his intensive legal and business activities have ensured that we never lose sight of him for long as a grown man, and often they place him firmly center stage. But his youth and his intellectual formation are for the most part a frustrating blank; we can trace with reasonable success the fortunes of his family as a whole during this period, but Miguel himself scarcely emerges from the wings. Even as an adult he eludes the microscopic psychological scrutiny open to the biographers of later writers, for he left no personal correspondence — none, at least, has been discovered, and it seems unlikely that anyone would have thought the letters of so seemingly unimportant a figure worth keeping — and the references his contemporaries make to him are scanty and on the whole formal. It was not yet the custom to use literature, particularly prose, deliberately and openly to explore one's own sensibilities and experiences, and any attempt to make very detailed assumptions about Cervantes's life on the basis of his work is consequently as unreliable as it is fascinating, as the many novelistic biographies of him show. That he wrote about university students does not necessarily mean he was ever one himself, any more than Don Quixote's devotion to the imaginary Dulcinea means that his creator too languished in hopeless pursuit of some ideal love. The direct insights into

Cervantes the man and writer that come from his own pen are very few: a verse letter written in captivity in Algiers, an affidavit concerning his activities as a prisoner during this difficult time, a partly autobiographical poem, and the prologues to his works, which, happily, are often frank and revealing. It is not that he was a very secret man; on the contrary his was an open, outgoing nature. It is merely that, owing to his circumstances and to the sensibilities of his age, the evidence has just not survived.

Biography, of course, is by definition a search, an attempt to capture the essence of another human being's experience. But in Cervantes's case, the search becomes full-scale detective work, in which scraps of evidence have to be carefully sifted and painstakingly fitted together to make a convincing whole. It is a demanding process; some pieces of the puzzle fit snugly nowhere, others are interchangeable. A pay slip, a christening certificate, a deed of attorney, a theatrical contract — these are the tiny details on which we often have to build our knowledge of the activities of one of the world's great geniuses. From them, however, a strange story gradually unfolds, a story of courage, mismanagement and poverty, of dramatic episodes in a humdrum, even slightly sordid, existence. Like his contemporary Shakespeare, and indeed like all writers at the time without wealth and status, or access through a patron to them, Cervantes had his living to earn. And this is exactly what he spent the major part of his life doing, first in the army, later in low-level administration. There was nothing unusual in a man of letters being involved in such things; the intellectuals and writers of the sixteenth and seventeenth centuries were men of the world and often "trailed a pike," went on missions abroad, or played a part in public affairs. What is different about Cervantes is that his efforts brought him such scant reward — never did he rise to the solid prosperity enjoyed by Shakespeare — and obscured for so long his literary talent. He certainly found time in intervals in his official existence, and in his leisure hours, to write. But it was necessarily a desultory activity at best, for his energies were most of the time directed elsewhere, and the bulk of his output and all his major publications, bar one, were concentrated in the last sixteen or so years of his life, after he had withdrawn from government service and started making a sustained and heroic effort to earn his living with his pen.

His life, as a result, is characterized by an unusual imbalance between living and writing (made worse by the absence of a reliable chronology for many of his works), with the publication of Part I of *Don Quixote* effectively marking the transition between the two. Before then, his life, dogged as it was by failure, disappointment, and disillusion, was in a sense a preparation for greatness, not a deliberate apprenticeship but an unselfconscious laying down of experience through the business of living without which *Don Quixote* would not have been born. Afterward, his art became the overriding preoccupation of his life. Distinct as these two phases seem, therefore, they are totally interdependent. Some biographers have tried to arrive more quickly at Cervantes the Great Writer by compressing these long years of preparation, of journeying toward genius, and concentrating instead on the more productive years. But, if we pass too quickly over the years of danger, hardship, and frustration — over the mutilated hand, the excommunications, the long depressing months in prison — then we shall never understand the making of the man who has achieved immortality with one inspired work. For that work, written when he was already in his fifties, is the distillation of the experience of these very years, the disappointments as well as the hopes, the optimism as well as the despair. *Don Quixote* could have been written only by a man who knew both, and through his experience arrived at an equilibrium between the two.

There are, in any case, great bonuses to be derived from subjecting Cervantes's life before the publication of *Don Quixote* to as close a scrutiny as the evidence allows, for he lived through some of the most dramatic years in a very dramatic period of Spain's history. As a soldier, he fought at the great naval battle of Lepanto, the battle that turned the tide against the Turks in the Mediterranean; as a prisoner of war, he spent five years in slavery in the most notorious pirate city of the age, Algiers; even his activities as collector of military provisions for the Crown took place against the backdrop of the Armada sent by Philip II to deal with England's recalcitrant Virgin Queen. His lifetime spans the apogee of Spanish power and influence in Europe and the New World and the beginnings of its decline. The transition from greatness to incipient decay, from supreme confidence to insecurity and despair, was registered by Cervantes and is echoed in the changing mood and tone of his writing. And just as the early years of Spain's decline mark the high point of its Golden Age in art and literature, so too Cervantes in his declining years took refuge from an inimical world in his art. Independent spirit as he was in many ways, the man and his age were in a very significant sense in close harmony, and it is entirely appropriate that Spain's greatest moment in history produced her greatest son.

In the narrative that follows I have tried not only to give as full and as accurate and unpartisan an account of Cervantes's life as modern research has made possible, but to relate the man to the works and both to the age that produced them. Where conjectures are made, as they have had to be at times, they are made, I hope, plainly and clearly, and then only when necessity or interest warrant their inclusion. Cervantes deserves more of history, but the past guards its secrets, at times too well.

ONE

The Early Years

A CAREFUL SIFTING of the history of Spain in the fifteenth century yields many prosperous and important men with the name of Cervantes — rich aristocrats, successful prelates, knights of the military orders — on the shoulders of whom Spanish biographers in the past have sought to build a suitably illustrious genealogy for their literary hero, Miguel de Cervantes Saavedra. Wishful thinking has played a more prominent part in this process of glorification, however, than proof.

The reality of Miguel's ancestry, although far from humble, is more prosaic. Of his mother's family we know little, other than that her grandfather was a magistrate who came of prosperous landowning stock in the Castilian village of Arganda. Of the Cervanteses themselves, happily, we know more. Miguel's grandfather, Juan de Cervantes, was the son of a cloth merchant in Córdoba in the south. He graduated in law from Salamanca in the 1490s and spent his life as a peripatetic magistrate, ending up finally in Córdoba as a judge of confiscated property for the Inquisition. A magistrate's life was not without its hazards. In one town Juan was sued on no fewer than twenty-one occasions for malpractice, in one instance by a man who claimed to have been arrested and tortured on insufficient evidence. Juan, no doubt, was not entirely innocent in all this, but as one reads through the mounting list of accusations, one senses the strong smell of conspiracy, and it comes as no surprise to learn that he had managed to cross a powerful superior.

But the work would seem to have had its rewards too. In the 1530s Juan and his family lived for a while in ostentatious comfort in the Castilian university town of Alcalá de Henares. Here they mingled with the wealthy and influential, the three sons living the glamorous lives of young men about town; on the strength of this, the eldest soon made an advantageous marriage, although he did not live long enough to benefit very greatly from it. Where exactly the money came from for the slaves and servants, the horses and rich clothing, one can only speculate — not long before, Juan's daughter María had been borrowing money on the strength of a pearl rosary and a gold-encrusted satin sleeve — and the family's affluence in the event was short-lived. Miguel's father, Rodrigo, however, the middle and least successful son, would never lose his taste for cutting a dashing figure.

The legal entanglements and the financial instability that lay behind the magistrate's respectable façade were to become permanent features of the Cervanteses' life. But there was already a seamier side to their life too, which would find a later echo in the sexual liaisons of Miguel's own sisters and daughter. For Juan's daughter María had some years before been seduced by Don Martín de Mendoza, the illegitimate half-gypsy son of the illustrious Duke of Infantado, then Juan's employer. Don Martín had proved a generous lover — hence the gold sleeve that María was later to pawn — but when Juan intrepidly sued the Mendozas for the dowry that Don Martín had contracted to pay María, who had borne him a daughter, Juan was hounded mercilessly by the Mendoza family on a trumped-up charge of professional corruption and daughter-mongering, and thrown into jail. He was subsequently declared innocent, and María eventually even got her dowry. The incident bears a quite striking resemblance to a painful incident in his grandson Miguel's life years later. The embarrassments that plagued the grandfather were always temporary, however — he lived and died on the whole a successful man of comfortable means. By no stretch of the imagination could the same be said of his son or his famous grandson.

Juan himself was largely responsible for this. Soon after his prosperity in Alcalá de Henares had begun to wane, some colossal disagreement severed his relations with the rest of the family, his wife included, and when he moved off again on his travels only his youngest son, Andrés, went with him. Left behind in Alcalá, the remainder of the family now embarked upon a steady descent into poverty. Miguel's father had no alternative but to forsake his finery and take up a trade to earn his bread and butter.

The trade he settled for was that of barber-surgeon, a calling decidedly humbler than his father's and a far cry from the professional and social status of a surgeon today: a surgeon at the time set bones, let blood, and staunched wounds, leaving diagnosis, prescription, and prognosis to his academically qualified superior, the physician — though many a sick person without money enough for a doctor depended for treatment on the local surgeon instead. In later years, Miguel's sister, Magdalena, would refer to her father in a contract as the licentiate Cervantes de Saavedra. But Rodrigo did not graduate from any university, although he may well have embarked upon the study of medicine at Alcalá before his father's departure compelled him to fend for himself and set up business with what expertise he had already managed to acquire. Magdalena invented the qualification for her own purposes; every shred of respectability is precious to those who live on the margin of poverty.

That Rodrigo himself shared his daughter's aspirations is obvious from the name she gave him. Grandfather Juan was plain Cervantes, and Rodrigo is referred to simply as Rodrigo de Cervantes in many contemporary deeds. But he styled himself Cervantes de Saavedra whenever the fancy took him, assuming dignity and social standing with the addition of a second name, borrowed from another, more illustrious, branch of the family. Of one thing we can be sure: had Rodrigo indeed been a licentiate he would have brandished the title before his name after the manner of the day. By March 1543, Rodrigo, still living in Alcalá, was married to Leonor de Cortinas. Since none of her family ever appears at the christenings of her children, it looks as though Leonor was considered to have married beneath her. The union was richly blessed with issue, if not with worldly prosperity, and in time seven children were born, five of them in Alcalá itself: Andrés in 1543 (named for Rodrigo's absent younger brother), Andrea in 1544 (a poignant indication that the firstborn had already died), Luisa in 1546, Miguel in 1547, and Rodrigo in 1550.

Alcalá was then a vital, thriving town. Its university, founded in 1508 by Isabella the Catholic's great reforming cardinal, Francisco Jiménez de Cisneros, had become the center of humanist learning in Spain, its printing presses among the most active in the Peninsula in the 1520s as they spewed out copies of Erasmus's work for Spaniards eager for the new learning and thinking. With Salamanca remaining as it did the bastion of medieval scholasticism, Alcalá, during the first half of the sixteenth century, was the very focus of Renaissance Spain. More than any other place it symbolized the intellectual exuberance and the ideological fervor which characterized that country until it turned in upon itself in the 1560s, after the triumph of orthodoxy and traditionalism at the Council of Trent. In no more appropriate town could Cervantes have been born.

Miguel de Cervantes (the Saavedra does not appear on the certificate) was baptized on Sunday, 9 October 1547,* in the parish church of Santa María la Mayor in Alcalá as his four elder siblings had been before him. The church was destroyed, alas, in 1936 during the Spanish Civil War, along with many other buildings in the town, by then a decaying backwater. No date of birth was recorded, but there are two strong possibilities: Thursday, 29 September, which was St. Michael's day, or 8 or even 9 October itself, babies being often baptized in those days of high infant mortality on the day of their birth. As to the house where he is thought to have been born, it survived down to the present century and even escaped the ravages of the Civil War. Then in the mid-1950s, not long after it had been identified as the probable birthplace of Spain's most famous son, it was, unbelievable as it might seem, reduced to rubble by the town council to make way for the grander reconstruction that now goes under the name of Casa de Cervantes and houses a Cervantes museum and library. Instead of facing the Calle de la Imagen, the house today faces the main street that runs at right angles to it — only the Calle Generalísimo Franco, as it is now called (though everybody still refers to it as the Calle Mayor), was at the time considered grand enough, obviously, to mark the spot.

The building itself has undergone the same process of

---

* In accordance with the usual practice, dates for the first three and a half decades of Cervantes's life are given as they occur in contemporary sources. Spain adopted the Gregorian calendar on 10 December 1582, which means that anybody wishing to arrive at the modern equivalents for old style dates before then must add ten days.

pious aggrandizement. The modest dwelling that housed the barber-surgeon and his young family, and probably his mother, his sister María, and her illegitimate daughter as well (the house may well have been María's, bought with the dowry wrested from her powerful lover), is now the beautiful and spacious house of a wealthy sixteenth-century Spanish gentleman. With nine rooms downstairs, seven up, and others behind locked doors, it is built round a charming small courtyard open to the sky, with stone pillars, picturesque well and soaring fig tree, and a gracious flight of stairs to the first-floor balcony. All is cool white walls, suitably worn red-tiled floors, strong, dark tables, chests and benches, and richly canopied beds, a superbly imaginative reconstruction in honor of a superbly imaginative genius, but poignantly misleading. Of the many-roomed house where the assiduous visitor is now allowed to wander, only a small part, opening onto the Calle de la Imagen, could have echoed to the first inarticulate cries of the child who was to become a master of the written word and that part, on an impoverished surgeon's earnings, can hardly have had the dignity and elegance of what we see today. Any courtyard, staircase, or well in the original building would have been shared with other families.

What little we know of Miguel's father during the years that followed indicates that the boy enjoyed neither a stable nor a secure childhood. The family moved frequently and was constantly in debt. This background of financial anxiety and strain was to dog Miguel's footsteps all his life, to such an extent that we are driven to conclude that he was as much his father's son in his inability to manage his finances as in his inability to acquire them in the first place. The resilient, resourceful partner of the marriage was Miguel's mother; tireless and inventive in her efforts to keep her family afloat, we shall see in due course to what lengths Leonor was driven in her efforts to compensate for life's misfortunes and her husband's ineffectiveness.

Soon after the birth in 1550 of Miguel's younger brother Rodrigo, the elder Rodrigo decided that the time had come for him to leave Alcalá and seek his fortune elsewhere. A university town which produced each year more medical graduates than it could absorb professionally — years later Cervantes would remark in his exemplary tale, *The Dogs' Colloquy*, that two thousand out of the five studying at Alcalá were reading medicine — was not a particularly propitious place for a struggling surgeon. And if he were already suffering from the deafness that afflicted him in later life, then the odds were even more against him. The Cervantes family, therefore, packed up their belongings and, like most people in search of their fortune, moved to the capital, then Valladolid. Rodrigo's mother and his sister María (her illegitimate daughter had by now married well) went with them. With his only surviving brother, Andrés, in Andalusia, the unfortunate Rodrigo was now head of a larger family than he was able to cope with, and the more capable and somewhat more prosperous María seems to have taken much of the initiative in the arrangement of the family's affairs.

Alas, Miguel's father soon discovered that the streets of Valladolid were paved with nothing but stone, and the following year, every expendable possession sold or pawned, his rent unpaid and his credit exhausted, his ineffectual handling of his affairs landed him in jail for debt. His claim to be exempt from imprisonment for debt on account of his genteel birth had not been accepted (throughout the case all mention of his surgeon's trade is carefully avoided) and his guarantors — his sister María and a hosier friend — had failed to meet their obligations. Accordingly, he was arrested, and María's goods and chattels, as well as his own, were seized. The notary's list of Rodrigo's goods mentions — apart from clothes, household linen, cushions, a sword, a guitar, a figure of the Christ child, a grammar book, and two medical books — only one chest, one table, some benches, and three chairs, two of them broken: not an atypical inventory for the time, but an eloquent commentary upon the prosperous elegance of the house in Alcalá that will masquerade for posterity as the young Miguel's home.

At this point Doña Leonor, Rodrigo's mother, stepped in and helped save the day. She petitioned that the goods confiscated from her part of the house were her own, not her daughter María's, and protested that as a minor María could not in any case be held liable for Rodrigo's debts. That she thought she could get away with the second claim says a lot for the middle-aged María's looks, but it was by any standard a daring move and the bravado of the first lie shrivels away almost to nothing in comparison. She would not be the only Leonor driven to subterfuge by the erring Rodrigo's ways, and indeed the frequency with which the Cervantes family, after the manner of the time, called upon the services of the law is no more remarkable than the blitheness with which it seems to have abused them. Anyway, the ruse worked, and María's goods and chattels were released. After seven months of litigation, during which time Rodrigo passed in and out of jail as the tussle swayed in favor first of one litigant then the other, his evidence of his gentleman's status — a clutch of statements from family and acquaintances rustled up in Valladolid, Alcalá, and Madrid — was finally accepted, and he was released at the end of January 1553. But the hardships suffered by his women and children — and another, Magdalena, was born while he was in prison — during the weeks they had somehow to live through without a breadwinner, are only too easy to imagine. How much of all this impinged on the five-year-old Miguel it is hard to say. There are several remarks in his works later on about the trauma of arrest and imprisonment, but he himself was to be no stranger to prison life and perhaps personal experience alone inspired them. Even so, his father's regular disappearances into jail at this time could hardly have failed to become a bitter family memory.

By the autumn of 1553, Rodrigo and his family were in Córdoba — evidently they had decided to throw themselves upon his father's mercy. Their welcome in that flourishing center of commerce was not as openhanded as they would have wished, however, and the end of October found Rodrigo buying cotton and linen on credit, presumably for shirts and underwear for his family. Certainly no reconciliation took place between the old couple, for the two households remained separate. Miguel by now was six and had probably begun, seated on the floor of some modest schoolroom, to learn the rudiments of grammar; we have his own testimony that he was a precocious reader. That both his sisters, Andrea and Magdalena, showed themselves in later life to be literate is an indication, in those days of low literacy and even lower female literacy, of the concern Rodrigo felt for his children's education, poor as he was. Miguel's stammer, freely admitted to by the grown man, while impeding, perhaps, the smooth recitation of things learned by rote, does not seem to have held him up, or indeed to have bothered him very much at all. In 1555, the first Jesuit college in Andalusia was established in Córdoba and possibly he was among its first pupils, for he refers with great warmth to the quality of Jesuit teaching in *The Dogs'*

Colloquy later on. Sadly, however, nothing about his intellectual formation is certain, and these years will almost certainly remain forever a tantalizing blank.

With Juan's death in March 1556, the Cervantes family lost whatever financial protection the old man had chosen to give them and what social standing they might have derived from their relationship to him. Within the year, old Doña Leonor was forced to sell her only manservant, "a slave of dark brown colour," for seventy ducats, which left her alone with her maid. Soon she had no need of her either, for Doña Leonor succumbed, in March 1557, either to old age or to the typhus epidemic then sweeping the city. How long Rodrigo stayed on in Córdoba is not known — he had little now to keep him there, except a tenuous connection with the Inquisition, which his father had probably obtained for him and which, if it was a stipendiary position, could not have been very lucrative. It is not at all unlikely that he sought at this point the protection of the only remaining prosperous member of his family, his youngest brother Andrés, perhaps moving to the small country town of Cabra — where Andrés would for many years be town mayor — to be near him and to use his influence to find work.

However, all that is certain is that seven years later, in 1564, seven crucial, formative years that constitute a yawning gap in our knowledge of the life of one of the world's greatest writers, Rodrigo turned up in Seville, then the largest city in Spain and third in size in Europe only to Paris and Naples. We assume, though we have no proof, that his family was there with him; Leonor seemed always to have been ready to accompany her husband on his wanderings, though the prospect of yet another move, in those days of excruciatingly uncomfortable travel, along the interminable, dusty, vagrant-ridden roads of Spain, might well have proved too much for a woman doughtier even than she. As for the children, the exotic attractions of the cosmopolitan southern city that had become the gateway to the riches of the New World — a city whose extraordinary inhabitants, like their Muslim forebears, were said to bathe regularly — were enough to excite the dullest imagination, and they would not readily have missed such an experience. Miguel was to spend a great deal of time in Seville in later life and to develop a very special affection for the city. Here, no doubt, now seventeen, he resumed his studies, presumably under the guidance of the Jesuit fathers of whom he speaks so warmly later on. His cousin Juan, Andrés's son, probably accompanied him to school: since Juan lived with the family in Seville for a while, one imagines it must have been for this specific purpose.

Rodrigo's own activities in Seville remain surrounded in mystery, a mystery born solely of our own ignorance. In October 1564, he signed a power of attorney enabling his wife to receive monies owing to him and sued for overdue rent the occupier of a house he had sublet; but these wheelings and dealings, whatever their nature, were pathetically inadequate, and the following year he was in debt once more. This time Andrea's goods were seized in error along with her father's — or so she claimed; but, remembering her grandmother's ruse, this may well have been another occasion upon which necessity bred invention. In her official protest she declared herself to be several years younger than she really was, perhaps simply out of vanity but more plausibly — since she was only twenty — in an attempt to arouse greater sympathy for her plight. Andrea all her life was to remain incapable of remembering her true age.

It was probably in 1564 that the young Miguel saw a performance by the group of itinerant players run by the famous playwright and actor-manager Lope de Rueda, a seemingly trivial incident that was in fact to be something of a landmark in his life. For it was to be Cervantes's lifelong ambition to become a successful dramatist. Rueda's daughter was baptized in Seville in July of that year, so clearly the troupe was performing there. Miguel could equally well, of course, have seen them at any time and in many places during his youth, for like other such companies they wandered around the towns and villages of Spain with their makeshift stage and their meager props and costumes, setting up their temporary theater one day and moving off along the road again the next. Whenever and wherever he saw them, the young Cervantes was vividly impressed, and many years later, in 1615, he referred to his experience in his prologue to a collection of plays he had written but never succeeded in getting produced:

> . . . as the oldest of those present I said I remembered seeing the great Lope de Rueda — a notable actor and a man of distinguished intelligence — perform. He was a native of Seville and a metal beater by trade, which means that he was one of those who manufactured gold leaf. He was an admirable writer of pastoral poetry and in this respect nobody then nor since has surpassed him; and although, being then a mere boy, I could not properly judge the worth of his verse, from those lines I can remember and am able to judge now as a mature man, I am sure that what I have said is the truth. In the time of this famous Spaniard, all an actor-manager's trappings fitted into one sack, consisting more or less of four white sheepskin coats embossed with gilt, four beards, four wigs and four shepherd's crooks. The plays were eclogue-like discussions between two or three shepherds and the odd shepherdess; he [Lope] would dress them up and spin them out with two or three interludes — about a negress, perhaps, or a bully, or a fool, or perhaps a Biscayan; for Lope could act these four

parts, and many more, with the greatest skill and accuracy imaginable. In those days there was no stage machinery, no battles between Christians and Moors either on foot or on horseback; there were no figures emerging, or appearing to emerge, out of the center of the earth from underneath the stage, which was made of four benches placed in a square with four or six planks laid on top and only four palm's widths therefore from the ground. Neither did clouds descend from the sky bearing souls or angels. The theater hangings were an old blanket, pulled by two cords from one side to the other, which formed the dressing room and behind which the musicians would sit, singing some old ballad without a guitar. When Lope de Rueda died, they buried the famous and excellent man in the church at Córdoba (where he died) between two choir stalls, where the celebrated madman Luis López is also buried.

What nostalgia for those far-off days of the theater's simple beginnings — free from the pressures of professional competition and the demands of literary precepts — can be detected in the reminiscences of the disappointed, aging playwright, overtaken and left behind as he was by then by dramatists more talented than himself and better geared to the requirements of the commercial stage!

Rodrigo's debts seem to have convinced him that Seville was not after all the place for a struggling barber-surgeon to live. Within a year or so the family had once more packed their worldly possessions onto a mule train and set off hopefully along the road to a better future, this time in Madrid — since 1561, by decree of His Catholic Majesty Philip II, capital of Spain.

Prior to 1561, Madrid, on the left bank of the river Manzanares, had been a large, flourishing, but relatively quiet provincial town. Far less important than Seville and Córdoba and even Alcalá, although it had housed the

Court temporarily on more than one occasion in the past, it was unlikely to attract the family of an impoverished surgeon seeking new opportunities and avoiding old commitments.

Raised to its new status, however, Madrid exploded into frenzied life, and as the Court inevitably generated its huge following of parasites and petitioners, to its teeming streets that tentacled their way into the surrounding countryside, there flocked the hopeful, the ambitious, the criminal, and the unemployed from all over Spain. By the end of the century it would boast five times the number of inhabitants it had when the Cervantes family arrived there. It was the logical place for Rodrigo, now in his mid-fifties, to make one last stab at success.

We know that the family was not complete, if only because his middle daughter, Luisa, had joined Saint Teresa of Ávila's order of Discalced Carmelites at the recently founded Convent of the Conception at Alcalá, as Sister Luisa of Bethlehem. Ironically enough, by opting out of the normal pressures of everyday life, she was to become not only the longest lived of Miguel's siblings but also, by the worldly standards of the day, the most successful, being elected Prioress of her convent the maximum number of three times. To all intents and purposes the Church was the only career, or at least the only respectable career, open to women at the time, and within its structure Luisa rose almost as high as one could go.

Her two sisters, Andrea and Magdalena, of whom we shall be seeing a great deal, and her three brothers, Miguel, the young Rodrigo, and Juan, almost certainly accompanied their parents to Madrid. By now Andrea had already embarked upon a very different path through life from Luisa's. Sometime in the mid-1560s, she gave birth to a daughter, Costanza, the result of an affair, probably in Seville, with Nicolás de Ovando, a young man of some social standing who was shortly to become gentleman-in-waiting to Cardinal Espinosa, President of the Council of Castile. Soon after her arrival in Madrid, she became involved with an Italian living in the capital, called Giovanni Francesco Locadelo. In June 1568, she received by deed of gift from Locadelo the sum of 300 *escudos* and a large quantity of cloth, clothing, furniture, and other household effects, ostensibly in recognition of Andrea's ministrations to him while he was a patient of her father's. The nature of the ministrations is not specified, but it is not difficult to guess: such devices to maintain respectability were habitually resorted to in deeds at the time, as we shall see later as we follow the fortunes of the Cervantes family. As for Magdalena, she too was to walk a worldly road, but as the youngest child but one, her adventures by 1566 had hardly had time enough to unfurl.

In the year they moved to Madrid, Rodrigo's mother-in-law died and the family prepared to do legal battle, if necessary, for their rightful inheritance: as far as we know, his wife Leonor was an only child. It looks as though they got whatever was coming to them, for the Cervanteses not long afterward entered upon what was probably the most prosperous period of their life together. In 1568, Rodrigo was in a position actually to lend a large sum of money to a friend. It was a generous gesture but an improvident one, for the money was never recovered, and the family's prosperity was accordingly short-lived.

And what of Miguel? By now he was almost twenty, but of his life at this time, of his plans and dreams for the future, we know almost nothing. Later he would claim to have been a voracious reader from a tender age and to have early on committed himself to his lifelong ambition to become a successful poet, an ambition virtually synonymous, since drama throughout Cervantes's lifetime and for long afterward was written in verse, with his later hopes for a career as a playwright. But of his earliest attempts at writing poetry, only one piece has survived — an uninspired and somewhat awkward sonnet addressed to Philip II's third wife, Elizabeth of Valois, which must have been written sometime in the mid-1560s. His formal education had certainly been interrupted by his family's wanderings, although this mattered much less then than it would now. Education was not yet conceived of as a graded program of learning, and pupils could, therefore, pick up and put down their studies virtually at will. The learning Cervantes was subsequently to display was wide-ranging, but so lightly borne as to make it impossible to tell whether it went any deeper than that of the average well-read man of letters of the time, who knew something of much — rhetoric, poetics, philosophy, and history — and acquired a great deal of that secondhand or in translation. A higher education was no prerequisite to this sort of cultural osmosis. A professor of rhetoric at Salamanca informed one of Cervantes's nineteenth-century biographers that he had seen Cervantes's name entered in the university register two years running as a philosophy student, and the dates 1582 through 1584 have since been proposed as the most likely ones for such a stay. But in 1582 Cervantes was thirty-five, a highly improbable age at which to embark on a university career, especially after the very eventful years he was to live through before then. Be this as it may, Cervantes's name does not now appear in the records of Salamanca University, nor for that matter in those of Alcalá, where he is more likely, perhaps, to have matriculated as a youth, given its closer proximity to Madrid, which itself did not boast a university. It is true that in two of his tales, *The Licentiate of Glass* and *The Feigned Aunt* (if this indeed is his), as well as in *Don Quixote,* Cervantes reveals a lively familiarity with student life at Salamanca, but student life then, as now, could not have varied all that much and was readily observed by the interested eye in any university town. The dangers of this kind of hopeful inference are obvious from the claim, based upon the mention of various such activities in *Don Quixote* and *The Galatea,* that Cervantes probably excelled at outdoor sports. By such a measure, Shakespeare, on the evidence of *Hamlet,* was a grave-digger.

What is fairly clear is that when Miguel moved with his family to Madrid he had by no means settled on a career. A literary bent, however pronounced, was no help in earning one's living, unless it were combined with some other occupation. The playwrights of the day often acted as well as wrote, and for a young man with a stammer this solution was impossible; it would not in any case have met with the approval of Rodrigo, who, while he counted theater people and many of humbler calling among his friends, rather liked to cut a figure as a gentleman. The obvious alternative was to secure a position as secretary to some nobleman who would appreciate his literary efforts; perhaps this was indeed what Miguel had in mind when he moved to the capital, cynosure now of the talented and rich. The city, however, swarmed with young men on the lookout for just such a job, and in the meantime Miguel seems to have done something rather more constructive than kick his heels.

The aspiring poet next appears in 1568. On 3 October of that year Philip II's adored wife Elizabeth, to whom Miguel had earlier written his sonnet, died. Shortly before, the child she carried — her third in as many years — had been stillborn. It had already proved a year of tragedy for Spain's austere King. On 24 July he had lost his only son Don Carlos — a vicious, uncontrollable, meddlesome young man of grotesque appearance and unsound mind, the pathetic product of Hapsburg inbreeding. He had died of self-inflicted excesses while under house arrest after plotting against his father. Now this second bereavement, a deeply personal crisis for the grieving Philip and a constitutional crisis for the country it left without a male heir, moved the young Cervantes, along with many other poets both aspiring and successful, to compose some verses in memory of the young Queen. In the following autumn of 1569, four of his compositions, including an elegy addressed to the Inquisitor General and President of Castile, Cardinal Espinosa (perhaps he hoped that his acquaintance with Andrea's erstwhile lover, Nicolás de Ovando, would stand him in good stead in that quarter), were published in a commemorative volume called *A Truthful History and Account of the Illness, Blessed Passing and Sumptuous Funeral Obsequies of the Most Serene Queen of Spain, Our Lady Doña Elizabeth of Valois.*

The volume was edited by a Madrid schoolmaster called Juan López de Hoyos, who in it calls Cervantes "my beloved pupil" and again "our dear and beloved pupil." Now López de Hoyos, a learned man with humanist leanings, had become headmaster of the Estudio de la Villa (City Academy would be the nearest translation) only the year before, in 1568, when Cervantes was already almost twenty-one, so what this reference to Miguel as his pupil means exactly is not clear. The Estudio's pupils would normally have been in their early to mid teens, although since it was the custom at the time to take one's education whenever one could, mixed classes of twelve-year-olds and twenty-year-olds studying the same text were not uncommon. Since the academy had been closed for part of 1566 and 1567, owing to the departure of the previous principal, Miguel could not have spent much time there before López de Hoyos's arrival on the scene. Perhaps he had been for a while a private pupil of López de Hoyos's, before the latter's appointment to the academy, or perhaps on account of his maturity he worked in the school for a time as a pupil-teacher, helping Hoyos with the teaching of grammar and arithmetic and at the same time furthering his own knowledge of Latin and Latin literature — Ovid, Cicero, Virgil, Seneca, Catullus, and Horace — under the guidance of his master. Through Hoyos he would certainly have made contact with Erasmian thinking and criticism. Whatever the circumstances, the warmth of the master's regard for his pupil was unmistakable, and from it we may safely conclude that something of Miguel's exceptional talent was already showing through; his poems reveal him to have been already a cultivated young man. We may also conclude, I think, that he was a young man of endearing disposition, for ability in itself rarely inspires affection.

Through López de Hoyos's good offices, therefore, the aspiring young poet had by the age of twenty-two reached print. He was not to reach it again, as far as we can tell, for almost twenty years, for, owing to circumstances very largely beyond his control, he was to spend his youthful maturity struggling with life rather than with words, laying down a bedrock of rich experience for future exploitation rather than living vicariously through his imagination and his pen.

This experience was already not inconsiderable — if only because poverty is an experienced teacher and genteel poverty an exacting one. Seville, furthermore, was not a city where a youth could live for long without learning much of life and something of the world; the bullion ships that sailed up the Guadalquivir to the Torre del Oro on the quayside, where their contents were stored, brought in their wake not only the seductive airs of a new and exotic world, but a cosmopolitan throng of people of the sort generated by every great port; the city was infamous already for its flourishing underworld. And now the capital, with the decorous glamor of its highly formal and elaborate court, its political intrigues, its endless jockeying for power, wealth, and influence, was, we may be sure, making its own special contribution. What he did there to fill his time and earn his keep, however, is a mystery, unless he did indeed supplement the family income by helping López de Hoyos in the school; his parents could hardly have afforded to support him for long, in spite of the recent legacy from his grandmother's estate. Most of this Rodrigo in any case soon managed to give away, as we saw. If Miguel's literary ambitions were already powerful, he may well have joined the throng of aspirants that swarmed round the court, living off hope and air as they waited for the patron who would take them up and guarantee them funds or a position. That he had already begun to make something of a name for himself as a poet we know from a sonnet written by a friend of his years later, welcoming him back to Madrid after his long absence.

Whatever his plans and hopes for a literary future, they were not yet to be realized. When we next come across him he is in Italy. The move from Spain, which was to prove fateful, was possibly not one that he made of his own free will; he would certainly not have made it had he known how long it would be before he set foot on his native soil again. But events in Miguel's life were beginning to achieve a momentum of their own, to develop a wayward and lasting resistance to ambition, hope, and purpose.

TWO

❧

The Hazards of War

AT THIS TIME a large part of Italy — the kingdom of Naples (which took in the southern half of the peninsula), Sicily, Sardinia, and the region around Milan — belonged to Spain, the Mediterranean arm of an Empire over whose colossal body the sun, by the boast of its King, Philip II, never set. Although his was essentially an Atlantic Empire, spanning Spanish territories in the Old and New Worlds, the Mediterranean played, and was to continue to play, a crucial role in Spanish affairs.

The country's European involvements in the second half of the sixteenth century were many and complex. To the north lay the growing maritime challenge of England under Elizabeth I, a challenge Philip had tried to forestall by marrying Elizabeth's Catholic elder half sister, Mary Tudor. Her death in 1558 left him a premature widower, without the hoped-for child to inherit the English throne. To the north again, but on the mainland, lay that other major Spanish possession in Europe, the Netherlands. This unfortunate province, situated so conveniently yet so perilously near England, became for Spain a seemingly bottomless pit into which Philip was to pour a never-ending stream of money and men in his ruthless and desperate attempt to fulfill his self-appointed role as sole defender of the Catholic faith.

To the east and south lurked the foreboding presence of a far mightier enemy, the crescent moon of the Ottoman Empire. And while the whole of Europe stood in dread of the growing Turkish menace, Spain, with its long, exposed eastern coastline, its proximity to North Africa and its Moriscos — nominally Christian but a perpetual aching tooth in the jaw of Spanish orthodoxy — lived constantly with the fear that Islam would try to wrest back from Christ the peninsula where it had once established a western caliphate to rival that at Damascus. It was, after all, only seventy years since the Catholic Monarchs, Ferdinand and Isabella, had obliterated the last, anachronistic vestige of Muslim Spain, with the conquest in 1492 of the Kingdom of Granada. And during the very years with which we are concerned, the Moriscos of the Alpujarras, a mountainous region in southern Spain, revolted for the second time against the repressive treatment the Morisco communities had consistently received at the hands of the authorities. The by no means extravagant fear of collusion between the Spanish Moriscos and their Muslim brethren around the Mediterranean was a perpetual hindrance to Spain's peace of mind. It was a hindrance that the country would not tolerate for very much longer. In 1609, a decree of expulsion would be proclaimed, and, in the five years that followed, 275,000 Moriscos would be ushered out of the country (where, in most cases, their families had lived for centuries) and handed over to the mercies of foreigners who happened to share the same religion. Had there ever been a chance of peaceful integration and coexistence, the threat of a Turkish-Morisco conspiracy, imagined or real, put an end to it.

In her central involvement in these various aspects of

the European scene, Spain was not alone, and here we reach the very crux of the matter. For in all these wheelings and dealings, an elaborate, devious, and constantly shifting battle of power politics was being waged with France and with the Papacy, in those days as much a temporal as a spiritual power. France lay between Spain and her possessions in the Netherlands, the Franche-Comté and Italy, which complicated considerably the whole question of overland communications and troop movements. France, moreover, itself had ambitions in Italy. Open hostilities, however, could prove disastrous; neither country wanted to see the other grow too strong, yet neither wished to drive the other too far into the arms of other major powers such as England or the Holy Roman Empire. As for the Papacy, Rome needed Spanish assistance to contain the French, yet bitterly opposed Philip's attempts to gain control over the Church in Spain. There was the weighty consideration, too, that both Spain and France would be essential allies in any all-out campaign against the Turk. This period, therefore, is a time of changing allegiances and constantly regrouping alignments, as each power's interests shifted and changed direction with the tide of events.

In 1556 Spain had actually gone to war with the Pope. Within the year France had eagerly grasped this golden opportunity and formed an alliance with the Papacy against Spain. As England's Queen was then Philip II's wife, England weighed in on Spain's side. But with the death of Mary Tudor in 1558, the unnatural alliance fell apart, and in 1559 France and Spain acknowledged the pointlessness of their struggle with a peace treaty. Each thereby both gained and lost. France ousted the English from the north of France, thus relieving the fear of English-Spanish encroachment. As far as Italy was concerned, however, the treaty constituted a triumph for

Spain, for France ceded Savoy and Piedmont to their Italian rulers and relinquished Corsica. That these states did not go to Spain itself was not important. The French threat in Italy was gone, the rest of the country was divided among its Italian rulers, and Spain, one of Europe's most powerful states, with over half the territorial extent of Italy in its possession, was effectively in firm control.

The Spaniard who left Spain for Italy, therefore, particularly those parts of it subject to his own King, went to a country where Spaniards felt at home — and had felt at home for a long time, for Spain's Italian possessions went back to the acquisition of Naples by the Aragonese in 1443. Add to this the glittering reputation Italy still enjoyed among men of education and letters in Spain at the time, and its popularity with Spanish soldiers who relished the good life Italy had to offer, and it is not difficult to see why a young man like Cervantes should have found his way there, especially if he had good reasons for not remaining at home.

The date of his departure from Spain is unknown. He might well have left before the publication in the autumn of 1569 of López de Hoyos's *History* containing several of his poems. The first hard evidence of Cervantes's stay in Italy occurs in documents, dated 22 December 1569, in which his father Rodrigo produced witnesses to affirm that his son, then in Rome, was legitimate and of pure Christian extraction, none of his forebears on either side of the family having been Moors, Jews, or conversos (converted Jews) nor ever convicted of any heresy by the Inquisition or of any other infamous crime. Clearly Miguel had sent for the affidavit, presumably in order to obtain a position of some sort, and the nature of the testimonial suggests that it was a position either with a Spanish or an ecclesiastical employer; anyone else was unlikely to require a deposition on oath as proof of Cervantes's purity of blood.

This phase of Cervantes's life is as blurred as his early years and, if anything, more confusing. But, where before the confusion concealed, we can be fairly sure, nothing very startling, it now springs from an episode of high drama. On 15 September 1569, the legal authorities in Madrid ordered the arrest of a student called Miguel de Cervantes who, having wounded a certain Antonio de Sigura in Madrid, had been sentenced to the loss of his right hand in public and to ten years' exile from the capital. The loss of a hand was the standard penalty according to the strict letter of the law for anybody who drew a sword or a knife within the precincts of the royal palace.

Now there is nothing to show that this Miguel de Cervantes then fled to Italy. Neither is there anything to show that our Miguel de Cervantes left Spain under such a thunderous cloud. Since there were certainly two Rodrigos de Cervantes (the other a keeper-of-accounts at the citadel of La Goleta after Tunis fell to Charles V in 1535), why not two Miguels? At twenty-two, Cervantes was somewhat old to be still a student, especially in view of his family circumstances, and although the description of student might have been loosely used, the odds are that the culprit was either known to be a student or was seen by witnesses wearing the student's customary garb of gown and four-cornered cap. Furthermore, the affidavit produced by Miguel's father Rodrigo in December of that year contains no whisper of any such disgrace.

However, there is a certain amount of circumstantial evidence to support the view, held by more than one Cervantes scholar, that the author of *Don Quixote* was indeed the offender referred to in the order of arrest. To begin with, the odds against there being two Miguels of roughly the same age in Madrid at around the same time must be very great. The fact that the incident must have occurred in or around the palace is not significant; Miguel could easily have gone there in the company of some more highly favored acquaintance or merely as one of the many supplicants who thronged there to present their petitions and memoranda. The timing fits. The warrant was issued on 15 September 1569. The culprit had by then very sensibly fled to Seville (if he were indeed a student, this would bring him immediately within the jurisdiction of the civil rather than the university authorities), and had accordingly been tried and sentenced in his absence. By December our Miguel was in Rome apparently looking for employment. As to the references he needed, the witnesses who testified in the affidavit procured for him by his father were careful to make no mention of criminal offenses in general (though Rodrigo states that this was required) and affirmed only the family's innocence of any Inquisitorial (heretical) offenses. This omission may be deliberate or it may be accidental, but it strikes one as somewhat odd that the three witnesses in turn neglected to meet this one requirement although the rest of the document is absolutely punctilious in its observance of the formalities of legal testimony. Then there are the hints — no more than that — provided later on by Cervantes's writings. In his exemplary tale *The Little Gypsy Girl,* a young man who with a friend kills two rivals in a duel flees to safety in Italy. In his play *The Gallant Spaniard,* the heroine Margarita tells how a suitor of hers, Don Fernando de Saavedra leaves for Italy after wounding her brother in a duel. Although dueling, illegal as it was, was not uncommon at the time — the Spanish dramatist Calderón and his two brothers actually killed a man in a duel in 1621 — and although young men left Spain frequently for no very pressing reasons, this combination of fictionalized incidents, identical name, and suitable chronology does begin to look like something more than coincidence. Cervantes's lifelong propensity to pack his writings with the details of his experience, together with the fact that in both novel and play the victims have brought their fates upon themselves, while their offenders are brave, generous, and noble young men who suddenly find themselves in dire trouble through love, only serve to strengthen our suspicions.

Did the young Cervantes become involved in a fight in Madrid — over a girl, perhaps, or over some insult leveled at his literary prowess or, more plausibly, at his family, possibly his sister Andrea, whose reputation was vulnerable to say the least? The image of honor-sensitive, sword-happy machismo that this conjures up ill fits the familiar picture of the mature Cervantes as a disillusioned, compassionate, and wry-humored observer of the human comedy. But at this juncture he had barely embarked upon the long road of chastening experience that was to lead to *Don Quixote,* and it is hard to expect the mildest man not to retaliate if attacked, which is more or less the situation in the incident in *The Little Gypsy Girl.* Those who wear swords tend, when provoked, to use them.

Any answer to the question, therefore, is pure speculation, but the question, given the evidence, has to be asked. Eleven years later, in 1580, Cervantes would return to Madrid without a sign of unease about any sentence hanging over his head. Of course the ten-year-exile sentence would by then have been well and truly complied with, and the brutal physical punishment might easily have been forgotten or, in view of Cervantes's war record and suffering in captivity, overlooked. Even so, Cervantes had actually set out for Spain — although he never got there — in 1575, carrying with him letters of recommendation with which he hoped to apply for a captaincy. He would certainly have needed to go to Madrid to press his claim. If he were indeed the Cervantes sentenced in Madrid in 1569, it is odd that he should have been so eager to return in 1575 to the place where punishment awaited him, and equally odd later that nowhere in the negotiations that led to his release from captivity in Algiers is there any mention of such an incident in his past — no anxiety expressed as to what might happen when he returned to Madrid nor any tentative seeking of assurances on the basis of his services to his country. Perhaps we shall never know how to regard the fact that he later, as a result of a battle wound, lost the use of his left hand. Was it an ironic quirk of fate or cruel poetic justice? Until it is established where Cervantes was in 1569, and when exactly he left for Italy, the safest course for us, since our suspicions and such evidence as there is will not allow us to follow legal practice and deem him innocent until proven guilty, is probably to declare the case "not proven," after the Scottish manner. If he were the Miguel de Cervantes who got himself into serious trouble in 1568 or 1569, he subsequently preferred not to mention the fact. Years later in *Journey to Parnassus* he would make a veiled reference to some imprudence in his past, which had affected the course of his whole life, but nothing more explicit than that ever escaped his pen.

Later on, both Rodrigo, Cervantes's father, and Miguel himself, on separate occasions twelve years apart, were to claim that he enlisted as a soldier in 1568. This would not necessarily clash with his request from Rome in 1569 for a testimonial of his faultless origins, since on his arrival he might not have been assigned immediately to a company. It would be unwise, however, to accept their statements uncritically, for on both occasions — as we shall see later on — it was patently in Cervantes's interest for his service record to appear as long as possible, and it is not even inconceivable, if Miguel were indeed Antonio de Sigura's assailant, that it was a device adopted by the family in retrospect to provide Miguel with an alibi for the year 1569.

Whether 1568 was the year of his enlistment or not, a soldier he became. It was a logical step for a young man with few ties and poor prospects to take; as a popular saying at the time had it, "There are three roads to success: the Church, the Sea [that is, the New World] and the King's Service." It was also an honorable one, the path taken by hundreds of young men to prove their mettle and their loyalty to God and country. Miguel's great poet-hero, Garcilaso de la Vega, Spanish epitome of the Renaissance gentleman, had been fatally wounded, at the age of thirty-three, while scaling a French fort at the battle of Le Muy in 1536. When young Andrés in *The Little Gypsy Girl* needs a pretext for leaving home with his father's blessing, he simply states that he is off to fight in Flanders (in fact he is off to join a gypsy band in their life of petty crime).

Nevertheless, with the New World and the Church competing with the Crown for the able-bodied youth of Spain, the drain on the country's manpower was enormous, and recruitment was necessarily brisk. In his exemplary tale *The Licentiate of Glass,* Cervantes describes the sort of recruiting patter for which he might well himself have fallen as an infantry captain tries to persuade the young licentiate to enlist:

> He praised the soldier's life; vividly conjured up for him the beauty of Naples, the comforts of Palermo, the rich plenty of Milan, the banquets of Lombardy, the splendid meals in the hostelries. . . . he praised to the skies the free

life of the soldier and the liberty of Italy. But he told him
nothing of the cold experienced by the sentries, the
danger of the attacks, the terror of battle, the hunger of
the sieges, the devastation of the mines, and other matters
of this kind, which are taken and considered by some to
be the additional burden of a soldier's lot and are in fact
the major part of it. As a result, so much and so well did
he talk that Tómas Rodaja's discretion began to falter
and his will to hanker after that life which lies so close
to death.

Perhaps, like Tómas and like many of the soldiers
throughout his works, the new recruit embarked at Cartagena. He certainly mentions several times in his writings the road to that ancient city, the New Carthage
founded during the Punic Wars by the Carthaginian
general Hasdrubal as a strategic base against the Romans.
Or he might have paid his own sea passage to Italy, either
from Cartagena or one of the other eastern ports that
teemed with soldiers, prostitutes, and criminals on their
way to the galleys, and then enlisted when he arrived
there. In *Don Quixote, The Trials of Persiles and Sigismunda* and the exemplary tale *The Two Damsels*, he
would describe Barcelona with an immediacy that suggests he had visited that city. But it seems more likely
that, if he went by sea, he went at the King's expense. Of
course he might have made the much longer but more
interesting journey overland through France, at the time
at peace with Spain; in *Persiles and Sigismunda* he refers
to France with vividness and warmth, and it is difficult to
see when else in his life he might have been there.

December 1569, as we saw, discovered him in Rome.
The details of the early part of his Italian career are
missing, but what scraps of evidence survive indicate that
by 1570, he had donned the bright plumes and popinjay
dress of the serving soldier. An ensign called Mateo de

Santisteban, used in 1578 by Cervantes's father as a witness in his attempts to raise a ransom for his captive son,
testified that he had been with Miguel at the great battle
of Lepanto in 1571 and that Cervantes had served in the
company of one Diego de Urbina since the year before.
Another ensign testified two years later in 1580 — the
year of Cervantes's release — that he had known him since
1570, and Cervantes himself, according to a third witness
testifying for Rodrigo in 1578, claimed to have been in
action on various occasions before the battle of Lepanto.

At the beginning of Cervantes's exemplary tale *The
Generous Lover,* the young captive Rodrigo bewails the
destruction of Nicosia, and his Turkish friend Mahamut
too laments the terrible change that had come over the
"renowned and beautiful island of Cyprus." But whether
this means that Cervantes took part in the abortive expedition of Spanish, Genoese, Venetian, and Papal vessels
that set out in September 1570 to relieve Cyprus — a
Venetian possession that had been occupied by the Turks
— we do not know. Even the evidence that should be
more reliable appears confused, for Diego de Urbina's
company, in which Cervantes is supposed to have served
in 1570, had been engaged against the Moriscos in the
rising in the Alpujarras and did not leave for Italy until
1571, only four months before Lepanto. Yet Cervantes
certainly mentions Urbina, a "famous captain from Guad-
alajara" in *Don Quixote,* and in all probability, therefore,
Santisteban's memory misled him. Cervantes could well
have transferred to Urbina's company in 1571, before
Lepanto, from one serving under a different captain.

That he saw action at the battle of Lepanto — and
enough of it to inspire the disillusionment of *The Licentiate of Glass* in any soldier — is indisputable.
Throughout the 1560s, the forces of East and West, of
Crescent Moon and Cross, had clashed repeatedly in the

Mediterranean as they struggled for supremacy. In 1560, a huge Spanish force moving to the relief of Tripoli — captured by the Turks in 1551 — had been routed by the Turkish fleet and forty-two vessels and eighteen thousand men had been lost, very largely because of the Spanish fleet's inability to protect its expeditionary forces once they had disembarked. Thereafter Philip II set about building up his Mediterranean fleet — largely galleys rowed by slaves and convicts — and improving his naval strategy, and by the mid-sixties the Spaniards were on the offensive in the western Mediterranean. When the Turks in 1565 occupied Malta, the island of the Knights of St. John (already ousted from Tripoli and Rhodes), the Spanish fleet, backed up by Spanish land forces from Italy, drove the enemy from the island. Philip, however, failed to follow up this victory; Catholicism was by now beleaguered on another front and a great part of his resources, both money and men, was being diverted to the Netherlands for the struggle against the Protestants. Fortunately for Spain, the Sultan, Selim II, for his own good reasons, signed a peace treaty with the Holy Roman Emperor, Maximilian II, in 1568, and there ensued a period of respite. After the invasion of Cyprus by the Turks in 1570, however, Philip came under increasing pressure from the Republic of Venice and the Pope to join forces in a move against Selim. The first, halfhearted attempt to save Cyprus, as we saw, failed abysmally. Events at home in Spain and in the Netherlands then suddenly conspired to make Philip more receptive to the idea of a major offensive against the Turk. That same year, 1570, saw the Morisco revolt in the Alpujarras, and Philip was quick to grasp the danger of having an enemy within the gates, a latter-day wooden horse for the Muslims outside. In the Netherlands, meanwhile, the Duke of Alba had established his ruthless and repressive hold over the Flemish insurgents and seemed safely in control.

Accordingly, on 20 May 1571, the Holy League was formed with Venice and Rome for a three-year offensive against Islam. Spain undertook to finance half the enterprise and to subsidize Venice, while Venetian trade routes with the East remained closed, by removing tariff barriers between Venice and the Spanish states in Italy. The King's handsome and dashing twenty-four-year-old half brother, Don John of Austria, was named commander in chief of the allied forces, comprising over two hundred galleys and twenty-eight thousand men. He immediately took the offensive, resolving to seek out and destroy the enemy.

The Turkish fleet lay in the Gulf of Lepanto near Corinth. Don John decided that this would be the perfect place to attack: the enemy, hemmed in by the Christian fleet, would be unable to make a run for it, and the proximity of land might even encourage the Muslim troops under attack to desert their vessels. On 7 October 1571, as dawn broke, the two armadas sighted each other. The Christians realized aghast that the Turkish fleet was far superior in number, and to bolster their sinking spirits Don John reviewed the fleet in a frigate, urging his men on, as he passed up and down, to sublime efforts in this Battle of the Cross, promising freedom to any galley slaves who distinguished themselves during the fray. Outnumbered as they were, however, the allies had two things in their favor: the huge Venetian galleasses (merchant galleys recently converted into warships) with their heavy firing power, and the renowned and extremely well-equipped Spanish infantry, then the best in Europe. In addition, Don John decided upon a brilliantly simple tactic, which was to pay off handsomely.

All galleys had an upturned spur at the prow which was used both as a ram and as a grappling device in close encounters. These spurs often impeded the galleys' maneuverability and had the further disadvantage of interfering with the main centerline bow guns. Don John, therefore, had the spurs of his vessels cut away at the last moment (they had been sawn through beforehand in preparation), not so the Christian galleys would ride lower in the water and thus escape the enemy shot, as many Spanish historians have with gravity-defying confidence maintained, but so their own guns could bear down with unprecedented and unexpected accuracy on the lower-lying Muslim galleys. The damage at close range was devastating.

In spite of their vessel strength, therefore, the Turks were crushingly defeated by the allies in a ferocious battle that marked the beginning of the end of Turkish supremacy in the Mediterranean. As Cervantes was later on to say in *Don Quixote,* the day was a happy one for Christendom, for "all the world then learned how mistaken it had been in believing that the Turks were invincible at sea." He was right in his assessment of the situation. While the Turks were by no means finished, the Christian victory, as the historian Braudel has pointed out, "had halted progress toward a future which promised to be very bleak indeed."

Cervantes was on board the *Marquesa.* On the day of the battle he was sick and feverish. According to the testimony of two witnesses, his captain and several of his comrades urged him to stay below deck and rest. This humane advice was vehemently rejected by Cervantes, who asked what the world would think of him if he failed to fight, declaring in time-honored fashion that he would rather die fighting for his God and King than go below. So eager indeed was he for action, that at his own request he was deployed in the thick of the fighting, in charge of twelve men in a long boat. Whether the long boat's function on these occasions was to maintain communications with the flagship is not clear; whatever its role, it was a dangerously exposed position to fight from.

The battle began at noon. The horror that ensued may easily be imagined from the fact that by four o'clock in the afternoon, when a crucifix and the head of Ali Pasha, the Turkish commander, appeared on the mast of the Christian flagship, the sea seemed to the exhausted, battleworn soldiers to run red with blood. Thirty thousand Turks were killed or wounded, and three thousand more taken prisoner. Of the allies, nine thousand died and twenty-one thousand were wounded. On the credit side, fifteen thousand Christian galley slaves were freed.

At that time naval warfare in the Mediterranean still followed the old pattern of head-on clashes between slender, infantry-laden galleys, essentially floating battlefields despite their strategic mobility. The day of the fast-cruising sailing vessel bristling all around with cannon and manned by sailors, however, was beginning to dawn, and Lepanto was to be the last great galley battle in maritime history. These galleys carried around 175 oarsmen (augmented to 200 at Lepanto for extra speed) and between 250 and 300 sailors and soldiers. And while all battles are at once brutal and pitiful, a sea battle between galleys was doubly so, for the oarsmen that propelled them were chained to their positions, with no choice but to sit and wait for the excruciating rending of iron, wood, and bone as the ram of the enemy vessel made straight for them and then, if they were still alive, to watch the water rising toward them as they sank, still in their chains. When Ali Pasha's enormous galley charged head-on at Don John of Austria's flagship, the battering ram penetrated to the third row of oarsmen. In Part I of *Don*

Quixote, Cervantes describes vividly what it was like to fight at sea from the far more favorable standpoint of the ordinary infantryman:

> ... if this danger seems but small, let us see whether it is equaled or surpassed by that occasioned by the collision of the prows of two galleys in the middle of the open sea; as they engage and lock together, the soldier is left with no more space to stand upon than two feet of plank at the stem of the prow; and even so, in spite of the fact that he is confronted only a lance length away by as many threatening ministers of death as the opposing side has cannon, and although one careless step would send him down to the bosom of Neptune, even so, with intrepid heart, impelled by the honor that drives him, he exposes himself to the battery of guns and attempts to cross the narrow passage to the other ship. And the most amazing thing is that hardly has one fallen from whence he will not rise until the end of the world but another takes his place; and if this one also falls into the sea, which lies in wait for him as if he were its enemy, another replaces him and another, before each has properly had time to die; no greater courage and daring than this may be found in all the hazards of war.

Cervantes knew what he was talking about. Forty-odd men aboard the *Marquesa,* the Captain among them, were killed. He himself did not survive the battle intact, receiving two gunshot wounds in the chest and a third in his left hand that deprived him of the use of it for life. It is often maintained that he lost the hand, and on occasions Cervantes too gave that impression, but it is quite clear that the hand, although badly maimed and rendered useless, remained. The injury, he was later to maintain in the Prologue to his *Exemplary Tales,* although ugly, seemed to him beautiful since he had sustained it "on the loftiest and most memorable occasion that had been, or ever would be, fighting under the victorious flag of the son [Don John] of that thunderbolt of war, Charles V of blessed memory." And the pride he took in the part he had played in that mighty battle against "Ottoman pride" — the battle no doubt commemorated in his play *The Naval Battle,* alas now lost — was to remain with him to the end of his days, a brief moment of heroic glory for his memory to caress as he wrestled with the bitterness and disillusionment of failure and neglect. The witnesses later produced to support the efforts made to effect his release from captivity all testified to the valor in battle displayed by Miguel de Cervantes. Never again would he live through an experience that would cause him in retrospect such unalloyed joy or bring him such unqualified praise.

The battle over, the victorious Spanish fleet made for Messina in Sicily for repairs. Cervantes must have received treatment for his injuries in the hospital there. With his chest injuries he was lucky to survive, for gunshot wounds were notoriously more difficult to cope with than the commoner sword or pike wounds: contemporary medicine was incapable of dealing with internal bleeding or blood poisoning. The company under the command of Diego de Urbina convalesced and wintered in Calabria, but Cervantes, clearly not well enough to travel, remained in Sicily. It is not firmly established whether or not Cervantes was indeed granted, at Don John's order, a small wage supplement in recognition of his bravery, as one of his military comrades later claimed, but he certainly received several sums of money in the January and March of 1572 to pay for his expenses during his recuperation. He was fortunate. No Spanish soldier at the time could rely on being regularly paid, and Miguel's payments were almost certainly advances on a much larger sum of back pay owed him. By April he was

deemed fit for service again and, in the general and pro-
longed reshuffling of the Spanish forces made necessary by
the losses sustained at Lepanto, he was assigned at a
higher rate of pay to a different regiment, that commanded by the famous general Don Lope de Figueroa.
When his superiors finally assigned him to a company, he
was sent to join that commanded by Manuel Ponce de
León, then stationed in Naples.

Sometime not long afterward he was joined in Naples
by his younger brother Rodrigo, now twenty-two and
also a soldier. There is some evidence that he too had
fought at Lepanto. Their pleasure at meeting up again
must have been intense. In July they both sailed with
Don John of Austria and the Spanish fleet to Corfu,
where the Christian forces were to meet in preparation
for another attack on the enemy, this time in the Levant.
But the allies, whose conflicting interests were now driv-
ing them apart, ineptly missed one another, the Turkish
fleet made a point of being elusive and the expedition
petered out. Not, however, before a skirmish near Nava-
rino (now known once more by its ancient name of
Pilos) in the south Polypenese between the Spanish ships
and some of the Barbary pirates whose depredations in
the Mediterranean were a persistent menace not only to
Christian trade and shipping, but to Christian coastal set-
tlements. In the course of the engagement, a galley captained by Hamete (or Mahamet Bey as he was otherwise
known), nephew of the famous corsaire Barbirossa, was
seized by the Neapolitan flagship, the *She Wolf*, under
the command of the Marquis of Santa Cruz. Let Cervantes tell us what is supposed to have followed:

> Barbirossa's son [*sic*] was so cruel and treated his captives
> so badly that when the oarsmen saw that the *She Wolf*
> was coming at them and was almost upon them, they all

with one accord dropped their oars and seized their
captain, who was standing upon the awning-support
shouting at them to row faster, and passing him from
bench to bench, from stem to stern, they tore at him with
their teeth so that scarcely had he reached the mast but
his soul had already passed into hell.

So speaks the Captive in Part I of *Don Quixote,* his adventures in large part parallel to Cervantes's own.

In February 1573, Cervantes and his company, after
wintering in Sicily, were back in Naples. Here he successfully applied for several dollops of his long overdue
wages. Clearly they proved inadequate to keep him
going, for shortly afterward he requested, and received,
another, larger sum. In March, Venice, unable to tolerate
any longer the crippling financial strain of open hostilities with the Ottoman Empire, left the League and reestablished relations with the Turks. Philip II, whose
heart, unlike that of his brother Don John, had been but
half committed to the recent campaigns in the Eastern
Mediterranean, was now free to turn his attentions to
that area of the war against Islam that concerned Spain
most closely — the African coast. The Cervantes brothers
were once again in Don John of Austria's forces when he
took Tunis in October of that year — although Miguel's
wounds, particularly his hand, were still troubling him.
His elation at participating in yet another symbolic victory over Islam is not difficult to imagine. But his joy was
to be short-lived. Nine months later, long after Don John
had returned with his troops to a rejoicing Naples, leaving Tunis in the hands of a Spanish garrison under a
native governor, the Turkish fleet retaliated and laid
siege to Tunis and to its citadel, La Goleta. In a verse
letter he was to write later in captivity, Cervantes would
regret not having stayed behind in Tunis to defend it.

But this feeling, expressed in the knowledge of what happened to the citadel, was born of the depression and hopelessness he was experiencing at the time of writing rather than of any desire at the time to stay in Africa. Had he done so, he would almost certainly not have survived.

Cervantes seems not to have gone with the other veterans of Don Lope de Figueroa's regiment to winter in Sardinia on his return from Tunis — or at least, if he went, it was only for a short time. For in the February and March of 1574 he was in Naples, though still receiving his military pay. The attractions over rural Sardinia of a bustling, cosmopolitan city like Naples — for a Spaniard virtually a home from home — especially for a soldier straight from battle, are easy enough to imagine. But Cervantes's motive for being there was probably a personal one. At some stage during these years in Italy, he met and fell in love with a girl in Naples — probably the "Silena" of his poetry (his own pastoral pseudonyms were Lauso and possibly Elicio) — by whom he had a son, Promontorio. If the testimony of his ballad "Jealousy" and of *The Galatea* can be relied on, Silena led him something of a dance and caused him not a little heartache. But no literary expression of love, we must remember, was complete unless obeisance was made to the pangs of jealousy and the icicles of disdain. If, as seems probable, the affair was now well under way, it makes sense that he should have sought permission to remain in Naples on his return from Tunis and during the ensuing lull in his military duties. An ordinary volunteer soldier's life was less organized and disciplined than that of the fighting man of later times. He wore no proper uniform, received no real training other than that thrust on him at the front, and could not always rely on receiving pay, clothing, or even food. He was often committed to no fixed length of service, moved between companies and regiments with some ease and frequency and, in compensation for his deprivations, was allowed his creature comforts as a matter of course whenever feasible. Hence the pages, servants, and baggage women who accompanied armies on their marches: each company was allotted its quota of whores. In the context of this far more casual military life, it is by no means improbable that Cervantes was given leave to winter away from his company, in Naples. Italy itself was peaceful, and troops were not normally mobilized in winter.

It is possible that in the late spring of 1574 he went with Don Lope de Figueroa's regiment to Genoa, where trouble with the French seemed to be brewing, for the city is described in considerable detail in *The Licentiate of Glass*. But if he did, he was certainly back in Naples in August when Don John arrived there from Spain to organize an expedition for the relief of Tunis. Miguel and Rodrigo, along with the rest of their regiment, sailed with it. On 3 October, however, news of the fall of La Goleta, Tunis's citadel, reached the expeditionary force at Trapani and the expedition was abandoned. The news made a painfully vivid impression upon Miguel, who had been there, of course, only the year before: the overwhelming odds, the advantages to the attackers of the surrounding sand, so easily scooped into trenches and platforms, the terrible casualties — all reappear in the post mortem on the disaster delivered by the Captive in Part I of *Don Quixote*.

This largely unaccounted-for year in Cervantes's activities in Italy offers a convenient vantage point from which to worry briefly at another bone of contention among Cervantes scholars. In the dedication to his pastoral romance, *The Galatea*, published in 1585, Cervantes refers in passing to a Cardinal Acquaviva whose chamberlain he had been in Rome. If only he had been a fraction more explicit, how much speculation could have been saved! Acquaviva visited Madrid in 1568 as Papal Envoy, partly to convey the Pope's condolences to Philip II on the death of his son Don Carlos (by the time he reached the Spanish court, condolences were doubly in order, for the Queen too was dead) and partly on diplomatic business. Many have fondly imagined that he met the young Cervantes during his stay there and was so impressed by his person and his wit that he took him into his service and carried him off to Rome. The theory, although appealing, does not convince, for it is difficult to see how Miguel, not at that time impoverished but certainly not wealthy, could possibly have met such a high-ranking ambassador. The fruits of Cervantes's first tentative literary efforts, however promising, were scarcely such as to compel the notice of the great. Another suggestion is that Cervantes joined the cardinal's household soon after he reached Rome but before his enlistment in the army. However, there are difficulties here too. The assumption, based on what Cervantes says in his prologue to *The Galatea,* is that Acquaviva was already a cardinal when Cervantes worked for him, and Acquaviva, we know, did not receive his cardinal's hat until May 1570, a year in which Cervantes claimed to have been already in action. Furthermore, if Cervantes had managed to obtain such an attractive position on his arrival in Italy, and before his enlistment, it seems unlikely, his patriotism notwithstanding, that he would have been quite so prompt in embracing the soldier's life. A number of high-born Spaniards joined the army, often as common foot soldiers, for the honor and glory, but the great majority of native recruits, like the foreign mercenaries who were recruited, enlisted because they were poor. As the Italian soldier in *Don Quixote* sings,

To the war I am driven by necessity.
If I had money, forsooth I would not go.

Perhaps Cervantes served the cardinal briefly later on
during a lull in his military activities, as has been suggested by others. For since Acquaviva died in July 1574 it
would appear, if Cervantes's master was indeed already
a cardinal, that Cervantes must have served in his household between May 1570 and July 1574. Yet from October
1571 (the date of the battle of Lepanto) to July 1574,
Cervantes was a serving soldier and there is no indication
whatsoever of his being in Rome; indeed it was probable,
as we saw, that he was already in action in 1570. The
likelihood of his interlude with the cardinal's occurring
during these years is not in my view very strong.

So where does this leave us? As far as I can see we have
to nail our speculations to the time when we know for
certain that Cervantes *was* in Rome. Not only was he in
Rome in the winter of 1569; he was also in need of a
testimonial of his unblemished origins. And this is when,
to my mind, he must have entered the cardinal's service.
The cardinal, after all, who was only a year older than
Miguel, is far more likely to have taken on as secretary-
cum-steward a young man straight from Spain with his
schooling and his burgeoning literary aspirations still
close about him, rather than a veteran soldier — one of
thousands — with a mutilated hand, especially if that
young man was an enlisted infantryman seeking a temporary position until such time as he was assigned to a
regiment and company. And Cervantes himself, for the
same reasons, is much more likely to have sought that
kind of position before rather than after he had entered
active service.

That Cervantes states that he had served "Cardinal"
Acquaviva is neither here nor there: it would have been

unnaturally punctilious — as well as less impressive — to specify in his prologue that Acquaviva, so soon to become a cardinal, had not quite reached that elevated position when Cervantes knew him, and very possibly Cervantes's period in his service overlapped briefly with his new status. The remaining possible objection is that Cardinal Colonna, to whom Cervantes dedicates *The Galatea* and of whom he claims Acquaviva spoke so warmly to him while he was in his employ, was probably only a boy of ten or eleven from 1569 to 1570. But I think we may take Cervantes's assertions in this respect as flatterer's license, based very likely upon some passing remark made by Acquaviva about the boy's precocity and promise; as Governor of Naples and, subsequently, commander of the Papal forces during the period of the Holy League, the boy's father was well known to Acquaviva.

We need not speculate, therefore, whether the nebulous year between the capture of Tunis in October 1573 and its fall was the time of Cervantes's service in Cardinal Acquaviva's household — the cardinal, it will be remembered, died in July 1574.

After the abandonment of the Tunis expedition, Cervantes's regiment was quartered in Palermo in Sicily under the auspices of the Duke of Sessa, then viceroy of the island. But by December, Miguel was back in Naples once more. From what followed it is clear that Cervantes had in his own eyes reached a point where some thought needed to be given to his future. He was by now twenty-seven years old and by his own testimony had been a soldier for four. He was still an ordinary infantryman, albeit a veteran receiving a veteran's supplemented pay, and he obviously considered that the time had come for something better. Why he had not already been promoted, to corporal or sergeant, if not to ensign (lieutenant), it is impossible to say. Certainly he had the experi-

ence and, on the evidence of Lepanto, he did not lack the
qualities necessary for the assumption of responsibility.
The theoretical term of service for promotion to ensign
was six years, but in practice promotion was often much
speedier — a fellow soldier and aspiring playwright, Andrés Rey de Artieda, although younger than Cervantes,
was already a captain. Perhaps Miguel had simply not
been well enough in with any of his successive captains;
captains promoted whom they pleased without interference from above as long as company numbers were observed, and habitually favored relatives and friends. Miguel was all his life a proud man, psychologically
incapable himself of sycophancy and contemptuous of
those who rose in the world by means of it. That he
considered himself suitable material for leadership is
clear, for during the months of respite that followed —
much of the time spent no doubt in the company of
"Silena" — he sought and obtained from Don John of
Austria in Naples and from the Duke of Sessa in Sicily
(who as Count of Cabra must have known both his
grandfather and his uncle, Andrés) testimonials of his
war record and general standing, to enable him to return
to Spain and petition the King for a captaincy in one of
the new companies constantly being formed for service in
Italy.

In his later writings he would feelingly stress time and
again the deprivations as well as the dangers of the soldier's life; and in the famous arms and letters soliloquy in
Don Quixote, Cervantes shows that any illusions he
might originally have cherished about the glory of military life were quite shattered by experience:

And we shall see that poverty embraces no one poorer
than the soldier, for he is a prisoner to the misery of his
pay, which arrives either late or never, or to what he

can swipe with his own hands at considerable danger to his life and conscience. And sometimes his nakedness is such that one slashed doublet serves as both finery and shirt, and in the middle of winter in open country all he has to protect him from the inclemency of the sky is his own breath, which issuing as it does from a void, naturally comes out cold, which is completely against Nature. At long last comes night, allowing him to recover from all these discomforts in the bed that awaits him; that bed, unless it be through fault of his own, he will never find too narrow, for he may measure himself out on the earth as far as he likes and wrap himself round in it to his heart's content without fear of getting tangled in the sheets.

Nevertheless, there can be little doubt that in 1575 he had decided to make the army his career, for the near future at least, and that he wanted to serve in Italy, generally acknowledged as a softer billet in all respects than the cold, hostile Netherlands, but with the additional attraction for Cervantes of being the home of his mistress, and their child, if already born. And it would be pointless to pretend that the soldier's life was all bad. In theory his daily bread was guaranteed, his wounds were cared for after a fashion, he was free of taxes and tithes and he was, in theory again, automatically ransomed by the army if taken prisoner. All of which meant that he was substantially better off than the thousands of poor trying to keep body and soul together back home. When his back pay at last came through, he could squander it on wine and women and on fine clothes and feathers as colorful and dashing as he pleased, leaving only his red sash and the cross on his chest to mark him as a soldier. And there was always, of course, the chance of booty; not a few soldiers returned to Spain with enough money to keep them in modest comfort for the rest of their lives. As for the man who made captain and thereby gained almost total control over the rank and file serving under him, including the distribution of their pay, the world was virtually his oyster: corruption, predictably, was rife. It is strange to think that but for the intervention of fate the author of *Don Quixote,* most famous of Spaniards, might have lived out his life a prosperous but unknown captain.

But Cervantes's military ambitions, like most of the other worldly ambitions he was to cherish, were destined to fail. That he was relying heavily on his record, particularly at Lepanto, to commend him to the King may be deduced from the fact that promotion to captain normally came after ten years of service and rarely to a soldier straight from the ranks. The warm letters of recommendation from two such prominent figures as Don John himself and the Duke of Sessa, however, must have given him high hopes of success. At the very least the venture was an opportunity for him to return to Spain and see his family — for, like all petitioners, to Madrid Cervantes would have to go. There he could play the conquering hero home from the wars, reveling in the horror and wonder his tales of battle with the ferocious Turk would rouse in his admiring family and friends, displaying with casual pride his letters from the great recommending to the King that Miguel de Cervantes be given a captaincy, no less, after six years of service. Those letters he would come to rue, but at this point they were his passport to success. Accordingly, on 20 September 1575, Miguel and his brother Rodrigo, who had obtained leave of absence to accompany him, set sail from Naples on the *Sun,* one of a flotilla of galleys destined for Spain. In those days of piracy, no vessel dared sail the Mediterranean alone.

THREE

❧

The Captive's Tale

FOR FIVE DAYS everything went smoothly. The little fleet
followed the Italian coastline north, never losing sight
of it for long, for the galley was not a vessel equipped for
long voyages in open seas. On the sixth day out, the *Sun*
and two other galleys became separated from the rest of
the flotilla in a storm. As they passed Les Saintes Maries
on the French coast, they were attacked by three Barbary
privateers under the command of an Albanian renegade
named Arnaute Mami who by renouncing his faith had
risen from captivity to become a Captain of the Sea in the
Ottoman Empire. The brunt of the attack, which was led
by another renegade, a Greek called Dali Mami who captained one of the enemy vessels, seems to have been taken
by the *Sun* itself. Those on board put up a spirited defense, fighting long and fiercely enough to prevent the
galley's being taken until the other Spanish vessels came
to its rescue. The captain died in the attempt. Abandoning hope of abducting the galley itself, the pirates settled
for human booty and made off for Algiers with a valuable
cargo of Spanish prisoners. Miguel and Rodrigo de Cervantes were among them.

In *The Galatea* Cervantes, always ready to transform
the stuff of his own experience into material for his

books, embroiders dramatically upon this already dramatic incident. The Spanish galleys become one sailing ship, the three Algerine galleys fifteen (this is not in fact as extravagant a number as it may seem, for the Barbary privateers often marauded in large groups), while the death of the Captain becomes in the romance that of everyone on board, except for the narrator Timbrio and his two beautiful female companions. The battle lasts sixteen hours, and the Turks succeed in boarding the ship only at the ninth attempt. But Arnaute Mami is here, commanding his fleet, just as he will be later on in *Don Quixote* and in the exemplary tale *The English Spanishwoman*. Since Cervantes was only just twenty-eight when he was captured — he probably celebrated, though the word in the circumstances can scarcely be appropriate, his birthday on board the pirate galley — it is hardly surprising that the event which was to deprive him of his freedom for five of his most vigorous years should have left an indelible impression upon him. The other detail in Timbrio's story that draws the tale close to Cervantes's own experience is the reason given for Timbrio's survival when all but he and the two girls are killed. These are spared on account of their sex and beauty and they then plead for Timbrio's life, playing on the pirates' greed by claiming that he is of noble birth and, therefore, worth a large ransom.

The prospect of a high ransom that saves Timbrio's life in *The Galatea* was to dog its author's footsteps during his captivity and actually lengthen its duration, for when Cervantes was searched by his captors they found on him the letters from Don John of Austria and the Duke of Sessa. And since only a man of standing, clearly, would have been granted letters of recommendation by men of their rank and reputation, the ransom subsequently placed upon his head was, by this ironical twist of fate, set far too high for his impoverished family to reach. Dali Mami, who took Cervantes on board, was much too shrewd to allow such a prisoner to slip through his fingers, and Cervantes accordingly became his slave. (In 1576 a fellow prisoner after his release stated that Miguel de Cervantes was Arnaute Mami's slave, but all the evidence contradicts this. He probably confused the two names.) On arrival in Algiers the despairing Cervantes was handcuffed, chained, and put into prison to await ransom, his protestations of poverty ignored. By his own admission (in his verse letter to Mateo Vázquez, written later on in captivity), when he first sighted the notorious corsair city, the tears, despite himself, streamed down his face.

The Algiers where Cervantes found himself was an extraordinary place. The headquarters of Islamic piracy and privateering in the Mediterranean, the town as Cervantes came to know it had sprung up in response to the hectic maritime activity generated in the Mediterranean in the sixteenth century by commercial prosperity and by political and religious hostilities. It boasted a good harbor, solid ramparts and stout defenses, and, as well as spawning privateers, it sheltered and serviced them and provided a market for their spoils. It was, as a result, one of the most thriving commercial centers in the Mediterranean — as its mint, its theological school, its hospital for the sick, and its splendid public baths (complete with hot and cold water) testified. Politically, it was very largely a law unto itself, part of the Ottoman Empire yet powerful enough and far enough away from Constantinople to enjoy a substantial degree of autonomy. Culturally, it was an exotic hybrid, teeming as it did with Christian slaves, expatriate Spanish moors, renegades, and adventurers from everywhere. To its port and market flocked ships from France, Spain, Italy, England, and Flanders, as well as vessels from the eastern Mediterranean; for although trade with Algiers was for the most part illegal in Christian countries, it flourished nonetheless. Like any frontier society living on the margins of conventional law and order, it was a place of opportunity, of quick profits, and unexpected promotions. Many a Christian captive solved the predicament in which he found himself by abandoning his faith, and many of those who did so prospered. The Beglerbey (or Pasha) of Algiers who took Tunis in 1570 and fought at Lepanto, Eujd Alí, had started life as a Calabrian fisherboy; in 1569, the Spanish, in an attempt to gain his support, tried unsuccessfully to bribe him with a marquisate. Such success would have been well nigh inconceivable had he remained within the rigid hierarchy of Christian society.

The commodity on which Algiers thrived above all was a human one, for the city was the hub of the Christian slave traffic in the Mediterranean. Captives were not merely brought back to Algiers by pirates who were based there, but shipped there by privateers from elsewhere who wished to sell them or offer them as payment for merchandise or supplies. Prisoners were thus a form of currency as well as a commodity. Their value was twofold: they could be ransomed for hard cash, or otherwise sold, or they could be put to work in the Algerine galleys or in the city itself. As a contemporary memorandum observed in 1564, "It is raining Christians in Algiers."

Cervantes's injured hand automatically kept him from the possibility of death, in battle or from physical exhaustion, in the galleys, but it was his spurious importance which, while ensuring he remained a slave, also ensured he remained alive. Captives of any importance or wealth were not as expendable as ordinary human beings. It was this prospect of ransom that for the most part decided the fate of prisoners in Algiers. Those awaiting their freedom were kept guarded and usually chained in the state prisons, called bagnios, where most domestic as well as government captives were locked up at night for greater security. Those considered less likely to be ransomed became slaves proper, either working in private households for their masters or, if they were "public" slaves, performing the various tasks involved in the servicing of the extremely well-organized city — sweeping, building, woodcutting, or tending the hundreds of luxuriant orchards and gardens surrounding the city to which the wealthier inhabitants retreated from the urban heat and dust in summer. Other than when they did a stint in the galleys these were not chained. A ball and chain, therefore, was a very mixed blessing: on the one hand a chaffing restriction on movement, on the other a symbol not only of importance but of hope. It did not always protect its wearer from hunger, cold, or even cruelty — a master's concern to protect his investment did not go that far and a contented prisoner would not press quite so urgently, perhaps, for his release — but it did save him from the hangings, the impalings, the ear- and nose-loppings, and other brutalities to which the wretched ordinary slaves were sometimes subjected by gratuitously cruel masters.

Not that life in the bagnios was, for most slaves, as harsh as it has often been made out to be by more partisan commentators. The slaves were regarded essentially as prisoners of war, and conditions were decidedly better than those in the public prisons of most countries at the time, and for long afterward. Even government slaves had Fridays off work and three hours a day free in which to earn money for extra food and clothes; basic issues of bread, clothing, and bedding were normally supplied from army stores. Galley service was limited to about three or four months in the year, whereas there was no such restriction operative in Christian galleys. There were taverns in the bagnios where slaves and guards drank and gambled together, mass was said every morning, and at the great religious festivals slaves were allowed to join in the celebrations. Some even managed to become involved in the sale of contraband goods forbidden under Muslim law, such as wine, tobacco, and spirits. Cervantes was less fortunate in his master than most. He was kept in chains and forced to find his own food. But he enjoyed the comradeship of his fellow ransom slaves, and together they spent their time talking, playing cards, negotiating for food, and, to judge from what the Captive says in *Don Quixote*, seeing how high they could jump in their chains. Cervantes, we know, also wrote poetry, much of it devotional. His muse had clearly survived the long confrontation with violence and death in Italy, and the enforced inactivity and resulting introspection of these years must amply have nurtured it.

The ransom trade between Spain and Algiers was brisk, with the most important prisoners fetching ransoms as high as fifty thousand ducats. Families were informed very quickly of the fate of their relatives — returning ex-prisoners were often entrusted with the messages — and of the amount of money needed to be found. This was normally then handed over to Spanish friars, at this period usually friars of the Mercedarian and Trinitarian orders, who specialized in ransoming activities. They carried the money to Algiers, effected the ransom, and returned with the freed prisoner, or prisoners, bearing with them for the families of new prisoners both bad news and the prospect of hope. Sometimes Christian slaves were exchanged for Muslim, for the Turks like the Christians were pledged to ransom their own soldiers. Alms had always been collected for the release of captives and later on various charitable organizations would be set up, centered in Italy, for the ransom of poor captives; but during the years Cervantes was in Algiers, poverty virtually meant permanent slavery with little hope of delivery. Cervantes himself was in the agonizing position of being deemed to be worth a ransom he knew his family could not easily pay. The ransoming of captives was a feature of all hostilities in the sixteenth century, and the proximity of Spain to the African coast ensured that it was a particular feature of the war, both formal and informal, between the Barbary states and the Peninsula. Captive Muslims became the slaves of Christian masters often as brutal as their Muslim counterparts, and the Christians were not above marauding expeditions of their own along the coast of North Africa. The shortage of convicts to man the galleys threatened to become crucial at times and by 1580 Algerine fishing boats — which were easy game — dared not put farther than half a league out to sea for fear of Christian privateers. The prospect of capture was, therefore, a constant threat to every soldier serving in the Mediterranean and to every traveler who voyaged its waters. The soldier, in theory at least, was ransomed automatically by the authorities, the traveler would expect to be allocated the sort of ransom his family could raise. The furthest thought from Cervantes's mind as he embarked for Spain must have been that the letters of recommendation intended to ensure a prosperous future for him would end up casting him into a limbo between slavery and freedom from which it would be five long years before he was delivered.

Reasonable as the conditions under which most slaves lived in Algiers were, overcrowding, hunger, and the inevitable physical brutality drove men to desperate action. Singly or in groups they frequently attempted to escape and sometimes they succeeded. Escape routes were set up with the help of renegades willing, for payment or for old times' sake, to forget their new allegiance for a while, or, less commonly, with that of Christian privateers. On one occasion years later, in 1595, a bold Valencian captain with a flourishing sideline in rescue operations would take on board no fewer than thirty-two refugees — Christian slaves, renegade Spaniards longing to return home, and Moors wishing to embrace Christianity — and carry them safely back to Valencia.

Cervantes's own exploits in this respect are worthy of the Scarlet Pimpernel himself. As a ransom slave he had little to do but brood on his predicament, witness the sufferings of his less fortunate companions, and dream of freedom. His dreams crystallized on at least four occasions into escape attempts, none of them successful and all characterized by their bold simplicity rather than by their cunning. There were two ways out of Algiers: by sea, which needed good organization and elaborate help, and by land, the simpler but more hazardous and less hopeful route.

Cervantes's first bid for freedom came early in 1576 and had little chance of success. He hired a Moor to guide him and some of his fellow prisoners along the coast to Oran, a Spanish possession. Once there they would without difficulty secure a passage to Spain. Cervantes does not tell us in the statement he signed on his release in 1580 whether the little group managed to divest themselves of their chains for the journey nor whether they carried sufficient supplies. He merely states cryptically that a few days after they set off the Moor disappeared. Since Oran was over two hundred miles away through difficult and hostile terrain, the Christians had no alternative if they wished to survive but to return to Algiers. Two features of this abortive flight from captivity are interesting. First, although the runaways included prisoners of higher military rank and social standing than himself, it was Cervantes who seems to have taken the

initiative in the escape attempt. Second, although simple in the extreme, the plan was not born of sheer bravado. As soon as their guide deserted them, the Spaniards
returned to Algiers and the survival it represented; presumably by giving themselves up, rather than allowing
themselves to be caught, they hoped to assuage their
owner's displeasure. In both respects this was to be the
pattern of Cervantes's subsequent bids for freedom.

In his statement of 1580, Cervantes claims to have been
"very badly treated" on his return, but as the Captive in
Don Quixote he holds he was never beaten or even
verbally abused by his master in spite of his provocative
behavior. Since in 1580 he patently wished to stress the
hardships of his captivity, and since it is difficult to see
why he should have later on wanted to gloss them over, it
seems likely that the rather vague term "badly treated"
referred to deprivations of some sort rather than to corporal punishment. We have it on good evidence that
throughout his captivity, Cervantes had to clothe and
feed himself, relying on the goodwill of Christian merchants with whom he built up large debts, so this neglect
was perhaps part of the punishment for his escape attempt. Certainly Dali Mami doubled his shackles, increased his guard, and restricted his movements more
severely. His time was still his own, however, and some
time before February 1577 he composed two complimentary sonnets dedicated to a fellow prisoner, an Italian
called Bartolomeo Ruffino who was whiling away his
captivity by writing an account of the siege and fall of
Tunis.

Meanwhile, back in Spain the Cervantes family had
not been idle. Their anguish on learning that both Miguel and Rodrigo were held captive in Algiers must have
been intense, not merely on account of the hardship and
possibly the danger of the young men's predicament, but

also on account of the excruciating difficulties it put them in. Finding one ransom would be difficult, finding two would be well nigh impossible. The family finances had deteriorated rather than improved, and in 1573 Andrea had set up as a seamstress to try and eke out a living, taking on a young girl as apprentice to help her. This was not the only way in which she was able to make ends meet, however, as we shall see.

The tenor of the Cervanteses' life while their sons were away fighting for their country can be gauged from a curious and complicated affair involving both Andrea and Magdalena. In the early 1570s Magdalena, then in her mid-to-late teens, became involved with a young gallant called Don Alonso Pacheco Portocarrero, son of Don Pedro Portocarrero, the man Don John of Austria left in charge of the garrison of La Goleta at Tunis after the Spaniards took the city in 1573. During their affair, or as a conclusion to it, Don Alonso promised Magdalena the sum of five hundred ducats, payable when he came into his inheritance on the death of his father. Since Don Pedro was in vigorous health, his son must have assumed that the day of reckoning was a comfortably long way off. When Don Pedro died in captivity in Turkey in the late spring of 1575 (after the fall of Tunis, Don John, wise after the event, claimed never to have thought much of him as a soldier), his son's bluff was called and in the May of that year Don Alonso signed a deed undertaking to pay the debt by 1 May 1576. By August, Magdalena had allowed herself to be talked into postponing the expiry date until Christmas 1580, although Don Alonso as a sign of good faith pledged the following month to pay his debt within two years, by September 1577. Whether Magdalena, by not suing Don Alonso, hoped to prolong the relationship or seek its renewal, who can say? Perhaps she was merely seeking to protect her reputation.

The whole plot thickens when we discover that on the very day — 1 August 1575 — that Magdalena signed her deed extending Don Alonso's breathing space to 1580, he signed another document before a different notary, acknowledging the debt of an identical sum of money — five hundred ducats — to Andrea, a debt incurred it seems in 1571, ostensibly over the purchase by Don Alonso of a gold necklace set with pearls, rubies, emeralds and diamonds, a heavy gold chain, a gold Agnus Dei, and a glass rosary. What are we to make of this? Did Andrea scrape a living when she had a young fatherless child to feed by selling jewels, as well as by taking in sewing? If so, was it through his business dealings with Andrea that Don Alonso met her younger sister Magdalena?

In the autumn of 1571, extraordinary as it may seem, Andrea had been involved in a law suit with Don Alonso's brother, Pedro, again over some money and jewels, though exactly who owed what to whom is not clear. The wording of Andrea's power of attorney suggests that Don Pedro was suing her, and perhaps it is not entirely fanciful to wonder whether Pedro was suing Andrea for the return of jewelry she had already sold to his brother. If true, this would imply that Pedro had been Andrea's admirer, at least, if not more. However, it may be unwise to take Alonso's jewelry explanation too seriously. Where would Andrea have come by the jewels (if not from Don Pedro) or the capital to buy them in the first place? It is well known that legal acknowledgments of debts, whether of usurer's debts or personal ones, were often couched in face-saving explanations and ambiguities, so is this a case in point? Many of Cervantes's commentators have taken Don Alonso's statement at face value, but if the debt was the result of a straightforward business negotiation, the wording of the deed is puzzling. It reads: "even if I were not obliged, as I am, to pay you the money, I freely grant it to you on account of my debts and obligations to you which amount to far more than five hundred ducats' worth." This surely smacks of something more than business. And had the debt been the result of some purely commercial transaction, would Andrea have been prepared to wait so patiently for payment? It is hard to see how, as a poor seamstress, she could ever have borne such a financial loss, were it indeed a real one. It was already four years since the debt had been incurred, and here in his deed of 1 August Don Alonso is promising to pay half by Christmas 1577 and half by Christmas 1578. In Magdalena's document that very same day, Christmas 1580 was originally Christmas 1578 too: Don Alonso hastily got it changed, obviously, when he realized how far he was committing himself. As far as we know for certain, neither sister ever got her money. Clearly Don Alonso was as close with his purse as he was free with his charms.

The fact that Don Alonso married in or around 1571 is perhaps significant. If he were having an affair with Andrea, as seems possible, the five hundred ducats were conceivably a peace offering on his marriage to another, more "suitable" woman. This is more feasible in my view than the conjecture that the jewels were real and a wedding gift to his bride. His fidelity to his wife subsequently appears as suspect as that to Andrea, for the debt to Magdalena is not easily susceptible of any explanation other than that soon after his marriage Don Alonso started seeing the teenage sister of the woman he had previously been involved with. Whatever the facts of the matter, whether Andrea had had an attachment with one of the brothers or both, it is not a very pretty picture that the fragmented evidence would seem to paint.

Years later, Cervantes implied that his two sisters — he calls them "maidens" — sacrificed their dowries to ransom him. It was a touchingly loyal view both of his sisters themselves and their financial standing. If the family was short of money, however, it was certainly not short on concern for the two young men or on energy in the struggle to secure their release. During 1576 Rodrigo *père* reported their capture to the Crusade Council, producing witnesses to give evidence of the brothers' service in Italy and their capture on board the *Sun*, in the hope of receiving a grant toward the ransoms. At this time the Mercedarian friars were in the very process of organizing a ransom expedition, raising money by collecting alms, and Rodrigo hoped to benefit from this and get his sons included on the list of captives to be negotiated for. In November, at the request of the authorities, he supplemented his statement with another containing further information.

The friars entrusted with the transaction set out from Spain at the end of March the following year. In the meantime, Rodrigo had been making strenuous but fruitless efforts to call in the debts owed him, including a substantial one of eight hundred ducats — the last vestige, probably, of Doña Leonor's legacy from her mother. The extent of the family's desperation may be deduced from the fact that Doña Leonor declared herself a widow in order the more easily to obtain sixty-odd ducats toward her sons' ransoms from the Crusade Council, which administered these grants. She was duly granted the money, with a year in which to produce proof that it was being put to the use for which it was intended; otherwise the money would have to be paid back. The situation was one of tantalizing agony, as overjoyed relief at obtaining some money, albeit under dangerously false pretenses, mingled with the anguish of knowing that unless enough, not just more, was found within the year, the grant would disappear and the outlook become as hopeless as ever. Doña Leonor's position was complicated by the fact that the sixty ducats were not hers to deploy as she wished, but designated to be allocated equally to both sons. However, the sixty ducats and the rest of the money the family had managed to scrape together by selling virtually everything they possessed were handed over to the Mercedarian friars to do the best they could with when their representatives left for Algiers in March 1577.

The negotiations for Miguel's release came to nothing. His master still clung to the belief that Miguel was an important man and the ransom money available was rejected as insufficient. However, Rodrigo's thirty ducats, together with what the friars were able to spare from their charitable funds, in the event brought the sum the family had managed to raise to the three hundred ducats needed to ransom him. A royal captive, his master the Pasha seems to have had a more realistic view of the Cervantes family's resources than Dali Mami. On 24 August 1577, therefore, Rodrigo with over a hundred other prisoners left Algiers for home, leaving Miguel behind for the Cervanteses to worry and scheme over. They reached the east coast of Spain five days later, and on 1 September attended a service of thanksgiving in the cathedral at Valencia.

Before he left for Madrid, Rodrigo, like every other released prisoner, obtained a certificate of ransom. This is what Doña Leonor needed to produce for the Crusade Council to show that the money she had been granted had been properly used. That she forgot to do so is clear from an order she received from the Council in February 1579 demanding the return of the sixty ducats; the wheels of Spanish administration, it will be seen, ground exceeding slow. Rodrigo's certificate she was able to produce, and she petitioned successfully for a stay of execution over Miguel's thirty ducats, with a view to their being transferred from the Mercedarians to the Trinitarians, who were shortly to undertake another ransom expedition. From her petition we discover that the ransom being asked all this time for Miguel amounted to almost six hundred ducats (five hundred gold escudos), twenty times as much as the grant from the Crusade Council.

On Rodrigo's departure Miguel must have realized that his chances of being ransomed in the near future were extremely thin indeed. It was probably now that he wrote his verse epistle to Mateo Vázquez, an acquaintance from his days in Madrid, by this time Spanish Secretary of State, asking for Vázquez's help. Rodrigo, perhaps, was entrusted with its delivery. Whether it ever reached its destination we cannot know. If it did it bore no fruit. Its tone, as it reviews his life, is one of deep depression. However, he could not have been entirely downcast, for he had worked out a plan of escape with the more fortunate Rodrigo before he left; it was a plan, in fact, of fairly long standing, to be executed probably by whichever of them escaped first. Cervantes's conduct in captivity appears to have been remarkably unselfish, but the ambitious nature of the plan arranged with Rodrigo must have been prompted as much by strategy as by goodwill. No one was going to send a vessel to rescue one or two prisoners; on the other hand, the prospect of a mass escape was one that might attract powerful sponsors. Accordingly, Rodrigo left Algiers bearing letters from two fellow prisoners, Don Antonio de Toledo and Don Francisco de Valencia, both Knights of St. John, addressed to the viceroys of Valencia, Mallorca, and Ibiza, asking for their support in organizing a frigate to sail to the Algiers coast and carry off a group of prisoners. According to Miguel later on, it was intended that these should include various leading Christians in captivity, gentlemen, professional men, and priests; men of a sort, in other words, to stir the interest of people back in Spain.

While Rodrigo worked to carry out his side of the arrangements, Miguel completed preparations back in Algiers. He had conceived the idea of a second escape attempt some time previously, deciding that he would need to find a place on the coast near Algiers where escaped prisoners might gather and, if necessary, hide until help arrived. Once this first major difficulty had been solved he would need to arrange for clandestine food supplies. The conditions under which he was by now living were less restrictive than they had been for a time after his first attempt at escape; perhaps he had deliberately lulled his master and guards into a false sense of security. As a result he managed to get in touch with a Navarrese gardener who worked on one of the beautiful and fertile estates along the coast, three miles or so east of the city. Here, on Miguel's instructions, fourteen Christian captives eventually gathered, escaping as and when they could. They sheltered in a cave in the gardens and with Juan the gardener's help, they were sent daily supplies by Cervantes, a Christian known as "El Dorador," or The Gilder, acting as intermediary. The risks involved in such a plan were very great, in spite of the fact that Dali Mami, now a Captain of the Sea, was absent from Algiers at this time, and the strain on Cervantes must have been enormous. By the end some of the runaway slaves had spent six months in their cave, emerging for fresh air only at night. Eight days before the frigate was due to arrive, Cervantes joined them.

All went according to plan. On the night of 28 September, the frigate, captained by a Mallorcan named Viana, himself a former slave, appeared offshore at the time arranged. The smell of freedom must have already been in the runaways' nostrils as they waited in the dark for the sailors to come ashore and pick them up. They waited in vain. Either the ship was seen from land by some Moors who raised the alarm, or the sighting of a fishing boat caused undue panic — both reasons are put forward by contemporary hearsay. Whatever the cause, the sailors took fright, and the frigate weighed anchor and made off. Two nights later it returned, and some of those on board seem to have gone ashore. They could not have seen the columns of Turkish and Moorish soldiers heading for the rendezvous. For El Dorador, either fearful of discovery or hopeful of a reward, had gone to Hassan Veneziano, the new Beglerbey or Pasha (Governor–General, strictly speaking, but King in all but name) of Algiers, declared his intention to renege and betrayed his fellow countrymen. The runaways were caught. So too were some at least of the rescuers; it is even possible that the rescue ship itself and all on board were taken, though Cervantes himself does not mention this.

After the elaborate preparations and the weeks of tension, Cervantes's sense of letdown and defeat must have been overwhelming. In the astonishingly brief space of four weeks, Rodrigo had managed to organize a rescue vessel to sail to the Algerian coast. It had arrived at the right place at the right time. Miguel for his part had successfully carried out his difficult and dangerous role, getting the prisoners too to the right place at the right time without discovery. That the whole operation should, by a hair's breadth of bad luck, have shattered into failure must really have persuaded him for a while that fate was against him.

Partly out of this fleeting sense of defeat, perhaps, he shouldered all the blame. Manacled hand and foot, he was taken before Hassan and interrogated, certain no doubt that this time he would not escape punishment as he had before and fully aware what that punishment would be — disfigurement or dismemberment, if not death. Hassan had the reputation of a brutal man. There can be no question that Cervantes's silence when ordered to reveal who had helped him carry out his plans saved the lives of a considerable number of people, although the poor gardener, Juan — obviously deeply implicated — was hung up by one foot until he died. Miraculously, Cervantes himself was again spared. His "importance" can be the only reason, for the view taken by some that Hassan was seduced into mercy by Cervantes's courage and attractive personality does not sit well with the Pasha's reputation; the execution or severe punishment of a man who carried letters of recommendation from Don John of Austria to the King of Spain might lead, after all, to serious trouble. Instead Cervantes was thrown into the bagnios to await suitable punishment and then handed back to Dali Mami.

It was either after this escape attempt or the next — the contemporary accounts are not at all clear — that Hassan bought Cervantes from Dali Mami for almost six hundred ducats. The ostensible motive for the purchase was to place the troublesome Spaniard under the strictest possible surveillance. Hassan, it is claimed, stated at the time that "as long as he had the maimed Spaniard in safe keeping, his Christians, his ships, and even the city itself would be safe, so greatly did he fear Miguel de Cervantes's tricks." There are, however, indications that he hoped to use Cervantes for another purpose. When Rodrigo's group had left for Spain the previous September, one of the Mercedarian friars involved in the ransom negotiations, Don Jorge del Olivar, had stayed behind as a voluntary hostage in exchange for some prisoners for whom a ransom was not forthcoming and who were consequently threatening to renege. Hassan Pasha desperately wanted to implicate the friar in Cervantes's escape attempt, probably in order to blackmail his order into paying an inflated ransom for him. Whether or not he was involved has never been established; probably not, in view of the fact that Cervantes makes no mention of his being so in the statement he made about his captivity in 1580. If he was, Cervantes resolutely denied it, and Don Jorge escaped the Pasha's wrath. That his position remained extremely vulnerable is clear from a petition sent by Cervantes and forty-two other prisoners to the Pope, Gregory XIII, and Philip of Spain in October 1578, begging that Don Jorge be ransomed. A similar petition to the General of his order bore fruit, and soon afterward Don Jorge was released for the sum of four thousand ducats down and another three thousand six hundred ducats in annual installments. Hassan's intimidation of the monk had paid off handsomely.

Long before this happened, Cervantes's disappointment over his own second bid for freedom had yielded to his natural optimism. Encouraged no doubt by his apparent immunity from severe punishment, five months after the cave episode, in early 1578, his indomitable will to escape led him to try again. This time he sent a Moor — an uncertain ally at best — along the coast to Oran with letters for the Spanish governor, Don Martín de Córdoba, and other dignitaries whose names were known to him, asking them to send a rescue party back to Algiers with the Moor to rescue him and three Spanish gentlemen from the bagnio. Simple and straightforward as the plan sounds, it was the least practical of all Cervantes's escape attempts, betraying a temporary loosening of his grasp on the realities of his situation worthy of Don Quixote himself, and poignantly reveals the power of his longing to be free. This attempt too was doomed to failure. The Moor was captured near Oran and taken back to Hassan Pasha in Algiers. He died, impaled, without breaking his trust, but Miguel's name was there on the letters for all to see and he was sentenced to two thousand strokes.

This was of course a death sentence, since a fraction of that number would have killed the strongest man. Cervantes's charmed immunity held and he received not one. The sentence and its remission were almost certainly a ploy on Hassan's part to force a ransom, at the highest possible price, and rid Algiers of the irksome slave. A similar ruse, as we saw, worked with Don Jorge del Olivar.

The problem was that Cervantes had no powerful and wealthy order behind him. We do not know whether news of the sentence hanging over Cervantes's head got back to his family in Spain, but it seems possible. Certainly in May 1578, Magdalena renewed her efforts to extract her five hundred ducats from Don Alonso Pacheco, who had obviously not paid up by September 1577 as he had promised. The official expiry date of the debt, it will be remembered, was to be Christmas 1580. But Magdalena and her father might well have been spurred by notice of Miguel's plight into trying to obtain the money sooner, although the fact that Don Alonso had remarried in the winter of 1577, after the death of his first wife, suggests, perhaps, that Magdalena's motive was a less magnanimous one. The family were undoubtedly doing all they could. Cashing in on her "widow's" status, Doña Leonor, with the help of a statement from the Duke of Sessa about her son's services to his country, even embarked upon an abortive and long-drawn-out attempt to raise money by acquiring and then selling at a profit a trading license for Algiers, trade with which was supposed to be severely limited and, therefore, closely controlled by the Council of War. It was a brave but foolish project, doomed to failure by Doña Leonor's poverty and inexperience, though she did succeed eventually, after her son's release, in finding a buyer for the permit. By June of 1578 a Valencian merchant, Hernando de Torres, had actually been commissioned to undertake Miguel's ransom. Andrea had committed herself to contributing two hundred ducats, possibly part of the five hundred she was still hoping to receive from Don Alonso, half of which should by now have been paid, the other half of which was due the following Christmas. The family had already deposited a much smaller sum with the Mercedarian friars for dispatch to Torres and, using all they possessed as collateral, they now bound themselves to pay back to Torres whatever money over and above these sums he should need to spend on Miguel's ransom. What prevented Torres from carrying out his commission is not revealed. If Andrea's money was not forthcoming, owing to Don Alonso's reluctance to pay his debts, perhaps the merchant felt he stood to lose too much by the transaction.

The sentence of two thousand strokes seems to have had a sufficiently chastening effect on Cervantes to persuade him to put thoughts of escape out of his mind for a time. Over a year passed by without incident, a year spent, like most of his time in captivity, in talking, dreaming, and writing verse, as well as in keeping himself alive by cajoling merchants to lend him money to survive. The news of the deaths, only two months apart in October and December of 1578, of his two heroes, Don John of Austria and the Duke of Sessa, must have been a bitter blow when it arrived. Don John's death in particular severely affected Christian morale in Algiers, and we have Cervantes's own testimony, in his play *The Traffic of Algiers,* that slaves were taunted in the streets with the hopelessness of their position, now that their glamorous young leader was gone.

By September 1579, however, Cervantes was once more thinking in terms of freedom, obviously believing with Don Quixote that escaping was the duty of the prisoner — "for liberty and honor one can and must risk one's life." He had met in Algiers a renegade from Granada, formerly called the Licentiate Girón, who was beginning, Cervantes had heard, to show signs of regretting his change of faith and wanting to return to Spain. Discovering that Abdaharraman (Girón's new Muslim name) was known as a man of reliable character, Cervantes seized his chance. At his instigation, Girón, with the financial backing of a Valencian trader then in Algiers called Onofré Exarque, arranged for the purchase of an armed frigate. Cervantes himself contacted some sixty fellow captives, once again people of some standing of the sort, one imagines, who could afford to reimburse the obliging Exarque, and bade them hold themselves ready. It was a sound plan and deserved to succeed. But once again the would-be runaways were betrayed.

Breakouts, successful and unsuccessful, as we saw earlier, were a commonplace of slave life in Algiers. Only the strange, hybrid flux of the city's population made them possible. It must be rare for a prisoner of war to find himself surrounded in the enemy's stronghold by fellow countrymen and coreligionists freely trading, by people of divided allegiance and by others with no allegiance at all except to Mammon. Not often is the city itself his prison, where he may move about, albeit manacled and guarded, in his daily work or in his negotiations for supplies. Yet the social, religious, and commercial stewpot of Algiers that made the escape attempts possible also made them hazardous in the extreme, as friends turned overnight into foes, confidants into traitors. And Cervantes enjoyed by now the reputation of a daring, resolute, and dedicated rebel. The testimony of his fellow prisoners shows that he was known, liked, and admired throughout Algiers, and such reputations breed envy and resentment. But exactly why the obnoxious Doctor Juan Blanco de Paz, an unfrocked Dominican friar from Sala- manca, should have hated Cervantes enough to betray him is unfathomable. Perhaps Cervantes committed the unforgivable offense of not including him on the list of his sixty candidates for escape. But betray him he did, first, according to Cervantes, by sending a Florentine renegade named Cayban to Hassan Pasha with the infor- mation, then later confirming it himself. Whether it was quite as overt and deliberate a piece of treachery as this is uncertain and unimportant; the end result was the same. Rumor in Algiers had it that Blanco de Paz was re- warded with a gold coin and a jar of lard.

In the hope of catching them all red-handed, Hassan did not flush out the conspirators immediately, but word got out that the plot was known. Blanco de Paz, in an attempt to divert attention away from himself, accused a Doctor Domingo Becerro of the treachery, and, in a show of righteous indignation aimed at giving his accusation credence, even threatened to strike him down. Cervantes claimed later that Exarque, alarmed at the possibility of being implicated by Cervantes, should he confess all under torture, offered to pay his ransom and get him out of Algiers on a vessel preparing to leave. Cervantes re- fused, reassuring Exarque that nothing would make him talk, and went into hiding instead. If true, these were brave, even foolhardy, words. Cervantes, we know for cer- tain, with the help of his protector Diego Castellano, who had been one of those intended for the escape ship, did go to the trouble of sending messages of reassurance to his fellow conspirators from his hiding place. Since Cervantes could not have been sure whether or not any names other than his own had been given to Hassan, it looks as though he had decided not to risk the consequence to his fellow countrymen of escaping himself. If he stayed instead to shoulder the blame, he might succeed, with his proven knack of avoiding punishment, both in staying alive himself and distracting attention from the others. If these were indeed his motives, they do him great credit. That they were is suggested by the fact that he gave himself up immediately when Hassan published a proclamation stating that whoever was harboring him would, if discovered, be put to death. Diego Castellano himself testified to this.

With his hands tied behind his back and a noose around his neck, Cervantes was subjected to a threatening and abusive interrogation by Hassan. The Pasha was unable to get him to admit anything other than that he, together with four other Christians now free (convenient but spurious scapegoats), had alone been involved. The renegade Girón accordingly got off with exile from Algiers and Onofré Exarque sailed away unscathed. As for Cervantes himself, thanks not only to the intercession of a friend of Hassan's, a renegade Captain from Murcia called Maltrapillo who was familiar with Cervantes's high reputation in the city, but also, on the evidence of one observer, to the bewildering bravado of Cervantes's replies, his life was spared. He was, however, laden with chains and confined to the prison for Moorish convicts in the palace, where he languished for the next five months. Removed now from the congenial company of most of his fellow Christians in captivity, a considerable number of whom had been men of learning and letters, awaiting he knew not what fate, his thoughts of Blanco de Paz must have been bitter indeed. But the unprincipled doctor had not finished with him yet.

At this juncture Cervantes's plight must have appeared to him quite hopeless. He had attempted and failed four times to escape; as a result he was regarded as a dangerous man, not likely to be given the chance to make another bid for freedom. To make matters worse, Hassan, he learned, would soon be leaving for Constantinople where he had been recalled. If he took Cervantes with him along with his other slaves, any chance of Cervantes's ever seeing Spain again could be forgotten. His state of mind may readily be deduced from a letter he sent on 6 November to the Sicilian poet Antonio Veneziani, a fellow prisoner to whom Cervantes had promised some verses in praise of the Sicilian's constancy in love, and who subsequently repaid his friend with a suitably grateful sonnet. The short epistle begins, "I assure you on my word as a Christian that I am so beset with imaginings that I have been unable to execute as I would have liked these lines I send you." He then proceeds with melancholy dignity to ask the recipient's pardon and to promise to write him, at a time of greater composure, some lines in praise of his mistress Celia.

By the time of the fourth escape attempt, however, things were at last beginning to move back home. Doña Leonor, as we saw, had succeeded in getting the grant of thirty-odd ducats for Miguel's ransom transferred to the Trinitarian friars, who were planning a ransom expedition. On 31 July 1579 in Madrid, Doña Leonor, still passing as a widow, handed over a total of two hundred and fifty ducats to the two friars, Juan Gil and Antonio de la Bella, who were to conduct the negotiations. On the same day Andrea was able to hand over another fifty ducats. The order would, they hoped, supply any amount outstanding from the alms collected for the expedition. That the Cervantes family had by now lost touch with Miguel is clear, for they assumed him to belong still to Dali Mami; they were not even sure he was still alive. On 4 September the Crusade Council handed over their contribution — four hundred and seventy-five ducats, not in the circumstances a very significant sum — to the expedition. The order continued to collect alms, and the friars eventually sailed for Algiers the following May, by which time Cervantes had been transferred from the palace prison back to the bagnios.

By 3 August 1580, one hundred and eight prisoners had been ransomed. They set sail on that day for Valencia with Antonio de la Bella, arriving there two days later in a prodigious storm. Juan Gil stayed behind to complete the negotiations. Between 8 August and 8 September he bargained successfully for seven more prisoners, and Cervantes himself acted as witness for one of the deeds of release. What anguish must he have felt as he did so! The ransoming friars always operated, understandably, on a basis of quantity rather than quality, ransoming as many slaves as they could with the money available. The operation was a complex one, with funds deriving as they did from so many different sources and destined as they were for different ends, and careful calculations and hard bargaining were necessary to spend the money to best possible effect. Juan Gil carried with him only three hundred ducats designated specifically for Cervantes, and the asking price was almost six hundred. Yet the plight of Hassan's slaves was becoming urgent, for he was to leave for Constantinople on 19 September, and so Juan Gil concentrated on bargaining with the redoubtable Pasha. Hassan, however, claimed that all his slaves were gentlemen and swore that he would not settle for less than six hundred ducats for any of them (insisting as usual on payment in gold escudos). He would, in any case, need galley slaves for the trip to Constantinople and was, therefore, not set upon selling them all.

For Miguel, the conclusion, when it came, was hair-raising in its closeness to disaster. On 19 September Cervantes, in irons, was taken on board along with Hassan's other slaves. As the sails were being raised, Juan Gil, unable to meet the sums being asked for some of the other Christians on board, turned up with the six hundred ducats asked for Cervantes, the family's contribution having been supplemented by two small sums from the private and general alms at his disposal and by funds destined for the ransom of Christians he had been unable to trace. But even now there was a hitch: Hassan was adamant that the money should be in gold. And so as the minutes ticked away Juan Gil had to use up more of his precious funds buying gold escudos from the traders at an unfavorable rate of exchange. At last, however, he was able to rush back to the galleys clutching his bag of gold coins. Cervantes, described in the deed of ransom as "of middling stature, heavily bearded and with maimed left hand and arm," was immediately set free. He had been a captive for almost exactly five years.

Another month was to pass before Cervantes sailed for Spain. In the meantime he had an urgent task to perform. After Blanco de Paz's betrayal of Cervantes, news of his treachery had not surprisingly raced like a forest fire through the Christian community in Algiers. Posing now as a general commissary of the Inquisition, he attempted to restore his own reputation by impugning Cervantes's character. In his assumed role as Inquisition investigator —for which, when subsequently challenged by the worthy Juan Gil, he could produce no proof although he had had titulary connections with the Inquisition in León before his capture—he set about preparing a file on Cervantes's activities in Algiers, trying to intimidate and to bribe witnesses into giving evidence against him. Blanco de Paz's motive is transparent. If he succeeded in slurring Cervantes's good name, then anything Cervantes said against him in Algiers or, if he were ransomed, in

Spain, would be attributed to spite and be dismissed as untrue. It was doubly important to Cervantes, therefore, that Blanco de Paz be stopped and that the truth about both men be firmly established. Working on the basis that attack would be the best form of defense, Cervantes decided to set up a private inquiry and accordingly spent his time after his release in organizing an official document of exoneration. First, on 10 October in the presence of Friar Juan Gil, he deposed with Pedro de Rivera, the notary apostolic in Algiers, an extended statement, consisting of twenty-five points, about his "captivity, life, and customs." Among other things it unequivocally accused Blanco de Paz of treachery. Twelve witnesses then testified to the truth of the deposition and finally, on 22 October, Juan Gil himself added his support, testifying to Cervantes's good character and to the reliability of the whole inquiry.

This document is the source of most of the information we possess about Cervantes's life in captivity. Ironically, Blanco de Paz's attempt to blacken his name not only ensured that these five years represent one of the best documented periods of Cervantes's life, but stamped him as a man of unquestionable integrity. The twelve witnesses differ in the length and depth of their acquaintance with Cervantes's story, and sometimes in the details they give, but they are unanimous in their depiction of Cervantes as a good and honorable man, stressing his popularity, his kindness to his fellow prisoners, and his unfailing courage in shielding them from punishment. The Spanish monk Diego de Haëdo, in his *Topography and General History of Algiers,* published during Cervantes's lifetime, claimed of Cervantes that "if his luck had equalled his courage, industry, and ingenuity, Algiers would by now be Christian, for he aspired to nothing less than this." In his admiration for Cervantes,

Haëdo allowed himself to get carried away. But however one looks at it, Cervantes's record in Algiers was a remarkable one. The repeated escape attempts, the resistance to intimidation and threats of torture, and the constant support for his fellow captives, reveal a character of unusual initiative, stamina and energy, persuasive as well as resolute, cautious as well as daring, realistic as well as optimistic, above all a character capable of standing up to adversity in a way few men can.

In fact his behavior at Lepanto and during his captivity in Algiers makes one wonder whether Cervantes was not one of that restless band of individuals who respond better to war than to peace, who thrive on challenge, adversity, and danger. His years in Algiers reveal him as a very special man and yet nothing in his life subsequently bears out the distinctive personal promise of these years, except perhaps the patience in adversity that he was later to see as the enduring legacy of his captivity. It is as if, deprived in his daily life of the right sort of stimulus, these outstanding qualities remained dormant, surfacing only in the imaginative world he created with his pen to compensate for the drab reality of his existence; as if the drama and richness of his experience in Algiers, the deep familiarity he acquired with all manner and variety of men, including himself, could find outlet and continuity only in a creativity which, while it fed off life, was superior to it.

Be this as it may, after the character inquiry was over and the deposition with its supporting testimonies had been duly made, Cervantes had no thought but to put the last five years behind him as quickly as possible and make for home. He sailed for Spain on 24 October with five other ransomed Christians. The ship put in at Denia on the Valencian coast a few days later. The moment he stepped foot on his native soil — unseen for ten years or more — must have been one of the sweetest of his life, and no doubt like his hero in *The Generous Lover* he fell and kissed the ground in an ecstasy of relief. As he says through the Captive's lips in *Don Quixote,* "there is in my opinion no joy on earth comparable to regaining the liberty one has lost."

FOUR

✿

New Beginnings: Of Love and Literature

BEFORE MAKING HIS WAY TO MADRID, Cervantes spent a month or so in Valencia settling his affairs; his captivity and his ransom had been heavily subsidized and arrangements for repayment had to be made. But mindful of his parents' anxiety as well as of the urgency of his financial responsibilities, he wrote to his family by way of a fellow ex-prisoner traveling to the capital. His father Rodrigo immediately initiated the proceedings necessary to petition for a grant from the Crusade Council toward the debts Miguel had incurred in Algiers. The sum involved could not have been a small one, for as well as the extra ransom money obtained for him at the last minute by the good Trinitarian friars there were the five years of loans by means of which Cervantes had kept himself in food. By mid-December Miguel himself was in Madrid filing his own statement and witnessing that of a friend in the same position.

By now the first flush of delight at being free must have evaporated and been replaced by more complex feelings. Cervantes was, after all, thirty-three years old, with nothing to show for the previous ten years but a mutilated hand and a depressing list of debts. The captaincy in pursuit of which he had set out for Spain five years before was now a hopeless dream: almost ten years had passed since Lepanto, and nothing suffers more from enforced inactivity than the reputation of the warrior. He had no professional training to fall back on. The future was consequently a worrying blank. Even his pleasure at being reunited with his family must have swiftly turned to something like dismay. Ten years leave their mark, and he found his parents showing the signs of age and anxiety, his father now distressingly deaf, and the family as a whole more impoverished than they had been before he went away.

In their struggle to live a decent life, of course, the Cervanteses were by no means alone, for the second half of the sixteenth century in Spain was a time of drastic inflation. The problem was a European one as the demographic pressure of rising populations increased the demand for food, housing, clothes, and other goods, but Spain, owing to the direct inflationary effects of the influx of precious metals from America, was more seriously affected than any other country, and in the course of the century prices increased eightfold. The precise social consequences of this economic crisis in Spain are not easy to determine, but the broad effect was that the gap between rich and poor yawned wider even than before. Property was concentrated in the hands of a small number of very wealthy aristocrats, and, as rents and prices rocketed, the great landowners and the most powerful merchants flourished; the great mass of the peasants, on the other hand, who bore the main burden of crushing taxation, saw the purchasing power of their wages fall remorselessly from year to year. The hardest-hit of all, however, were probably those in the middle — the small traders and landowners, the minor officials, the lower clergy and professional men, those whose incomes failed to keep up with the prices of the commodities they depended upon, and whose former standards of living consequently melted away before their eyes. By May 1581, soon after Cervantes's return to Spain, the situation was bad enough to provoke an engineer of repute to state: "The prices of goods have risen so steeply that *seigneurs,* gentlemen, commoners, and clergy cannot live on their incomes." The inevitable result was a flight from the land and a corresponding increase in the number of destitutes, in the shape of beggars, prostitutes, and rogues, who swarmed round the towns like wasps round an empty jam jar. Cervantes's emaciated hidalgo hero and the tricksters, thieves, and ruffians who people his exemplary tales and his one-act plays are the products as much of observation as imagination.

As a surgeon, dependent on other people's prosperity insofar as he worked at all, Cervantes's father belonged to one of the worst affected sections of society. For him and his family, life was an unremitting and exhausting struggle against the insidious effects of poverty upon a gentility that was swiftly degenerating into a hollow sham. The record of their life is that of an endless battle to repay and recover debts. For Miguel's brother, Rodrigo, the solution to the future had been a straightforward one: he had resumed his life as a soldier and was to remain one. Andrea since the summer of 1577 had been living on her own with her small daughter in a rented house, the more easily, one assumes, to lead her life of tangled involvements. At some stage before 1605, she would become the wife and then the widow of an unidentified Florentine called Sante Ambrosio. As for Magdalena, who since 1575 had been going under the name Magdalena Pimentel de Sotomayor — how she came by it has never been established — Cervantes returned home to find that she had embarked upon a relationship with a Basque named Juan Pérez de Alcega. Alcega had been deputy controller to

Philip II's fourth wife, Anne of Austria, until she died in October 1580, and he subsequently became controller in the Infantas' household. However deep Magdalena's emotional attachment to Alcega, it is clear that as a bachelor in his position, although no longer young, he represented a very good match indeed, and she did in fact receive and accept a promise of marriage from him. By the summer of 1581, however, he had changed his mind. Undaunted by this reversal of her hopes, Magdalena threatened to petition the Vicar–General of Madrid to compel Alcega to marry her. Alcega, evidently as determined now to avoid the match as Magdalena was to enforce it, offered financial compensation of three hundred ducats for his breach of promise, and Magdalena cut her losses and accepted. She received one hundred ducats down and the promise of payment of the rest within the year. The Cervantes sisters were singularly unfortunate in their choice of men, and the pattern of their financial dealings with the philanderers they took for lovers strongly suggests that gullibility rather than greed was the key to their liaisons.

Doña Leonor's submission of Miguel's certificate of ransom to the Crusade Council in February 1581 closes the door for us on a crucial period of his life. For him the door cannot have closed, for his Algerian debts survived to rob him of his peace of mind. Their existence made employment imperative. Without his letters of recommendation for a captaincy — even if he had managed to hang on to them they would have been five years out of date — the idea of resuming his military life as a common soldier did not appeal. In 1580 his brother, Rodrigo, had marched to Portugal with the Spanish army sent to secure the Portuguese throne for Philip; soon he and the army would be sailing for the Azores to deal with the last vestiges of resistance from the Portuguese and their French allies. But Miguel, six years older on his return from captivity than his brother had been and with a damaged hand, obviously felt that for him the footloose, carefree life of the soldier was over.

That he did, however, try his luck with the King on the strength of his war record and his Algiers document is clear. For he followed Philip to Thomar in Portugal, where the Spanish monarch was formally recognized as King in April 1581. There Cervantes petitioned for a post, only to be fobbed off with a temporary appointment as King's messenger. On 21 May 1581 he received fifty ducats on account to enable him to sail to Oran to pick up dispatches. By 26 June he was back in Cartagena, where he received the remaining fifty ducats due to him for expenses before setting off to report back to the King in Lisbon, described by Cervantes in *The Trials of Persiles and Sigismunda* as "the greatest city in Europe." For several months he hung around the court in Lisbon hoping for something to turn up, possibly whiling away the empty days working on what was to be his first major publication, the pastoral romance *The Galatea*. He applied for a post in America and in late 1581 or early 1582 was sent by an influential official of his acquaintance to Madrid to petition the Council of the Indies for a post in the New World. He was assured, however, that there were no vacancies at present, though the next caravel might conceivably bring news of one. But no news to Cervantes's advantage ever arrived from the other side of the Ocean Sea and for the time being this ended Cervantes's career as a public servant.

At this point Cervantes disappears for a while from sight, though fragments of information here and there allow us to piece together a rough picture of his and his family's activities during the next few years. In August 1582, Doña Leonor was still trying, with the help of a merchant friend of Miguel's in Valencia, to dispose of the trading license she had obtained to help with his ransom. The merchant, Juan de Fortuny, was almost certainly one of those to whom Miguel owed money; and Doña Leonor was presumably hoping in this way to reduce her son's debts. Miguel himself was in Madrid during these years but how he lived we do not know for certain, though it seems likely that he concentrated his efforts largely upon writing for the stage. In 1583, at Magdalena's request, he pawned for thirty ducats five rolls of furnishing taffeta given her years before by Giovanni Locadelo (she was to sell the taffeta to the pawnbroker two years later for over four times as much), so obviously the family circumstances continued much as before. The news that Rodrigo's military pay had been supplemented in recognition of his bravery in action in the Azores boosted family morale a little; even more so his promotion soon afterward to second lieutenant. Miguel's own pleasure at his brother's success must have been tinged with some regret for his own lost hopes of military success, but by now Cervantes, disillusioned with the rewards of heroism and public service, had thrown himself into a very different sphere of activities. He was renewing old literary acquaintances — Francisco de Figueroa, Pedro Laínez, Juan Rufo — making new ones and gradually, perhaps even unconsciously, committing himself to a life of literary involvement.

This period of his life, however closed to us where his routine existence is concerned, was in many ways an extremely full and productive one. Around this time he had an affair with a young married woman called Ana de Villafranca, or Ana Franca de Rojas, as she was sometimes known, who subsequently gave birth to his only daughter, Isabel de Saavedra, brought up by her mother and putative father, Alonso Rodríguez. The dates of the affair are obscure. In June 1605 Isabel would give her age as twenty, but since in 1639 she would swear to being only forty years old (having obviously inherited the Cervantes women's poor memory), her evidence is not entirely reliable. However, if Isabel was not twenty in 1605, we can be certain she was older, not younger; this means she was born between 1581, when Cervantes returned to Spain, and 1585. However, on 12 December 1584, Cervantes married another woman, and since it is unlikely, if not impossible, that a man with a new bride would immediately embark upon an affair with someone else — and Cervantes's nature was certainly not that of the philanderer — Ana almost certainly predated Cervantes's marriage. As this took place at the very end of 1584, Isabel's claim to be twenty in 1605 would fit in with the conjecture that her conception, perhaps even her birth, preceded Cervantes's commitment to his fiancée: if she were born in late 1584 (the feast of St. Isabel was on 19 November) she would still have been only twenty in the June of 1605.

The nature of Cervantes's relationship with Ana is unfathomable, although liaisons of the sort were run-of-the-mill among the theatrical people whose company Cervantes was keeping at the time. She does not seem to have found her way into his poetry, but then love poetry was never an absorbing interest of his. And although it would be highly dangerous to assume from this that love played no important role in his life, it is nevertheless true that the relationships he depicts in his writings tend to be either highly romanticized or sordidly materialistic, as though he himself never managed satisfactorily to combine reality and dream. With his stutter and his shattered hand, of course, he was not cut out to play Lothario.

As for his wife, the traditional view is that Cervantes's marriage to Catalina de Salazar y Palacios was not a love match, a view based on the fact that the pair for long periods of time led relatively independent lives. But even if we grant the probability that time soon revealed an incompatibility that matured eventually into the "calm, secure companionship" which Don Quixote recommends as being preferable to the unsuitable love match (Part II, chap. xix), it is difficult to see why Cervantes should have married Catalina at all if not for love, or something which for a while resembled it.

Certainly Catalina was no great social or financial catch. She came of respectable, moderately prosperous country stock, of genteel descent on the paternal side; but her ineffective father, although he owned a house in nearby Toledo, could not even sign his own name (neither could her mother, but that was normal) and he had died in 1584 laden with debts. Cervantes's own eligibility, of course, was decidedly unimpressive, and Catalina's mother could not have been overjoyed at the prospect of her daughter's marrying a struggling writer from the capital, impoverished, maimed, and but three years short of forty. On the other hand, in the eyes of a widow with two young sons of seven and three to bring up, no respectable suitor who could provide the standard marriage settlement of one hundred ducats could have been unwelcome. There is no proof that the couple married without their families' blessing, as is sometimes suggested. On the contrary, Catalina's uncle, Juan de Palacios, officiated at the ceremony.

Catalina, for her part, had two things obviously in her favor. First there were the small parcels of land she had inherited in her native Esquivias, a flourishing, wine-producing village of some twenty-eight dwellings, to the south of Madrid in La Mancha. Then there was her youth — she was eighteen years old when Cervantes married her in the village church on 12 December 1584. But while her property must certainly have seemed a welcome bonus — and one day, after her mother's death, there would be more — it is not easy to believe that the man who had not long since completed a pastoral romance exploring the intricacies of a spiritualized concept of perfect human love would have sold himself for a small orchard, a few olive trees and vines, some furniture (including a cradle, never to be used), food and linen, four bee hives, a cockerel, and forty-five hens. The income from the land was in any case negligible. Catalina's youth, one suspects, was a different matter. To Cervantes, at thirty-seven, with years of hardship and disappointment behind him, living surrounded by the sordid sophistication of the capital and emerging from a very unspiritual relationship with a married woman, the simple attractions of rural life and of a fresh young face and body must have seemed to offer a promise of renewed hope and vigor. His courtship of Catalina followed the completion of *The Galatea* — it is highly unlikely that she actually inspired it as many have claimed — and Cervantes's exalted state of mind and his mood of fervent aspiration as he traced the tortuous loves of his pastoral heroes and heroines, must surely have lingered on to affect his vision of Catalina and the life she offered. His decision to marry her may well have been an impetuous one, for there is no record of his ever having been in Esquivias before the September of 1584, when he went there to help Doña Juana Gaitán, widow of his poet friend Pedro Laínez, arrange the publication of a *cancionero,* or song book, edited by her late husband. Who knows, perhaps Doña Juana acted as matchmaker.

At the time of the wedding, *The Galatea* had been finished for about a year. It passed the censor on 1 February 1584, and four months later Cervantes had found a publisher, Blas de Robles, who paid him 1,336 *reales* outright for the manuscript and copyright. For an unknown writer this bizarrely precise sum was by no means a negligible one, but if Miguel had no other means of support, it was far from being an adequate income to live on, and most of it probably went toward payment of the endless debts which alone made life viable for so many people at the time. There was subsequently the marriage settlement too to find, of course, but perhaps some timely financial recognition from Cardinal Colonna, to whom Cervantes dedicated the work, helped here. Ascanio Colonna was a young Italian Maecenas and scholar, then resident in Alcalá and later on to become viceroy of Aragon. In dedicating *The Galatea* to him, Cervantes was angling, perhaps, for the sort of patronage enjoyed by his friend, the poet Luis Gálvez de Montalvo, who had recently entered Colonna's employ. If so, he angled in vain. As for Blas Robles, his willingness to pay Cervantes such a sum in advance of publication is an indication both of his belief in the book's worth and of the standing enjoyed by the pastoral genre at the time. He knew it would sell and sell it did, albeit modestly.

The time has come to say something of this, Cervantes's first real publication. Of all his works it is the most remote and on the face of it may strike us as an odd vehicle for the pent-up outpourings of a middle-aged man recently restored to a normal existence after ten years of experience of a life that was at best rough and ready, at worst primitive and brutal. Yet for this very reason it was in a way perhaps a necessary exorcism of the past, a healing journey away from the worst in life into the best, an examination, after seeing how low man can sink, of how high he may reach. *The Galatea* is in its way a celebration of love and friendship, and Cervantes had seen his fill of the consequences of hate and enmity, real and purely formal.

Around the middle of the sixteenth century the pastoral romance had replaced the chivalric romance as the darling of Spanish *littérateurs,* although the vogue for the chivalric was to survive almost unabated among the Spanish reading public for another fifty years or so. Ever since the publication in Italy in 1504 of Sannazaro's *Arcadia,* the vogue for the pastoral, in prose and poetry, had gathered momentum in Spain. The secret of its appeal, almost incomprehensible to modern taste, lay in its combination of two of the principal preoccupations of the Renaissance — nature and love. According to Neoplatonic theory, love was the controlling force of a universe (quite literally what made the world go round), which in its beauty reflected the divine love responsible for its creation. Fascinated by the problem of exactly how love between man and woman fitted into this exalted scheme, writers explored the concept of an idealized human love against the harmonious backdrop of an idealized nature, casting the shepherd — as became the gentle and relaxed nature of his calling — as protagonist, and drawing for support on whichever theorist best suited their particular purpose. The shepherds and shepherdesses, as they listen to one another's stories of tragic or unrequited love, ponder the seemingly indissoluble conflict between human nature and human aspiration, between the theory and practice of perfect love. The mood is one of self-preoccupation and frustration, the tone is languid yet emotionally charged, the overall effect is cerebral, for the characters, their experiences, and their words are all the prefigurations of a controlling idea. The shepherds and shepherdesses bear no resemblance, needless to say, to any that ever guarded sheep. They certainly do not spend "most of the day delousing themselves or mending their sandals" in the way real shepherds do, as Berganza disarmingly points out in *The Dogs' Colloquy.* For the most part, they are the author's own literary friends and acquaintances, thinly disguised with pastoral pseudonyms; the pastoral romance, in other words, was a *roman à clef,* another reason for its appeal.

The best, fully developed pastoral romance in Spain is Gil Polo's *Diana in Love* (1564), the continuation of a highly successful romance, *The Diana* (1559?), by Jorge de Montemayor, who propounded a view of love that Polo considered misleadingly self-indulgent by purist Neoplatonic standards and, therefore, decided to correct. Cervantes's contribution to the debate, while serious, is in the main unremarkable. He supports Polo's contention that love to be perfect must be subject to reason, but is less austere than his predecessor in his view of the relationship between true love and suffering: for Polo, true love was by definition totally serene. Like the others of its kind, the book's prose is interspersed with verse — over five thousand lines of it (the songs often summing up the theory of love being acted out by the characters), and its structure is the usual one of a succession of stories and interludes featuring various pairs of lovers, held loosely together by the relationship between Galatea herself and the shepherd who loves her, Elicio. While most of the verse is at best competent, at worst flat-footed to a degree, the prose, though sometimes wordy, is fluent and clear; and, straightjacketed though the dialogue is by the convention Cervantes follows, it betrays occasionally something of the penetration and insight we associate with the great Cervantes. The narrative is controlled and reasonably well-sustained, if ultimately frustrating: it closes with a cliff-hanger that is never resolved, for the continuation Cervantes promised was never written. So that even at the conclusion of the sixth and last part, Elicio and Galatea, far from enjoying the proper reward of their pure and faithful love, are still beset with troubles, faced

with the prospect of Galatea's enforced marriage to another shepherd — and a Portuguese shepherd at that.

The Galatea was not only Cervantes's first real bid for
recognition as a serious writer but also his first attempt at
an extended prose narrative, and although it deals with a
subject — love and marriage — in which Cervantes was
very deeply interested throughout his writing life, it is
clear from his prologue to the work that he regarded it in
part as a sort of apprenticeship, especially in his mastery
of language. This prologue in fact reveals him as being
already a self-conscious writer of serious stylistic purpose,
aware of the enormous richness and fecundity of his native tongue and determined to be part of the contemporary movement to dignify it. It also reveals him to be
alive to the painful dichotomy that every true artist
knows to exist between self-expression and self-exposure,
between the need to communicate and the desire to do
himself justice. His own mood here seems to be one of
optimism, of modest satisfaction with what has been accomplished, and quiet confidence that better things are to
come.

He implies in this prologue that the book had been
finished for some time before he submitted it for publication and it is not at all unlikely that he had conceived the
idea of writing it — and even scribbled down jottings for
it — while still in captivity. If he did embark upon it after
his release, then his enforced leisure yielded ample time
for literary activity. These years represent in this respect
a crossroad in Cervantes's life. Had he managed to secure
a position of sufficient permanency on his return to
Spain, the course of his career might well have been a
very different one. As it was he found himself with time
to read, to write, and to mingle in literary circles, to
reacquire the habits of mind and develop the interests
that his ten years as a soldier and slave had inevitably inter-

rupted. *The Galatea* itself reveals a sound familiarity with Neoplatonist theory as well as Ciceronian rhetoric and its very existence presupposes a close acquaintance with the pastoral genre and probably with Sannazaro himself, whose work Cervantes after his years in Italy would have been able to read in the original Italian. The complimentary sonnets to the author which, after the manner of the day, precede the text of *The Galatea*, as well as the references to him we come across in the work of other poets, show that Cervantes was well known to other literary practitioners; and the extended survey he gives, in "Caliope's Song" in the book, of the poets of his time — many now forgotten — clearly reveals that poetry was an absorbing interest. On the basis of a remark made by Cervantes in his prologue, *The Galatea* would appear to be, like other pastoral romances, a roman à clef, and efforts have been made to identify the romance's characters with various of his literary contemporaries. Some of the owners of the names put forward — the famous statesman/poet Diego Hurtado de Mendoza, who died in 1575, for example — Cervantes could have known only by repute; but that he was beginning to establish himself in literary society there can be no doubt. In a work published shortly before *The Galatea*, Pedro de Padilla's *Spiritual Garden*, he is even referred to as "one of the famous poets of Castile," though no doubt gratitude as well as admiration inspired this excessive praise: Cervantes had contributed some complimentary verses to the volume. At the time the poet's standard way of promoting his own interests was to praise his rivals, in a ritual of reciprocal back-scratching.

It is significant that several of the poets mentioned by Caliope in her song are known to us now as dramatists. Any devotee of poetry was almost by definition a devotee of the theater, which was poetry in action, and Cervantes's commitment to the idea of a theatrical career dates back to these years after his release when he mingled with poet-dramatists and actors and no doubt frequented the theater as a spectator himself, as strongly drawn still to its power and glamor as he had been as a boy when he saw Lope de Rueda perform. How early this commitment bore fruit is not certain, but on 5 March 1585, soon after his marriage, he undertook to provide a theatrical company manager named Gaspar de Porras with two plays, one to be called *The Comedy of Confusion,* later judged by him to be the best he wrote, the other *The Treaty of Constantinople and Death of Selim.* He was to receive twenty ducats each for them, twenty down and twenty on completion. Neither play has survived in its original form, and indeed the second may never have been written; it was normal procedure for plays to be commissioned by a theater manager, then bought by him outright on delivery. Cervantes probably went to Porras, sold him the idea of two plays he had already roughed out, and then went off to complete them, though, since he had to deliver *The Comedy of Confusion* within a fortnight, one at least must have been well on the way. Years later, in *Don Quixote,* Cervantes would complain of the effect upon the quality of plays of the merchandising atmosphere in which they were written. But the theater in Spanish cities, above all Madrid, was fast becoming a commercial proposition. By 1585 there were two permanent theaters in the capital (essentially, specially converted interior courtyards), owned by charitable brotherhoods who ran them as a business to finance their hospitals — as the lease of the fruit and water concession for the theaters two years later amply illustrates. Public support was enthusiastic — the fact that female parts were played by women and not by boys, as they were in Shakespearean England, was an added attraction — and the turnover of productions very rapid. Theatrical companies, therefore, were eager for material. Nonetheless, it seems unlikely that Porras would have committed himself to paying Cervantes for the plays in question unless he had already seen some of his work. It is probable, therefore, that the two early plays by Cervantes which have come down to us, *The Siege of Numancia* and *The Traffic of Algiers,* were by now already written. Certainly Cervantes claimed they belonged to the beginning of his checkered career as a dramatist, though there is nothing to show that they were written almost immediately after his release from captivity, as has sometimes been inferred from their subject matter.

If we are to believe Cervantes, and there is no reason why we should not, his career as a dramatist started successfully enough. *The Comedy of Confusion,* he later claimed, went over admirably in the theaters. The fact that on 1 August 1585 he witnessed a financial deed for a well-known theater-company manager called Jerónimo Velázquez seems to imply that Gaspar de Porras's company was not the only one with which Cervantes had professional dealings. As the titles of the plays mentioned indicate, Cervantes, not surprisingly, was drawing fairly heavily on his experiences in Algiers for inspiration. Such material was clearly of interest to Spaniards of the time, as indeed was the story of Numancia, the Iberian city whose inhabitants, rather than give in to the Romans, committed suicide by hurling themselves from the city walls. Thus far his theater was calculated to appeal to its prospective audiences, and those plays of his that did reach the stage were doubtless as well received as Cervantes claimed they were, as well received certainly as those of many other dramatists of the period. So what happened?

What happened — and Cervantes himself is as clear on

this point as posterity — was Lope Félix de Vega Carpio, the young poet warmly praised by Cervantes in *The Galatea,* who started writing for the Madrid theater in the mid-1580s and who within a few years had taken the capital by storm. Enormously prolific, with an extraordinary facility for penning verse that is rarely less than competent and frequently superlative, he sifted the best from the theater as he found it (a mixed bag of pastoral and religious drama, Italianate tragicomedy and Senecan tragedy) and on the basis of this created a popular drama — action-packed, nationalist in inspiration, and untrammelled by respect for classical precepts like decorum and the sacred unities of time and place — that was to dominate the Spanish theater for a hundred years. For a long time the horrified literary theorists were adamant in their disapproval, and a few dramas of the classical type continued for a while to be written. But the people paid, as Lope realized, and before long Lope and his disciples reigned supreme on the stage. The theorists themselves for the most part came around eventually, though their criticism had not in fact proved entirely sterile, provoking the playwrights into a more stringent approach to the technicalities of their writing. Like many another struggling dramatist, Cervantes succumbed in the face of this onslaught and after Lope had become firmly established he never had another play performed.

His bitterness at this abrupt end to his career as a dramatist emerges in the first part of *Don Quixote,* published in 1605. Here, in chapter forty-eight, the Canon and the Priest pour scorn and disapproval on the contemporary theater and the way in which it had sacrificed art to profit:

And although I [the Canon is speaking] have sometimes tried to persuade the actors that they are mistaken in thinking as they do, and that they would attract more people and more fame by performing plays that followed the precepts of art than they do by performing rubbish, they are so set and fixed in their opinion that there is no reasoning or proof that will move them.

The theater's blithe rejection of the classical rules of decorum and unity particularly incense them, and we can safely assume that the worthy pair voice their creator's first reactions to the new drama. Like the Canon, Cervantes had tried to persuade the commercial theater of the superiority of the pre-Lope drama, *his* drama, desperately urging upon managers plays they were no longer interested in buying. No doubt, again like the Canon and the Priest, Cervantes saw the managers and actors themselves — the entrepreneurs and middlemen of the theatrical world — as being largely responsible for the prostitution of the noble art of drama. The poets themselves are not to blame, says the Priest, "for since plays have become a commodity, they claim and they claim truthfully, that the managers would not buy [their plays] if they were not written in the usual way; and thus the poet tries to fit in with the requirements of the manager who is to pay him for his work." Cervantes had recognized that with the level of literacy still low, the theater, inevitably, was the area where the commercialization of art and leisure had taken root most quickly and powerfully. The solution he proposed, if the Priest can indeed be taken as his mouthpiece here, was a form of centralized aesthetic censorship which would prevent bad plays from being performed and thus raise the quality of dramatic workmanship.

His resistance of the temptation to jump onto Lope's theatrical bandwagon, along with most other playwrights, when he must have been badly in need of money, testifies both to his stubborn pride and to his instinctive distaste for an art that pandered to public taste. The slowness to detect the merits of the new theater is harder to fathom, seeming as it does to reveal an uncompromising, even reactionary streak strange in a man who was to produce a work of fiction unlike anything that had gone before. However, the explanation of Cervantes's blindness to Lope's appeal, to the realization that Lope was not merely following public taste but molding it, lies, I think, in his lack of any sure sense of the truly dramatic where the full-length play was concerned. The two early plays that have come down to us are, like *The Galatea* and the best of his verse, competent pieces in their different ways, with some very solid merits. *The Siege of Numancia,* which was highly praised in its day, even has a few sublime moments of truly epic grandeur. But it has them precisely because Cervantes's real gift as a writer is narrative, not drama, his true milieu character, not action. Thus, worthy as they are, these plays do not "take off" dramatically in the way Lope's earliest plays do, sloppily written as some of these undoubtedly were. Cervantes's pieces are overweighted with characters, they lack pace, and they have a stiffness, an air of the exercise about them, that betokens the dramatist who follows his theories rather than his instincts and fails to give those theories dramatic power. Even his later plays, which betray a considerable mellowing of his attitude to Lope's drama, could not compete in the commercial theater with Lope holding sway, hungry as the companies were for new plays. In the circumstances one feels that Cervantes's intentionally double-edged description of Lope as a "monster of nature" was commendably mild. A successful career as a dramatist would have guaranteed him a modest income, if not a fortune. As it is, the whole question of profit looms very large in his discussions of dramatic theory and practice.

But in 1585 this hammerblow of fate still lay in the future. Cervantes claims to have written twenty or thirty plays during the eighties (of which only nine titles and two texts have survived), all staged and all received, he says with endearing wryness, "without cucumbers or other missiles" and "without whistles, shouts or uproar." Grandly vague as this estimate is, he may well be right. Since the dramatist usually sold his manuscript to a theatrical manager who then used it as working copy, many Spanish plays of the period have not survived. Whether Cervantes was as innovationist in these early plays as he claimed later on to have been is another matter. Certainly the two surviving examples of his early theater do not bear this out, but it would not be just to disregard his claim on the basis of such a small sample of his work; the experimental streak in his nature is, after all, well attested to elsewhere.

In *The Traffic of Algiers* Cervantes draws directly on his experiences in Algiers. In fact he figures in the play himself as a captive soldier named Saavedra — the epitome of the resolute fearless Christian — at one point actually reciting in slightly altered form the letter in verse he had written in captivity to King Philip's Secretary of State. There are other familiar names as well: King Hassan, for example, Arnaute Mami and the two friars, Juan Gil and Jorge del Olivar; for Cervantes, throughout his life, was consistently to use in his writings the names of real-life people he knew or had heard of. The documentary aspect of the play doubtless lent the play a flavor of authenticity that contemporary audiences found attractive. Certainly Lope years later was to use the play as the basis for one of his own, *The Slaves of Algiers,* even "borrowing" some of its details — a sure indication of the plot's interest. But the inclusion by Cervantes among the characters in this play of contemporary realism of two called Necessity and Opportunity — he would later on claim proudly that he was the first to introduce "moral figures" into the secular theater — is an eloquent testimony to the unreliability of his dramatic sense. This same combination of personified abstractions and "real" people recurs in *Numancia,* but here the epic grandeur of the theme makes it less incongruous.

However well received Cervantes's early plays were, his literary earnings were not substantial enough for him and his wife to live on, even in the country. The death of his old father in June 1585 (leaving Doña Leonor the widow she had been claiming to be for eight years) could have done nothing to ease his financial circumstances, though at least Rodrigo left behind no debts for his family to pay, or so he claimed in his will. The money he had borrowed for Miguel's ransom had clearly been repaid. Cervantes divided his time after his marriage between Catalina's home in Esquivias and Madrid, where he stayed with his mother, Doña Leonor, moving frequently between the two places. Relations between the two families were close enough for Rodrigo to name the two mothers, Doña Leonor and Doña Catalina de Palacios, as his executors. Cervantes's increasing physical restlessness suggests that his confidence in the possibility of a career as a dramatist was already beginning to falter, in spite of Gaspar de Porras's commission. In December 1585 he turns up both in Seville and, shortly afterward, in Madrid, as a business representative negotiating financial deals on some unknown person's behalf. The following summer, after another visit to Seville, he is back in Esquivias making a marriage settlement of one hundred ducats upon his young wife, signing a receipt for her splendidly practical dowry and receiving from his mother-in-law power of attorney to act as her representative and administrator —

possibly to enable him to go to Toledo to collect the rent on the family's house there, which was leased to a cousin.

Cervantes continued, however, to write his earnest verse, contributing complimentary pieces to works published by friends. And in all likelihood his literary ambitions led him to join in 1586 the newly established Imitatoria Academy, the first of many literary salons launched by wealthy patrons in Madrid in the years that followed. But poetry, for all his intellectual commitment to it and in spite of his occasional successes in the poetry jousts of the time (a first prize in 1595, for example), was for Cervantes not so much a natural as a cultivated activity. Rarely does he resort to it as an instrument of truly personal expression and nowhere does he reveal through it anything distinctively his own. Of all the Spanish writers of the time, he is, after Lope de Vega, the one who displays himself most readily through his pen, yet it is not poetry, that traditional vehicle of self-expression, that lures him most frequently into genuine self-revelation, but prose. That, *Journey to Parnassus* apart, he should have reserved his innermost self and his profoundest thought for this medium in itself, perhaps, betrays in him an increasing awareness of his inability to make rhythm, rhyme, and meter correspond to the movements of his own thoughts and feelings.

In 1614, when he published *Journey to Parnassus,* a survey in verse of the writers of his time, this self-knowledge is ruefully and movingly brought out into the open when he describes himself toward the beginning of the work as,

> I who ever sleepless strive
> To manifest the poet's grace
> That Heaven has denied me.

Despite the assiduous attempts of Cervantes scholars to persuade us that the words were written in a spirit of irony, it seems clear from the context that Cervantes was in earnest. Why, after all, should his judgment be any the less reliable than posterity's? Cervantes was well aware that whereas he could string lines of verse together as well as most of his poetaster contemporaries, and indeed better than many, his poetic gifts were not of the divinely inspired sort. In his prologue to his *Eight Plays and Eight New Interludes,* published the following year in 1615, he wryly reveals that the true nature of his talents was no secret: "At that time [when he was trying to sell his plays] a bookseller told me that he would have bought them off me had a theatrical manager not told him that much could be expected of my prose but nothing of my verse." Apart from the autobiographical asides in *Journey to Parnassus,* the nearest he came to anything that could be called a personal poetry are four poems in Spanish ballad meter — "Jealousy," "Elicio" (the authenticity of which is in dispute), "Galatea," and "Disdain." The use of the pastoral convention and of pastoral pseudonyms like Elicio and Galatea as a distancing technique to conceal and dignify the poet's own experiences, moods, and thoughts was a standard one of the day, but there is nothing in these poems of Cervantes's, even in "Disdain," written in the first person, to make one *feel* that they are in any real sense the reflection of a lived experience, however autobiographical they may in fact be.

In 1587 Cervantes's growing realization that his literary activities were not going to provide him with a livelihood crystallized into action. And at this point his path crosses the stage of European naval history for the second time, although in a far more mundane way than when he fought heroically at Lepanto as a young soldier.

The idea of the Enterprise of England was a hugely

ambitious one, first conceived, in the early 1580s, of Spain's newly acquired strength (through the annexation of Portugal) in the Atlantic, and born very largely because of the execution on 18 February 1587 of the Catholic Queen of Scots, Mary Stuart. The plan had all the brilliance of simplicity: a large fleet was to set sail from Lisbon, proceed to the English Channel to meet up with the Spanish army in Flanders, embarked for this purpose, and escort it to the south coast of England. Essentially the armada would act as convoy to the landing forces, but if the English fleet were to prove troublesome, the Spanish ships would then engage and destroy the enemy.

But from the start things went wrong. The very notion of the Armada's invincibility was a fantasy inspired in Spanish hearts by the vast scope of the enterprise; ironically, the official title initially was *La felicisima armada,* the Supremely Fortunate Fleet, and long before its ultimate catastrophic defeat, the irony of that grandiose and optimistic title was cruelly revealed. The task of assembling enough vessels, men, and supplies became a nightmare for the man Philip had chosen to command the Armada — the Marquis of Santa Cruz, Captain General of the Ocean Seas and hero of Lepanto. In every dispatch the King pressed for speed, and eventually Santa Cruz despairingly finalized as best he could his totally inadequate arrangements and prepared to sail. A week before the sailing date he collapsed and died. After Santa Cruz's untimely death, the Armada was committed to the reluctant command of one of the highest grandees in the land, the Duke of Medina Sidonia, who by his own open and dignified admission knew little of warfare and nothing of the sea: "I am always seasick and I always catch cold," he wrote honestly to the King. Soon after it had put out from Lisbon, the fleet was battered by storms and had to flee to Corunna for repairs. Even the best of the motley collection of vessels were badly designed and undergunned, the crews were untrained, and a great part of the food supplies perished even before the fleet weighed anchor in Lisbon. Nevertheless, the fiction of invincibility was maintained; Spanish morale had to be kept up, and God, after all, as King Philip knew, was on their side. The fleet that eventually left Corunna comprised one hundred thirty vessels and some thirty thousand men.

The estimates originally projected for the size of the fleet had been even higher. The supplies needed for such a force, it was realized, would be enormous, for the men would have to be victualed not only during the expedition itself but throughout the weeks of preparation beforehand. A massive requisitioning campaign was thus inaugurated in the late spring of 1587. Soon the coastal towns of the southwest began to hum with the activities of preparation and the interior to ring with the clattering wheels of heavily laden wagons. Cervantes by now was urgently in need of employment, and there was certainly none to be found in Esquivias; the charms of village life must in any case have been beginning to pall. The opportunity came unexpectedly, and was grasped with an impetuousness that smacks of desperation. On 23 April, there arrived in Esquivias a small company of travelers who had been entrusted with the transport to Toledo of the remains of Saint Leocadia, brought to Spain from Flanders the previous year. At Toledo, on 26 April, they were to be received with great rejoicing and elaborate celebrations in the presence of the King and the royal family and most of the Court. The little group, in the charge of a Jesuit priest, spent the night in Esquivias and next day were seen off by a procession of excited villagers. Some followed the cortège all the way to Toledo, and it is very likely that among them went Cervantes. Certainly he was in Toledo on 28 April, partly on business perhaps but principally, no doubt, in order to witness the celebrations and to meet up with all his friends from Madrid. On the 26th there had been processions, illuminations, and music, and on the 27th a solemn mass in the cathedral — an occasion, in other words, which a man of Cervantes's lively curiosity would have been loath to miss.

At this point things seem to have moved very quickly. For on the 28th, Cervantes signed in Toledo a full power of attorney for his wife, who had remained in Esquivias, indicating both that he anticipated being away for some time and that he did not intend to see her before he went: otherwise he would have waited until he got back to Esquivias to visit a notary. There can be little doubt that he had discovered during the festivities that the Quartermaster General to the Armada, Antonio de Guevara, was about to start requisitioning operations in Andalusia, based in Seville, and had accordingly determined to go immediately to the southern capital and try his luck. That he should have decided to avoid the short delay necessary to return to Esquivias to say goodbye to his twenty-one-year-old wife speaks volumes. Catalina would almost certainly have opposed the plan, and Cervantes obviously decided he would not give her the chance to do so.

When he got to Seville, Diego de Valdivia, a member of the Crown Court in Seville, who was deputizing temporarily for Guevara, appointed him to a post as commissary to the Armada. It is taken for granted by all commentators that Cervantes would have needed influence to secure the position, and of course he could well have met Valdivia himself, or acquired mutual friends, in the course of his earlier business transactions in the city. That influence was necessary to obtain a temporary position as uncongenial as this — the commissary's job after all was to extract from people what they were reluctant to give — is an eloquent pointer to conditions in Spain. And just how unpleasant and difficult a position it could be, Cervantes was soon to discover. But although it has all the distasteful associations of the tax-gatherer, it would be wrong to assume that the position, in theory at least, had no attractions. It offered an income (and for the unscrupulous the possibilities for graft were endless) and it offered status; it also offered the opportunity to travel the south, an opportunity welcome to Cervantes if his previously unsettled state is anything to go by. But perhaps most important of all for Cervantes, it offered him the chance to feel part of what promised to be Spain's greatest achievement since Lepanto. He took a lifelong pride in the part he had played in that glorious battle and was quite clearly a man of deep patriotism.

There is no doubt that the Enterprise of England, its awesome dimensions apart, possessed a dramatic appeal that stirred the imagination of most Spaniards. At last His Most Catholic Majesty would bring to her knees the Protestant Queen who sat upon a throne that had almost become Philip's and whose sea dogs had for too long disported themselves with Spanish shipping. Francis Drake's daring raid on Cadiz on 29 April 1587 may have singed the King of Spain's beard, but it also set alight a flame of enthusiasm for Philip's plans for England that would be extinguished only in the waters of the English Channel the following year. In his exemplary tale *The English Spanishwoman*, published years later, Cervantes portrays Elizabeth in a flattering light, which suggests that the story was written after the peace treaty signed with England in 1605; but in 1587, as we know from the two solemn patriotic odes he wrote after the defeat of the Armada the following year, his feelings toward England were as hostile as those of any Spaniard. Had he been a younger man we can be sure he would have joined the great expedition. As it was, the idea of functioning as agent to the enterprise must have afforded him no small sense of involvement. The fact that while he traveled the dusty cart tracks of Andalusia requisitioning corn and oil Lope de Vega sailed with the Armada to England, cannot, however, have done anything in the years to come to soften his feelings toward the glamorous young dramatist.

FIVE

Of Corn and Oil: The King's Commissary

THROUGHOUT EUROPE, the year 1588 had long been designated by mathematicians, astrologers, and scholars versed in biblical numerology as a year of doom and disaster. Some even pronounced it to be the Day of Judgment itself. Not surprisingly, therefore, when news of Philip's plans started to seep out around the middle of 1587, Spain began to buzz with excited speculation. It looked as if the King was deliberately provoking catastrophe; and, of course, he was, though in his eyes the catastrophe that would fulfill the woeful prophecies was to be a Protestant one. For Catholicism, 1588 would prove a glorious year. Leaving Toledo around the end of April, Cervantes spent the summer in the heat-baked southern capital waiting for the requisitioning operations to get under way. He stayed, we are fairly sure, in the large and comfortable inn owned by a friend of his, Tomás Gutiérrez, a one-time actor and theater-company manager. And here, as in almost every other inn and tavern in the country, the table talk centered constantly, no doubt, on the great expedition being mounted against the English.

Exactly when Cervantes secured the promise of appointment we do not know. Certainly he did not start work until September, after the harvest was over. Then Guevara sent word to his deputy Valdivia that the requisitioning of supplies should begin, instructing him to arrange for collections of barley and wheat from Écija and three other towns.

Cervantes was sent to Écija, sixty-odd miles along the road to Córdoba, for wheat. At his inn he would have gained some inkling of the ominous facts that Écija had already that year handed over large supplies of cereals, for which the town had not yet been paid, and that there were still outstanding debts from previous years. He could not have been unaware either that the harvest had been bad. His misgivings as he embarked upon his new venture must consequently have been acute. He can have had no idea, however, as he set out along the dusty road to Écija, that he was setting out upon seven long years of tedium, trouble, and frustration. These years do not make exciting reading. Far from it. But they have in their irksome monotony a certain undeniable fascination for anyone interested in the way in which experience is imperceptibly transmuted into the fertilizing mulch of genius. The tale has its general interest too, illuminating as it does one of those myriad shadowy corners of which history is really made. When we think of the Spanish Armada and other great military enterprises of the past, we tend to linger on the surface of history, sparing little thought for the human detail of the administrative effort that went into them. But every bureaucracy is compounded of small personal tragedies, and the huge, unwieldy bureaucracy which Cervantes had just joined was no exception.

The commissary's powers and responsibilities were extensive. He had to requisition the cereal and arrange for it to be stored until payment arrived. It then had to be weighed and dispatched to its destination. Finally, his assignment completed, the commissary had to report back to the Quartermaster General in Seville. In the pursuit of these duties he wielded judicial powers: he could use force if necessary, he could confiscate goods and order arrests, he could commandeer transport. For the payment of the varied and elaborate expenses involved in all this — though not for the payment of the cereal itself, which was normally made directly by the government paymaster on submission of the commissary's receipt — he was entrusted with a substantial sum of money for which meticulous accounts were to be kept. The fact that the commissary himself was paid in arrears as and when government funds allowed, and yet had somehow to meet all his own personal expenses during these operations, was a hair-raising complication almost calculated to cause trouble.

It is impossible to believe that Cervantes was temperamentally suited to his new responsibilities. The ruthlessness and insensitivity essential in an efficient commissary, the ability to threaten and intimidate desperately anxious people, sometimes, after bad harvests, on the brink of starvation — these are not qualities which find any echoes in what we know of his life or what we read in his writings. It is easier to imagine him employing persuasion rather than force, reminding people of the fines they might incur for noncompliance, or trying to convince them that in view of the glorious nature of the enterprise the sacrifices they were being asked to make were worthwhile. For he grew to know as well as they that, given the state of the Spanish Exchequer, they might never be reimbursed. That he found some formula is clear, for time and again he produced what was required of him. The financial side of the work was altogether a different matter, and time was to show that Cervantes was not of the cast of mind necessary for the meticulous control of intricate bookkeeping. That many commissaries were more than a match for the financial challenges of their situation is apparent from the way they prospered — the opportunities for graft and swindle were enormous. And Cervantes has hard words to say about his former colleagues on more than one occasion in his later works. He himself was to find it difficult to keep his accounts straight, let alone make an illegal profit on the side.

In the event, Cervantes started his new commission already in debt. Since his hasty departure from Toledo had left him no time to organize funds, the months of waiting in the summer had been subsidized by his landlord-friend Tomás Gutiérrez — so too the personal expenses of his first commission. Cervantes, thanks to the unhurried workings of the machinery of Spanish government, therefore, set off for Écija considerably worse off financially than he had been when necessity drove him south in search of employment four months before.

Cervantes's first visit to Écija, where he arrived around 20 September, is recorded in a municipal document that states with some pathos that his intention was to take away all the town's corn, "leaving them only enough to eat and to sow," in other words, effectively depriving them of their livelihood. The town's council at once resolved to write in complaint to the King. Cervantes's first days in the town, however, were not entirely uncongenial. The crown representative in Écija, though now coming to the end of his turn of office there, was the Licentiate Cristóbal Mosquera de Figueroa, a Sevillian poet whom Cervantes had warmly praised in "Caliope's Song" in *The Galatea* and who was possibly a personal acquaintance from Cervantes's earlier days in Seville. Their brief encounter — Mosquera vacated his position on 26 September — must have afforded Cervantes considerable pleasure, especially since Mosquera showed him a treatise he was writing, or had already completed, on military discipline. This incorporated an account of the expedition to the Azores in 1582, and we can readily imagine Cervantes's gratification on discovering that his brother Rodrigo, promoted for bravery during the campaign, as we saw, was mentioned in the narrative. Before Mosquera left, Cervantes found time to write a complimentary sonnet for the work (which was not published until 1596) and Mosquera, we can be sure, returned Cervantes's goodwill of long standing by giving him good advice about how best to go about his difficult and distasteful task.

He needed it. Cervantes had arrived in the middle of what was already a fraught situation: a few days beforehand, the town had received official notification from Antonio de Guevara that it was to be deprived of its crops for the second time that year. But the good citizens of Écija had no intention of handing over all their grain without a struggle, especially since they were at the time in the middle of their *feria,* their sacrosanct period of annual festivities that began on 21 September and ended on 6 October. On 26 September the town council agreed to try and persuade Cervantes to satisfy himself with the smallest possible consignment of grain and sent a letter to this effect to Valdivia, who was himself collecting grain in the town of Andújar, to the east of Córdoba. Valdivia in reply merely ordered Cervantes to proceed with the collection.

Cervantes's position was an impossible one, caught as he was between sympathy for the plight of the townspeople and the need to carry out his orders. That he tried to achieve some compromise solution is clear from the way the situation dragged on through October, in spite of constant pressure from Valdivia. But finally, toward the end of the month, he set about requisitioning the corn he had been ordered to collect. As it turned out, a large quantity of the corn taken came from stores belonging to the Dean and Chapter of the Cathedral at Seville. The Church was not exempt from the requisitioning process, and Cervantes was within his rights to take what he did. While an experienced commissary, however, would have proceeded more circumspectly, Cervantes was imprudent enough to apply the logic of justice and take most from those with the fullest granaries. As a result of the uproar that ensued, Cervantes, the innocent middleman, was excommunicated.

Within a month or so of taking up his new employment, therefore, he found himself not only in debt, but excluded from that area of life in Spain to which every Spaniard was compelled by law to belong. Such excommunications were not uncommon and he could, of course, appeal — indeed by law he had to. Nonetheless, this was an extremely worrying development. What it signified to him in spiritual terms we cannot know. But throughout his life and work Cervantes gives us no reason to believe that he was not as true a son of the Church as he was fervent a patriot. In matters of religion, while in no sense a fanatic, nor showing any excessive reverence for the Church establishment itself, his beliefs and prejudices were the standard ones of the Spain of his day. He claimed with satisfaction to be the grandson of a familiar (official) of the Inquisition (the lawyer Juan de Cervantes), he speaks warmly of Jesuit education in his exemplary tale *The Dogs' Colloquy,* while the Canon and Priest in *Don Quixote* are amiable men employed partially as Cervantes's mouthpiece in their views on drama and literature. And there is no motive, other than wishful thinking of a foolishly anachronistic sort, for holding that his antagonism toward Moors and Moriscos was a spurious one or that Don Quixote's famous remark, "We have come up against the church, Sancho," means anything other than that the pair have bumped into the building in the dark. A mild wryness is the most that could be legitimately detected here.

The eminent Spanish scholar Américo Castro, for whom caste and race are the twin keys to the interpretation of Spain's culture and history, some years ago suggested that Cervantes was of *converso* origin and that this explained the lack of allegiance in his writings to any absolute values, religious, philosophical, or moral. The evidence he put forward, however, was by any standard strained. Castro started off from the conviction that Cervantes's wife, Catalina, had *converso* blood in her veins. In the early seventeenth century, two wealthy relatives of her family in Esquivias — the Quijados (an earlier Quijado is thought to have been the model for Don Quixote) — when they applied to join the knightly military Order of Santiago, were denounced as racially impure by Catalina's own brother, Francisco, by then a familiar of the Inquisition. There was a feud of long standing between the Quijados and the Salazars, for all that they were related, and coincidentally or not the Quijados had become known locally as judaizers. After long and exhaustive inquiries (in one case lasting twenty-one years), the two Quijados' names were cleared and their applications accepted. This is not by any means a guarantee that they were of pure blood, but they were in any case only cousins by marriage several times removed of Catalina's family itself. Since Catalina was clearly a *conversa*, Castro concluded, Cervantes was probably one too. The fact that *conversos,* unlike Jews, often went out of their way to marry "out," for tactical reasons, in itself makes this assumption a highly unreliable one. But Castro saw supporting evidence in the facts that Cervantes's father was a surgeon, his mother a doctor's daughter, and his grand-father at one time a cloth-merchant — traditionally Jew-ish occupations, although by no means exclusively *converso* ones after the Expulsion of the Jews in 1492. Castro detected further corroboration in Cervantes's lack of wordly success — promotion was denied him because of his suspect origins. But this conjecture is particularly un-convincing. Many men with *converso* blood in their veins reached positions of influence and wealth in society at the time in spite of the obsession with purity of blood, and reasons for Cervantes's failures may readily be found elsewhere. At no time were any suspicions of this sort raised about Cervantes in spite of the several routine in-vestigations into the family's origins that he and his fa-ther instigated at different times. And none of the several scurrilous attacks to which he was later subjected men-tion such a possibility. It is wishful thinking to envisage Cervantes as a free thinker and absurdly romantic to think that a few drops of distantly dissident blood, even if he possessed them, could turn him into one. The lives led by him and his family were the orthodox, devout ones of his day. If he declares allegiance to no absolute values it is because he took them for granted.

Even with the notice of his excommunication posted on all the parish church doors in Écija — which did noth-ing to improve his standing in the town — Cervantes had to continue with the collection of grain. On 2 November, the town council decided to write in protest to Valdivia. The letter succeeded only in bringing him hurrying to Écija himself. On his arrival an agreement was at last reached over the total quantity of grain to be taken, with the town itself left to decide who should contribute what. The town council's protracted resistance to the whole operation is largely explained by the fact that so far most of the grain had been extracted from the largest and wealthiest landowners of the community. Most commissaries, to give them their due, did their best to spare the poor.

While the inhabitants of Écija sorted out their problem, Cervantes and Valdivia passed northeastward to La Rambla in the province of Córdoba. Here all the recent unpleasantness in Écija promised to repeat itself. At least twice already that year, royal commissaries had visited La Rambla in search of corn, bacon, cheese, beans, and chickpeas, and there were unpaid government debts dating back to 1579. Valdivia, this time in more conciliatory mood, agreed to allow the town council to organize the collection itself and hand over an agreed quantity of high-quality grain within twenty days. In this way those who had contributed earlier in the year could be spared a second depletion of their crops. The inhabitants themselves, however, considered their council pusillanimous in conceding so readily to the demand for supplies, and soon made their antagonism felt. Skeptical about their intentions of ever completing their part of the bargain, Valdivia then blatantly broke his promise and ordered Cervantes to start the collection immediately. He himself left for Córdoba, leaving Cervantes to bear the brunt of the unpleasantness that followed. This time there was real trouble, and Cervantes, in desperation, was forced to commit several townspeople to prison. The severity of this measure had its effect and the town council wrote to Valdivia begging him to order the release of the prisoners and promising to hand over the corn required within twenty days. The letter, dated 22 November, reveals that another of Valdivia's commissaries, the very one who had carried off large quantities of grain the previous February, was also back in town looking for more. No farming community, however prosperous, could withstand these repeated depredations upon its stocks, and it is quite obvious that what Cervantes had to cope with was, in some cases at least, the resistance of real hardship. He managed within five days to make the necessary allocations and arrangements for the collection, but the last of the grain itself would not be handed over until the beginning of the following year.

Cervantes, meanwhile, on Valdivia's orders, proceeded to his next port of call, Castro del Río. Here again a man went to prison, this time a sacristan, and here as in Écija ecclesiastical supplies were appropriated. We can be sure that sheer necessity alone drove Cervantes once again to the Church's storehouses. When a commissary arrived in a new town it was to collect a specified quantity of corn and if most of the corn available belonged to the Church then he had no alternative but to take it. Excommunication was in this situation the Church's only weapon against the state, and it did not hesitate to use it. Within a very short time Cervantes was, as a result, excommunicate not only in the diocese of Seville but in that of Córdoba as well.

From Castro del Río Cervantes moved on to Espejo, another small country town, leaving an assistant behind in Castro del Río to complete the business there. At Espejo things seem to have gone smoothly for a change. That Cervantes found time to visit his uncle's family in nearby Cabra is clear, for when he returned to La Rambla to see how the collection there was proceeding he took his cousin Rodrigo with him as assistant. Indeed, when Cervantes toward the end of December received notification of his next commissions from Valdivia, he left Rodrigo at La Rambla — where some of the townspeople were still proving recalcitrant — to oversee the collection and storage of those supplies which were still outstanding.

After a short stay in Córdoba and its outlying towns

and villages, Cervantes by 10 January 1588 was back in Seville, his first tour of duty accomplished. With almost four months back pay due him, he must inevitably have taken stock of his new career at this juncture. He could not have been enjoying its problems and this respite, from them and from the saddle, was a welcome one. Constant journeying on muleback along bad roads in winter, even an Andalusian winter, would be few people's idea of pleasure. It is difficult to subscribe to the view that what kept him going on his travels, now and subsequently, was the search for material for some future great work of literature. Without question his work as a commissary, his stays in wayside inns, his encounters along the road, afforded him rich insights into human life and character which were to prove invaluable later on. Without question his experiences were helping to shape the mind and imagination of the man who would write *Don Quixote.* And without question they were earning him a wide knowledge of the physical face of Spain upon which he would draw, as he drew on his experiences in general, when he returned to his pen. But to attribute to his activities during these years a motive as self-conscious as the willful accumulation of what is known as "experiential material" seems absurd. He traveled the south requisitioning supplies because he needed a job and this was the one that had presented itself. And he continued to do so, in spite of the tedious and disagreeable nature of his duties, for the same reason. If he stored away in his memory as he went along the faces, anecdotes, incidents, and images that struck him as being rich in artistic potential, then he did no more than any would-be writer does. Genius lies not in what a writer observes but in the quality of his observation and of the use to which he puts it, and for this it is impossible to prepare.

Cervantes was now, in a very real sense, a prisoner of

circumstance. Just as the long credit-consuming wait in Seville the previous summer had rendered a post as commissary doubly essential, so now the discovery that the Paymaster General in Seville had no funds from which to pay Cervantes's wages meant that escape was out of the question. He needed that money to pay his debts, and unless he stayed on he might never get it. At the same time he had to go on paying his way. We know almost nothing of his wife's and his family's circumstances at this time, except that in the summer of 1587 the mysterious Andrea acknowledged in Madrid the repayment of a large debt owed her by a woman in Seville. But if Cervantes had hoped by now to be sending money home, that hope was sadly gone. For his own expenses he must have continued to rely on the generosity of his old friend Tomás Gutiérrez.

That the excommunications still hanging over Cervantes's head were not taken overseriously by his superiors is obvious. On 22 January 1588, the Quartermaster General, Antonio de Guevara, now in Seville, renewed his commission and ordered him back to Écija, this time in search of olive oil. Clearly he was considered to have measured up well to his new duties.

His powers to extract supplies, to commandeer transport, and to commit the uncooperative to prison remained the same as before, but, powers or no powers, Cervantes could not have been overjoyed by the thought of returning to the town where his very reappearance would be regarded as a calamity. And again the town protested to the King, begging to be spared and asking for payment of what was already owed them. They claimed that the taxation and requisitioning to which they had recently been subjected had brought the area to the very brink of ruin, with people going hungry and fields uncultivated. Even if we allow for a little tactical exaggeration, they clearly were in difficulties. However, no war can be fought without supplies, and their plea for a time went the way of so many others that reached the King, only to be rejected or ignored. Nonetheless, Cervantes had to be content with half of the consignment of oil required, either because there was no more or because he just did not have the heart to remove it. That he carried on him money to pay the muleteers he hired to transport the oil is clear from the receipt that still survives, but these seem to have been the only people involved in these transactions who, while bound to cooperate, could expect to see promptly the color of their money — an eloquent indication that whereas supplies may be embargoed, mules more often than not respond to no voice other than their master's.

His second assignment in Écija completed, Cervantes followed the oil to Seville, unaware that on 9 February the Marquis of Santa Cruz, commander in chief of the expedition for which all the supplies were destined, had died. When the news of Santa Cruz's death spread, the prophecies of a doom-laden 1588 which had been rippling through western Europe to Spaniards suddenly seemed prophetic indeed.

Word reached Seville around 23 February. Cervantes must have been deeply dismayed to learn of the demise of one of the last surviving heroes of Lepanto. If he had received any inkling from Guevara, who had been in close touch with Santa Cruz and with the King himself, that all was not well with the preparations for the expedition, he could not have been much cheered subsequently to learn the identity of Santa Cruz's successor, the Duke of Medina Sidonia. Cervantes's high opinion of Santa Cruz is made plain by the fulsome praise he lavishes upon the Marquis in the sonnet he had written months before for Mosquera de Figueroa's military treatise; and later he would pay homage to his memory in *Don Quixote,* where the Captive describes the old general as a "thunderbolt of war" — the highest military accolade in Cervantes's vocabulary. As for Medina Sidonia, apart from a few routine complimentary flourishes in Cervantes's first ode on the Armada, all he would receive was a withering comment in a scathing sonnet Cervantes wrote after the sack of Cadiz in 1596.

Affected as he was by the bad news, Cervantes had a pressing problem of his own on his mind. By now he should have taken steps to have his first excommunication annulled; and why he had not done so when last in Seville in early January is unclear. The mechanics of appeal, however, while not complicated, were expensive, and in all likelihood Cervantes in January had quite simply not been able to find the necessary money. Now, on 24 February 1588, he signed a power of attorney authorizing one Fernando de Sevilla to act for him in petitioning for absolution. The appeal was eventually granted, perhaps on the strength of Cervantes's own defense or, more probably, after the ecclesiastics concerned had received payment for their grain later in the year.

At the beginning of March, Cervantes was back once more in Écija, collecting more oil and negotiating over the as yet unpaid-for stores of wheat. Later in the month, rather oddly, he changed hats for a brief time when nine of the inhabitants of the town empowered him to receive payment on their behalf for wheat handed over by them in previous years. The arrangement was possibly occasioned by another of Cervantes's visits to Seville where the Paymaster General had his headquarters. Whatever the reason, Cervantes had clearly managed by now to establish reasonably good personal relations with the town where he was spending so much of his time. Soon afterward, on 5 April, Cervantes set about getting his second excommunication lifted — perhaps he had received word from Seville that under the care of Fernando de Silva things there were going well. Since he was liable to be sent away at short notice by Guevara, he needed a representative in Écija too to seek the "accustomed graciousness" of the Church on his behalf. His cousin Rodrigo, still resident there, was the obvious choice, and so it was arranged. To be excommunicated twice over in different dioceses was by any standard singularly unfortunate, and Cervantes must have been very relieved to have his extrication from both these embarrassments under way.

How much news of Cervantes's difficulties in the south had found its way back to Catalina at home in Esquivias we can only guess, but it was probably very little. Catalina could not have been pleased by her husband's sudden departure the previous summer, and letters full of problems and woes, reporting not just one but two excommunications, would inevitably have provoked recriminations as well as anxiety, both of which Cervantes would have been eager to avoid. On 1 May, while Cervantes was still in Écija, Catalina's situation was substantially affected by the death of her mother, Doña Catalina de Palacios. It left her not only with one third of the family house and some land, but two young brothers to look after. That Cervantes's departure the previous year had earned him his mother-in-law's severe disapproval is clear. This modest inheritance of Catalina's — that owing to the family's vast debts did not actually materialize until 1604 — was by the terms of the will, signed on 17 November 1587, not to be sold or given away, partly in case Catalina herself died without issue (in which case the brothers would inherit) but partly also to prevent Cervantes himself from benefiting from it. The resentment implicit in these quite explicit instructions shows that Cervantes's relationship with his mother-in-law had gone sour, and the baldness of the will's wording — with no attempt at any consideration for Catalina's feelings — suggests, perhaps, that the mother's resentment found an echo in the daughter. Since Doña Catalina de Palacios died without enough ready money to pay even for the legal fees, her son-in-law's failure, while she was still alive, to send money home to his wife could not have failed to rankle.

By the time news of Doña Catalina's death caught up with Cervantes, the funeral was long over. In any case he would have had neither the time nor the money to travel home. As it was, Catalina had to cope with her grief and her mother's affairs with the help of the uncle who had married them four years before.

With the Armada's new sailing date approaching, Cervantes spent most of May in Écija winding up his business affairs. What proportion of the supplies he had spent the past months trying to extract from people ever reached the historic fleet it is impossible to say. The oil from Écija almost certainly arrived at Lisbon, but whether any of the grain saw a mill in time is extremely doubtful. Most of it lay molding in store awaiting payment. Cervantes can hardly have avoided a growing sense of pointlessness and frustration. A successful outcome would have made all the harrying and persuasion, the endless journeying, the excommunications, seem worthwhile; as it was, there was virtually nothing to show for all his efforts, not even a salary.

Toward the end of the month he left for Seville. From there, however, he did not make for home. Still unpaid for his services in the government's employ, he decided to stay on in the south after the Armada had sailed, presumably in the hope that the money would come through. In the light of subsequent events he might have done well to

cut his losses and depart. The decision could not have
been an easy one to make, but the prospect of returning
to unemployment and rural boredom in Esquivias and
there getting involved in his wife's family's financial
affairs was probably incentive enough for him to stay on
in the south and let things take their course. Accordingly,
on 12 June 1588, two friends stood as guarantors for him
in a new contract with Antonio de Guevara in which he
undertook to account for his actions, whenever necessary,
to attend any proceedings taken against him, and to pay
any fines to which he was sentenced. Read with all the
wisdom of hindsight, the words of the contract strike an
ominous note, but the stipulations were clearly sensible
ones aimed at curbing the activities of unscrupulous officials. A few days later, the first payment for the Écija corn
at last arrived, and Cervantes was commissioned to return
to Écija to organize its transport to the mills for grinding
and thence to the biscuit manufacturers. There is still no
mention of his salary, but presumably Cervantes had extracted some promise from Guevara before he accepted
reappointment. And indeed on 1 July, two days before
setting out through the summer's heat for Écija (dubbed
with good reason "the frying pan of Andalusia"), he did
at last receive some pay — slightly more than one month's
salary of the ten due to him.

During the months that followed, life must have borne
a pronounced sense of déjà vu for Cervantes. Orders arrived to start collecting new supplies of wheat, forcibly if
need be, only to be followed by a repetition of the pleas,
disputes, and refusals to which Cervantes was by now
only too accustomed. His minor expenditure accounts for
this period (which are, it should be said, entirely correct:
he was not by any means as innumerate as he has sometimes been made out to be) mention, along with paper
and ink, brooms, candle oil and bolts, several sums of

money paid out to locksmiths for dismantling locks. Clearly Guevara would not believe that the granaries of Écija, overflowing as they normally were, were quite as empty as the town claimed. News of events in Écija spread through the region, carrying with it the reputation for intransigence which Cervantes, through no fault of his own, was rapidly acquiring. The discovery that a great deal of the grain amassed so painfully the previous year was infested with weevils and therefore unfit for milling, could only have exacerbated his increasing sense of frustration.

The wrangles continued. Cervantes signed certificates and receipts, hired locksmiths, bought supplies, rescued grain from the rain, and poured yet more metaphorical oil on troubled waters. From time to time he traveled the road between Écija and Seville — familiar by now with every hamlet, every inn, every tree even — reporting to Antonio de Guevara and collecting funds. In turn, dispatches from Guevara arrived in Écija with new commissions and demands, but rarely with funds to finance them.

The tidings of the Armada's fate, as they began to filter through, must have been greeted in Écija with almost as much bitterness as disappointment. All the urgings to self-sacrifice in the name of the great Enterprise — described by the Jesuit Pedro de Ribadeneyra in a rousing address to the men who set sail as "the most important undertaking by God's Church for many hundreds of years" — now seemed cruel indeed. Far from reaching the ships, their grain had lain uselessly deteriorating throughout the winter, and what was left of it would now disappear into the great anonymous maw of the Council of War's general stores.

Like many of his fellow countrymen, Cervantes found it hard to accept the rumors of defeat, and it was now that he wrote his first ode to the Armada, full of patriotic fervor and loyal protestations of confidence in the brave sword of Catholicism. With images of bloody death and destruction, splintered masts and drowning men, he urges the invincible Christian troops on to prophetic victory over the "West's biggest Pirate," the "vicious Lutheran." Spain, he bids Fame tell the army, is already celebrating its glorious triumph. When confirmation arrived in a stunned Spain that the great expedition had indeed ended in disaster, Cervantes found time to pen a companion ode, not recriminatory or defeatist at this crushing blow to Spanish morale, but consoling, compassionate, and protective in tone, and full of faith in the future. If Heaven has lifted up the perfidious English, it is only that they may have further to fall when evil at last is punished; when the bull, he points out, retires from the fray, it is to gather strength for a second, deadly onslaught. Patriotic set pieces as the poems are, they exude the kind of measured optimism that characterizes much of Cervantes's work, the optimism that steers bitter disappointment away from despair. Could he have realized what a turning point the defeat of the Armada would prove in Spain's fortunes, even he might not have been able to summon up any words of comfort.

In Écija the battle continued. In August 1588 the King himself responded at last to the town's pleas to be relieved of the demands of the Quartermaster General and his commissary, and provided its spokesmen in Madrid — who appear to have pressed for action on their own initiative — with an order urging restraint on Guevara. From the wording of the order it was clear that Cervantes had not been spared by the town's representatives in their attempt to paint as black a picture as possible of the situation. Fearing the royal order might not be effective enough, the town council even called upon the Church to pronounce on the matter. Its ruling was that it was not possible to extract wheat from those who had none, wealthy as they might be, and on the strength of this wise finding the town continued its fight. For his part Guevara politely but firmly continued to insist that his orders be carried out, and Cervantes himself appears to have become somewhat skeptical by now about all the protestations of poverty.

In September, Cervantes and his mule train wended their way along the cart track that served as a road to Marchena, to buy oil for which as usual he had no money to pay. Clearly he spent much of his time there brooding over events in Écija, as his concern for his good name — the same concern that had driven him to launch the private inquiry concerning his behavior in Algiers — asserted itself. On his return to Écija he lodged an objection against the misrepresentations made to the King concerning his behavior. Four days later he received what was effectively an apology from the embarrassed town council, which claimed that the accusations had been made without their knowledge or approval. They stated that in their view he had always carried out his duties "with great rectitude." A subsequent reassurance described him as proceeding with his work "diligently and well." These statements, unequivocal as they are, confirm the general impression that here in Cervantes was an honest man carrying out an extremely unsavory task with as much tact and fairness as the situation allowed.

Later that autumn, as more money became available — though never for him — to pay for the previous year's harvest, things became easier in Écija and Cervantes was able to continue his work of gathering new supplies in a more relaxed atmosphere. But with commissions for both oil and grain to fulfill, he was hectically busy as he moved ceaselessly around the town and surrounding countryside that autumn and winter. In December, even the Castro del Río supplies were paid for; and if Cervantes were still excommunicate, then this surely restored him to the Church's bosom in the diocese of Córdoba. Sometime during that month he and his assistants, tired of living in inns and hired rooms, rented a house for themselves in Écija.

His troubles in the south, however, were by no means over. In the New Year of 1589, one of the town officials who had been reprimanded by the town council for misrepresenting the situation in Écija to the King and who had obviously been nursing a grudge against Cervantes on account of this, accused him of having taken more grain than the quantity agreed between Guevara and the town. Highly indignant that the propriety of his procedures should again be in doubt, Cervantes, on 23 January, wrote a strong letter of protest to the town council, pointing out that so far he had collected less, not more, wheat than had been arranged. He demanded that this be corroborated by the grain owners in question, who should be summoned by the town crier to give evidence. Along with the letter, he submitted his own accounts for examination. That Cervantes was indeed incensed by this continuing hostility is made quite clear by the threat with which he ends his letter: if the town did not cooperate in the collection of the corn outstanding, he would take it by force and indiscriminately. He had had enough of the town's evasions and double dealings.

In its turn, this latest row died down and the year continued its predictable and monotonous course. More wheat was collected, more was milled and transported, more wages and debts were paid. In February, Cervantes made two lightning visits to Seville to present his accounts and to collect funds; then sometime in April, his commission in Écija completed, he settled in Seville for the time being. Here no doubt he relaxed and sloughed off the cares and irritations of the previous months, delighted to be back in the bustling, cosmopolitan city. At the end of June, he was actually able to settle accounts with Tomás Gutiérrez, repaying him for all the generosity and hospitality the innkeeper had so unstintingly given him. Where he found the money to do so is an unsolved mystery, but the suggestion that he won the money gambling seems an entirely plausible one. Cards were a craze in Spain at the time; everybody, men and women, high and low, played. As a former soldier, Cervantes would certainly be an old hand at them and it is clear from his writings that he was familiar with all the various card games. To try his luck at cards would have seemed an obvious solution to a man badly in need of money to pay his debts, especially if he were about to leave the city.

Cervantes's credit at this time was certainly good, for on the same day he settled up with Gutiérrez he acted as guarantor for a woman renting a house. There has been much speculation about his relationship with this Jerónima de Alarcón. It is true that Cervantes is described in the deed as living in the same quarter of Seville as she did, rather than where Tomás Gutiérrez's inn was located, and it is true that he had not seen his wife for almost two years. But while it would not surprise us if Cervantes had found a refuge in Seville from his cares in Écija, the evidence is so scant as to be capable of any interpretation. The woman might simply have been his landlady.

Still on the same day, Cervantes signed two other documents, one advancing an assistant a large part of the salary owed him — apparently out of his own pocket — the other authorizing this same assistant to act on his behalf both in his personal and his business affairs. And it is all this activity that has led biographers to believe that Cervantes was preparing to leave Seville, perhaps on the following day. It does seem likely that Cervantes at this juncture journeyed home to Castile. If he did, no doubt after spending some time in Esquivias with his wife and nephews, he traveled on to Madrid to see his ailing mother, his sisters, and his niece and to look up old friends and acquaintances. Whether he might have called on the recently widowed Ana Franca to see his growing daughter we can only guess, but it would be nice to think so.

If Cervantes was hoping to find in Castile some means of escape from the disheartening grind of commissary work, he was unsuccessful. Six months later, in February 1590, he was back in the south, in Carmona, Écija, and elsewhere, requisitioning olive oil destined for the fleet, then anchored off Corunna. In Carmona he must have encountered an echo from his more exotic past, for there at the time lived the poet-prince Muley Xeque, son of a former Sultan of Morocco deposed in 1576 by the Abd-al-Malik who appears both in Cervantes's play *The Bagnios of Algiers* and in the Captive's tale in *Don Quixote*. Who knows, perhaps it was hearing about Muley Xeque — soon to be baptized and made a grandee of Spain — that stirred up the memories that inspired these works, both of indeterminate date? In March and again in May, Cervantes appears in Seville signing receipts for arrears of salary — obviously his financial situation was easier than it had been, though he had still not been paid for his first Écija commission.

At this point Cervantes decided he had had enough; enough of poverty, enough of thankless hard work and constant wrangling, enough of dusty, rutted roads. And his discouragement with his prospects was such as to turn his thoughts beyond Spain, to that new land of riches and opportunity for the sixteenth-century Spaniard — America. Many men — adventurers, soldiers, administrators — had gone there seeking their fortunes, and an impressive number had found them. The wealthy *indiano,* or Spanish émigré to America, returning home to flaunt his riches, would soon be a familiar character in the Spanish drama. If the road ahead of Cervantes was closed at home, then why not follow in the *indiano*'s footsteps? Accordingly, when he discovered in Seville that there were at least four eminently desirable posts about to fall vacant — the accountantship of the kingdom of New Granada, the governorship of the province of Soconusco in Guatemala, the paymastership of the galleys of Cartagena (in modern Colombia), and the magistracy of La Paz (in modern Bolivia) — he decided to apply for them. His memorandum went to the Council of the Indies on 21 May with a résumé of his career to date and all the evidence he possessed of his long and faithful service to the Crown, including the report of his years in captivity in Algiers and the certificate his mother had obtained from the Duke of Sessa in 1578 concerning his military service. In his eagerness for success he stretched the truth a little, wording his own account of his career in such a way as to imply that he had lost his hand, rather than the use of it, and that he as well as Rodrigo had fought in the Azores. Even so, the evidence was not deemed sufficient, and on 6 June the Council rejected the application with the terse comment, "Let him look for something over here," scribbled across the bottom of his memorandum.

It is pointless to cry corruption or indignantly denounce his rejection as a personal insult or deliberate mockery, as some have done. The competition for the vacant posts at a time when jobs were scarce must have been fierce and must have included men with far more influence in high places than Cervantes. Furthermore, it has

to be said that at least two of the positions in question —
the governorship and the magistracy — were way out of
Cervantes's reach, and that even the other two could be
expected to go to men of greater authority and experience. What, after all, were Cervantes's qualifications? He
had been a good soldier and had fought at the battle of
Lepanto; he had been a courageous slave who had kept
faith with his God; and he had collected supplies effi-
ciently in Andalusia. In personal terms it was a com-
mendable record, but hardly impressive in the context of
a career in administration. Doubtless had the Council of
the Indies known that the man they were considering
would turn out to be Spain's most famous son, they
would have ensured the approval of posterity and given
him a job. As it was, they had no option but to judge his
case on its merits as they saw them to be. No doubt brib-
ery and favoritism were by now playing as large a part in
government appointments as outraged contemporary
commentators maintained, but even had the Council
proceeded with scrupulous impartiality their decision
would in all probability have been the same. And we
should be grateful, for, had Cervantes been swallowed up
by success in overseas administration, he would almost
certainly never have written *Don Quixote;* another book
perhaps, but not that one.

Cervantes himself, of course, inevitably and naturally
saw the rejection as a victory for official corruption over
personal worth. His intense disappointment echoes in the
Duke's words to Sancho in *Don Quixote,* "there is no
high office that is not obtained by some form of brib-
ery." But ground down as he was by the tedium and
worry of his work, and alive as only he could be to the
memory of the hardships and dangers of his eventful past,
his view of what was open to him was a supremely un-
realistic one. As we saw when tracing his adventures **in**

Algiers, desperation sometimes weakened his grasp momentarily on the realities of his situation. While in no way arrogant or presumptuous, Cervantes had a very pronounced sense of his own worth, and he had been goaded by frustration and probably by a feeling of panic at the passage of time into a bid for success, which, like his third escape attempt in North Africa, was doomed to failure. The insight into the workings of the distorting power of the human will with which these moments in his life in retrospect afforded him was to make a crucial contribution to the conception of Don Quixote. No one who had not himself acutely experienced the divide between the dream world and the real, between what the ego seeks and what it finds, and profited from the experience, could possibly have created the Knight of the Sorrowful Countenance. And Don Quixote in winning his way through to sanity and wisdom at once must reflect and chart his creator's own triumph over disappointment and disillusion.

Despite this setback, like so many others duly absorbed though not forgotten, Cervantes continued with his work. A power of attorney signed on behalf of his wife and his sister Magdalena in July indicates that he entertained no hope of returning home in the near future. His visits to Seville at least must have helped make life more tolerable, mixing, as he did there, we know, with writers and artists. His literary fervor had certainly not been dimmed by his humdrum life in the farming towns and villages of Andalusia. For out of his hard-earned and infrequently paid salary he purchased some costly books, part of the estate of a local dignitary recently deceased: four books in French with gilded covers — which indicate that he either knew the language or intended to learn it — and a history of Saint Dominic, by its price a very handsomely bound volume indeed.

However trying his commissary work had proved up to now, his real troubles were only just about to begin. On 27 August 1590, in Seville, Cervantes presented his signed accounts for all the grain he had requisitioned during the previous three years. They were out by a substantial amount. This amount Cervantes, by the terms of his appointment, accordingly "owed" the Exchequer.

In the light of this and of what was to ensue, we have to ask ourselves whether Cervantes might have deliberately misappropriated government funds. Many other commissaries, after all, were doing so. Very shortly a major scandal would break involving many of Guevara's high officials based at Puerto de Santa María on the coast, all of whom would be imprisoned pending charges of extreme gravity. Guevara himself would be removed from office. But while Cervantes was later to see the inside of more than one prison on account of his so-called debts to the Exchequer, he was never at any time charged with fraud or with abuse of his position. We must assume, therefore, that there was no evidence at the time of any serious misdemeanor against him.

It is a subject that puts Spanish scholars, not surprisingly, on the defensive. Surely the great Cervantes could not have fiddled the books? We nurture the belief that in our geniuses art and life should move together in one continuous flow of perception and integrity. But because there is so much to admire in Cervantes, it does not follow that he was in all things totally admirable; the rich wisdom of *Don Quixote* is compounded as much of personal lessons learned and follies duly reckoned with as of observation and insight, of humor and compassion, and it is no service to its author to regard him as some sort of saintly martyr to life's misfortunes and to human envy. Assuming, therefore, that it is not impossible that he did embezzle government money, where does the evidence point?

As we have seen, there seems no doubt that for a commissary his stock was high. Guevara trusted him (for what that was worth) and as far as the town council of Écija was concerned, his behavior, given his unpleasant duties, was impeccable. The gambling explanation proffered for his sudden prosperity in Seville in the July of 1589 is an obvious attempt to fend off suspicions of dishonesty, but given the slowness with which government funds came through it is in fact extremely difficult to see how Cervantes could possibly have amassed, out of the money entrusted to him, the sort of sum necessary to settle his accounts in Seville and lend money to his assistant. Since some other explanation seems essential, gambling is probably as good as any. Furthermore, if Cervantes had for some time been misappropriating the money entrusted to his care, would he have openly presented unbalanced accounts? Had he been adroit enough to carry out all his instructions and commissions and at the same time salt away money for himself, he would surely have been adroit enough to fudge his accounts to avoid detection.

That he was held responsible (as was normal) for the missing money but never charged with fraud indicates that the government deemed his crime to be incompetence rather than dishonesty. This is certainly where the evidence now available leads us. The way in which the financial side to the requisitioning of supplies was conducted was, as we saw, calculated to produce the maximum confusion. Cervantes handled large sums of money — for running expenses, for salaries, equipment and supplies, and on occasion for payments for the embargoed commodities themselves. Often the money was paid out by him in arrears, often only in part, and sometimes, when there was not enough, he paid out of his own (or rather his creditor's) pocket. In the meantime, for months on end, he and his assistants had somehow to pay their own personal expenses — board, lodging, and travel, not to mention such minor considerations as clothes — on little or no salary. By the time Cervantes presented his accounts in Seville in August 1590, he was the only participant in the Écija saga, the suppliers of grain included, who had not been paid. He could not possibly have survived unless he had used his funds on occasion to meet his own expenses, and clearly he had no alternative but to treat his petty cash as a general expenses fund whenever necessary. Subsidizing his official expenditure from time to time from his own pocket as he had to, he presumably felt justified in reversing the procedure; he kept a scrupulous account of small items of official expenditure and in theory all would eventually come out in the wash. When the government saw fit to pay his salary, he could settle any outstanding sums — he knew, after all, that he would be held accountable. There was really no other way in which he, or any other commissary, could have survived.

Had this been the extent of his commitment, all might have been well. But Cervantes was answerable not only for his handling of the funds entrusted to him, but for the supplies collected as well. If he stated he had collected ten tons of grain and ten tons on his certification were eventually paid for, then ten tons there had to be; he was financially accountable for any discrepancy at the rate the government had paid for the grain. In view of the way in which the harassed commissaries were expected to operate, the very notion of their keeping honestly balanced books seems a pipe dream, and it is a testimony to Cervantes's honesty, almost certainly, rather than to his dishonesty, that his own were so clearly unbalanced. That the sum he was deemed to owe the government was in the event somewhat less than a quarter of what the government owed him, must have made the discrepancy in his accounts seem in his own eyes less than criminal.

Having presented his grain accounts, Cervantes turned his attention to his olive oil accounts, which dated from 1588, submitting them for inspection in October. In this case the government ended up owing him a small sum. In November he bought himself some cloth for a new suit on credit, his faithful friend Tomás Gutiérrez acting as guarantor. That he was indeed short of money is possibly suggested by his appointment the following month of a proxy to represent him at the examination of his accounts in Madrid. Had he been able to afford the journey, he would presumably have taken the opportunity to visit his family — unless of course the prospect of the examination itself intimidated him. Time was certainly not the obstacle. The dismissal of Guevara and the arrest of his officers in Puerto de Santa María had brought a halt to requisitioning activities for a time.

Cervantes waited in Seville, and perhaps took the opportunity of this lull in his affairs to write. That year an anthology of poems printed in Valencia included his poem "Jealousy," the ballad of which, to judge from remarks he makes in his *Journey to Parnassus,* he was most proud. If he knew about this it must have given a small boost to his morale.

In March of 1591, he managed to persuade Juan de Tamayo, an obliging associate of the Government Paymaster in Seville, Agustín de Cetina — then in Madrid for the investigations into Guevara's organization — to advance him as a personal favor the salary still outstanding from his early days in Écija, authorizing Tamayo to seek reimbursement from Cetina. It was an extremely prudent move and had he not made it he might never have received his arrears of salary. As it was, he calculated wrongly and asked Tamayo for the wrong amount, doing himself out of a small sum (in his official statement of accounts, happily, he made no mistake). At this point Cervantes could have taken his money and run, home to Castile. But he stayed. Perhaps he considered that a salary constantly in arrears was better than no salary at all; perhaps he had resigned himself to life as a government official; perhaps he merely judged it prudent to stay well away from the Exchequer in Madrid.

In April Cervantes presented yet another of his accounts, by no means the last. By now Guevara had been replaced, and in the middle of the month Cervantes started work again, now, however, in spite of his service and his experience, on a slightly reduced salary. The scandal over the corrupt officials had rebounded to the detriment of the honest. This time Cervantes explored new pastures, among them Jaén, Úbeda (where Saint John of the Cross had taken refuge and was soon to die) and Baeza. In each case, he wrote in advance to warn the inhabitants of his arrival and to ask them to decide among themselves how the burden should be shared. In Úbeda he probably looked up a friend from his slavery days, Diego de Benávides, who was a native of that town; they had shared lodgings in Algiers during the period after their release. By the middle of October, Cervantes was back in Seville presenting more accounts. In November he was in Montilla, home in *The Dogs' Colloquy* of his "most famous witch in the world," *La Camacha of Montilla,* who "miraculously restored maidens who had been careless with their virginity" and who "in December had fresh roses in her garden." Here he encountered some familiar problems as well as the local folklore; but the arrival of his immediate superior, the chief commissary, to sort things out at least brought with it the bonus that he carried with him Miguel's arrears of salary, dating back this time a mere eight months.

In January 1592, when Pedro de Isunza, the new Quartermaster General, wrote to the King disclaiming authority over a substitute commissary in the Córdoba district who had been accused of serious abuses, he stoutly defended his legitimate commissaries, Cervantes among them, calling them "honorable and highly trustworthy men." But his men were still not finding their work easy, as is plain from a letter sent by Cervantes and a colleague to Isunza. In strong terms it complained that the royal mandate that supplies should not be removed before payment had been made was proving a serious obstacle. As far as we know, this was the only official complaint ever submitted by the long-suffering Cervantes about his conditions of work.

In early 1592 his commissions sent him and his assistants roving the Andalusian countryside through the provinces of Seville, Córdoba, and Jaén, encountering the usual obstacles and difficulties: on 29 January in Cabra, a reluctant muleteer and his train had to be conscripted on Cervantes's orders. It was a far from heroic or romantic existence for a potentially great writer, but it was with such petty problems that Cervantes had constantly to deal. The monotony must often have been formidable. The immediate rewards were small and painfully slow in arriving. In Seville, at the end of May, he received his pay for January and February, but this was soon eaten up and at the end of June he authorized his immediate superior, Diego de Ruy Saenz, to collect the residue due to him from the Quartermaster General in Puerto de Santa María. He also authorized Ruy Saenz to collect a sizable little debt owed him by one of his own assistants then working in that area; hard-up as he was, he had obviously found the wherewithal to help out a friend.

Not long afterward a storm that had been brewing for some time broke round Cervantes's head. At some point in 1591 (or so Cervantes asserted in August 1592, though years later he would ascribe the incident to the early spring of 1592), the very assistant to whom he had lent money, Nicolás Benito, in his search for corn, had forced open the doors of a granary in Teba near Málaga, removed quantities of barley and wheat, and dispatched them for processing into ships' biscuits. The grain, it emerged, had been earmarked for payment of state taxes. The official in charge of the grain, Salvador de Toro, who would have to answer for the deficit in his supplies, not unnaturally demanded payment from Pedro de Isunza, the Quartermaster General. When no payment materialized, he obtained from the Exchequer an order of execution against Isunza himself. Still Isunza did not act. Why he remained so obstinate is unclear, perhaps purely out of professional irritation. It was at this point that Cervantes became directly involved. On 5 August in Seville, to enable payment to proceed, he signed a statement confirming what Benito had done, and, three days later, he signed another statement describing what had happened to the grain. Nothing, however, came of this, and the government proceeded against Isunza's personal estate. The affair, in which Cervantes remained involved, was to drag on for years.

Meanwhile, Cervantes stayed on in Seville. There is some tenuous evidence that he was ill and confined to his lodgings for a while. On the day he signed his second report on the Teba affair, a figure from his past materializes — Juan de Fortuny, the Valencian merchant to whom Doña Leonor, Cervantes's mother, had entrusted her export license in 1582 in an attempt to ransom her son. Fortuny, still deeply involved in charitable lending to Christian captives in Algiers, was suing a debtor whom he had financed, and Cervantes, in recognition of his past kindness, stood surety for him. He could scarcely afford to, in reduced circumstances as he was: neither his salary back to March nor his loan to Benito had been paid.

At this worst possible moment — hard up and possibly ill — he received word that the examiners of his Écija accounts had found his vouchers and receipts inadequate to cover the sum of money he claimed to have spent on the transport of grain. The deficit, although not enormous, was the equivalent of almost eighty days' salary, and since he had received no salary for six months, Cervantes could not pay. As a result, there now occurred one of the most unfortunate episodes of his career in the south. Every commissary — so great was the mistrust in which they were held by the state — had to provide guarantors in every single town from which they operated. How they managed this, arriving as they often did in places entirely strange to them, goodness only knows, but manage they did. Accordingly, since Cervantes could not pay, and since the Exchequer showed none of the patience with its debtors that it expected of its creditors, it demanded its money from Cervantes's guarantors in Écija, one of them a widow. His embarrassment must have been acute, and he obviously made haste — probably by calling once again on Tomás Gutiérrez's generosity — to put things to right, for, since he was soon back working in Écija, renewed sureties must have been provided.

It seems possible that during 1592 Cervantes's thoughts had been revolving round the feasibility of combining his commissary work with a return to writing for the theater. His friend Tomás Gutiérrez was a well-known retired player and at his inn in Seville — a flourishing center of theatrical activity — the acting companies often gathered. On 5 September in Seville, Cervantes signed a contract for no fewer than six plays with a theatrical manager called Rodrigo Osorio. In the contract, Cervantes promises to deliver to Osorio six plays on subjects of his own choice, neatly written out, on condition that each one be performed within twenty days of delivery, that payment be made within a week of performance, and that any not performed within twenty days be nonetheless paid for. If it emerged that any one of the plays were not among the best ever performed in Spain, on the other hand, payment would be forfeit. As to the amount of payment, this was fixed at fifty ducats a play. His price had risen since the 1580s in Madrid, but then so too had the cost of living; nevertheless, fifty ducats was a respectable fee for a successful dramatist at that time. Not that Cervantes ever saw the money, for the plays were certainly never performed and almost as certainly never completed. The contract's wording has all the provocative flavor of a wager, and it is not at all unlikely that the whole idea was a gesture of bravado made over a jug of wine, in response to some argument, perhaps, or in support of some hasty boast. Cervantes possibly found time to write a speech or scene or two, incorporated perhaps into the plays he wrote later on, but the preoccupations and problems of his everyday existence could have left him little time, and even less inclination, for the demands of art. At least one of his literary offspring saw the light that year, however: the ballad called "Disdain," which was published anonymously in an anthology printed in Burgos.

In any event, what happened two weeks after the brave contract was signed must have driven all thoughts of the theater right out of his head for a while. The *corregidor,* or Crown representative, in Écija, Don Francisco Moscoso (the proximity of whose name to *mocoso,* meaning *snotty,* must subsequently have provoked Cervantes to many a jest at the *corregidor's* expense), had been, for reasons that remain obscure, conducting a consistent campaign against the government commissaries who fell within his jurisdiction. In his complaints and actions against them he had so far exceeded his authority that Pedro de Isunza had been driven to protest to the King about him. It seems likely, in fact, that the whole affair was provoked by professional antagonism (Isunza, it will be remembered, was already involved in one interdepartmental row), with Moscoso aiming through his accusations against Isunza's men at bringing the Quartermaster General himself into disrepute. The upshot was that in September, Cervantes, by then back at work, was arrested at Castro del Río, where some years before he had himself exercised his judicial powers and committed a sacristan to prison. He was accused of having allegedly sold wheat without authorization, of having appropriated a further small quantity of grain without providing certification, and of a minor irregularity involving ten days' salary, which he might or might not have entered as such in his accounts — the *corregidor* was not absolutely sure of his facts.

On 19 September, sentence was passed. He had either to return the corn (which was obviously impossible) or its value in money. In addition, he was fined and ordered to meet the costs of the case, which amounted to four days' salary and expenses for the judge and his officers. In view of the nature of the accusations, the sentence seems excessively severe, and clearly Cervantes's previous troubles had not helped. He duly appealed, and was let out on bail pending further investigation. On 28 September, Isunza, probably anticipating that he was going to need Cervantes's support for his own problems in the days to come, authorized payment to him of sixty days' salary. Five days before that, Guevara, on the very brink of disgrace (it was announced that his arrested officials might well end up on the gallows), had departed this life, and

Cervantes must have thanked his guardian angel that he had had the wit to extract his earlier arrears of salary from Guevara's accommodating colleague. By November, he was back requisitioning oil in Écija and elsewhere; then sometime in the late autumn he traveled to Madrid with Isunza to give evidence in the investigation into the Teba incident. The seriousness of the affair had now grown, with Toro implying that the grain taken had not been put to government use, but sold privately.

In Madrid, on 1 December, Cervantes made a third deposition relating to events in Teba. Two days later he wrote to the King a letter in Isunza's defense. It stated the facts of the case, and unequivocally accepted responsibility for issuing the orders that Benito had merely followed (whereas it seems quite clear that Benito in the event acted rashly). He denied that the corn had been sold for private profit, and even offered to stand surety himself in the matter if the case against Isunza's estate could be withdrawn: Cervantes's prudence was never a match for his generosity. As a result, judgment on the case was suspended — the issue after all was largely one of departmental demarcations — although this was by no means the last Isunza or Cervantes was to hear of the case. Cervantes was still being required to give evidence as late as 1598, after Isunza's death.

While he was in Madrid helping Isunza, Cervantes's own difficulties were, unbeknown to him, assuming more ominous proportions. The government auditors, after spending more time on his accounts and examining his salary payments, decided he owed the Exchequer over a year's salary. Since they cannot just have arbitrarily changed their minds and since Cervantes's guarantors had already paid the sum previously declared to be owing, this new, larger sum would seem to have been composed mainly of the value of the grain he had been accused by

Moscoso of having sold without proper authorization. At
the very most, this constituted a paper debt, since Moscoso had never suggested that the proceeds had been kept
by Cervantes. But obviously Cervantes's accounts did not
run in the clear straight lines the auditors expected, and
they deemed him to be in debt. They even disputed his
early salary receipts and docked him in retrospect of
twenty-six days' wages, which meant that this small sum,
too, formed part of the amount declared to be owing.
None of this, however, could he have learned until his
return to Seville, and by then the danger was over. For
while in Madrid, with Isunza there to support him, Cervantes appealed to the Council of War (guaranteed to
champion whenever possible the collectors of its essential
military supplies) against the sentence passed on him in
Castro del Río, and his appeal was granted. He must have
embarked on the return journey with a comparatively
light heart. Isunza, who was not a young man, had fallen
seriously ill — the investigation into his affairs had taken
its toll — and Cervantes made the journey alone, arriving
in Seville in the middle of December. On the way there
he stopped off at Écija to provide Moscoso with evidence
of his discharge. It is not difficult to imagine the relish
with which he did so.

The auditors were still worrying away at his accounts,
however, and in January 1593 he was required to make a
deposition concerning oil and other supplies he had collected three years before. It is clear from what they
wished to know that the auditors were often as incompetent at following accounts as the commissaries were at
keeping them. This time Cervantes and his superiors
were able to make things clear to the Treasury without
too much trouble. But it took them a year to do it nonetheless, and the news that on 22 December the Puerto de
Santa María officials had indeed been put to death for

their crimes — admittedly very serious ones, including the misappropriation of supplies destined for Spanish garrisons in North Africa — could not have made him sleep any more soundly in his bed at night. That his own problems were, if not inevitable, certainly a run-of-the-mill part of commissary work, is plain from the fact that now, as before, he resumed his duties.

But not immediately, for Isunza, although by now back in Puerto de Santa María, was still ill and unable to attend to the organization of military supplies. Cervantes remained in Seville, not in Tomás Gutiérrez's inn — an inn of some reputation and style he could not always afford — but in various other lodgings. But his relations with his old friend continued to be close, and when, in the late spring, Gutiérrez sued one of the religious confraternities in Seville for blackballing him (or rather blackbeaning him, for the vote was conducted with broad beans), Cervantes was able to return one of the many favors Gutiérrez had shown him by testifying in his favor. As a former actor-manager and as an innkeeper, Gutiérrez could not be admitted, the confraternity held, "without scandal." Respectability, rather than wealth or status, was the key to membership. Catalina, Cervantes's wife, in spite of her straitened circumstances had been admitted to a confraternity at Esquivias several years before, and the Seville confraternity, as Gutiérrez scathingly pointed out, was full of cobblers, handymen, and tavern keepers; there was obviously a subtle but crucial distinction between those landlords with beds for hire and those without. But theatrical people and innkeepers, however prosperous, were simply not respectable enough it seems. In his statement, Cervantes testified to the superior nature of Tomás's inn, describing it as luxuriously appointed, the sort of place where "princes, gentlemen, and judges slept," and to the respectability of all serious actors, such as Tomás had been. His authority in this he claimed to derive from having himself written many plays and *autos,* though if he wrote any of the latter (one-act religious plays), none of them has come down to us. The case dragged on through the summer, with Gutiérrez producing a succession of witnesses in his support. Even when the Church authorities found in Gutiérrez's favor, the confraternity persisted in its refusal and was accordingly excommunicated and fined. The confraternity then appealed to Rome, the appeal was disallowed and, eventually, in the early spring of 1594, after the entire membership had been excommunicated, they gave in. Within five months, Tomás Gutiérrez was a pillar of the brotherhood.

In the meantime, on 24 June 1593, Pedro de Isunza the Quartermaster General had died. His deputy, Miguel de Oviedo, replaced him and, on 7 July, Cervantes was issued with a new commission to collect corn in the immediate vicinity of Seville, and with some urgency. The weather the previous winter had been so bad that many towns, Seville included, had been flooded, and crops and animals destroyed, and supplies were consequently very low. On 8 July, Cervantes received sixty days' back salary for his work in Écija the previous November, and four days later he made the usual arrangements to delegate his power of attorney, should the need arise. Then, with a hundred ducats in his saddle bags for official expenses he set off once more on his travels, faced with the impossible task, in a wet year when supplies were low and prices correspondingly high, of extracting good grain in large quantities on credit and at half the going rate. To make matters worse, owing to Isunza's illness, the whole operation was late in getting started and much of the available grain had already been sold.

By the receipts he left in his wake, we can roughly

chart his journeyings round the small towns and villages of the province. On 18 August, owing to the dearth of wheat, his commission was extended to include the district round the Badajoz. After making the necessary arrangements in each place as he went along, he then retraced his steps to collect the grain which he hoped would be waiting for him in store. In September he was so busy he had to send for an assistant, and after a short visit to Seville in December, the new year of 1594 found him still hard at it.

In Seville, if not before, he received the news that on 19 October Doña Leonor, his mother, had died suddenly in Madrid. She was seventy-three. Sadly, after a lifetime of hardship and struggle, Doña Leonor had died just as things were beginning to improve for herself and Magdalena, with whom she lived. Not long before they had taken a new house, a modest two-story dwelling rented from a tanner and sandwiched between a laborer and a cordswain. Since Doña Leonor had paid her rent in advance, clearly mother and daughter had managed to make themselves moderately comfortable. Magdalena was very probably taking in sewing and possibly even Doña Leonor, energetic woman that she was, had found some way or other of making a respectable penny. Cervantes must have been very deeply affected by the death of the mother who had fought so resolutely and ingeniously to free him from captivity, though never does he mention her in his writings — family relations, even wives, were not the stuff of which literature then was made. It is perhaps significant nonetheless that the few mothers who do make an appearance in his work are loving and supportive. The only one who figures boldly, Doña Estefanía in *The Force of Blood,* is strong, compassionate, and true, for she was "a woman and a noble one, to whom compassion and pity come as naturally as cruelty to a man." The words might well have served as his mother's epitaph.

The news that his uncle in Cabra, Andrés, had also died shortly before cast a further gloom upon a dismal winter. In February, Cervantes was still collecting wheat, unaware that Philip II and his advisors were rethinking the whole provisioning organization and that their deliberations would very soon put him out of a job. For a long time there had been dissatisfaction with the way in which supplies were collected and distributed — the complex negotiations and payments, the great distances between the source of supplies and their destination — but the recent scandals and squabbling, the increasing confusion over accounts, and the rising crescendo of complaints from towns clamoring for exemption or payment, or both, finally settled the matter. In April 1594 it was decided that, in future, money for supplies would be released in advance and that the supplies themselves would be paid for and transported on collection. The complicated system of certification and centralized payment was therefore discontinued; Oviedo, the new Quartermaster General, was dismissed and his whole organization dismantled.

On 14 June, Cervantes once again presented his accounts. This time, happily, they were judged satisfactory. Then, shaking the chaff of Andalusia off his heels for ever, he made his way back to Madrid. At the age of nearly forty-seven he found himself once again contemplating a future that gazed blankly back at him.

SIX

A Man and His Time: A Period of Crisis

CERVANTES HAD SPENT seven years of his life gathering military provisions in Andalusia, one of the small army of men he describes so vividly in his interlude, *The Divorce Court Judge*:

> ... with a rod of justice in his hand and seated upon a small, emaciated, and cantankerous hired mule, without an attendant muleteer — since these mules are never hired out other than they be decrepit and stubborn; with his saddlebags at his side, in one a collar and a shirt, in the other some cheese, some bread and a wine-skin; with only leggings and a single spur to render his ordinary dress fit for traveling; and with a commission and a tingling in his breast, he trots over that bridge out of Toledo, the evil ways of the lazy beast notwithstanding; and but a short time later sends home the odd leg of ham and sundry yards of rough linen — in short the sort of things that go for a song in the villages where his job takes him and in this way he supports his family as best a poor sinner may.

That period of his life was now over. Tedious and frustrating as it had been, it had immeasurably enriched his experience of human life, adding to the more specialist perspectives of his time in the army and his five years of slavery an intimate acquaintance with the ordinary and the routine, with the abundant variety of urban and rural life. In particular it had drawn him into close contact with his own country, with its high civil servants and muleteers, with wealthy landowners and goatherds, with church prelates and serving wenches; and with their prejudices and pretensions, their fears and beliefs. Its effect on his writing, particularly on *Don Quixote* with its panoramic view of the rich tapestry of Spanish society, was enormous. And he himself evidently perceived this for time and again later on he would declare travel to be man's ablest mentor. To call him a literary writer is, although true, in a sense misleading; for, while he did indeed feed freely off literature, life itself in all its specific historical detail gave him equal nourishment. For him the world of fact and the world of fiction were both legitimate pasture grounds for the artist.

However, it must merely have seemed at the time that another unrewarding chapter in his life was closed. Once in Madrid he wasted no time in looking for further employment in government administration, the world he now knew best. Agustín de Cetina had been promoted to royal auditor and, probably on his recommendation, Cervantes received an appointment with the Exchequer itself, as a collector of taxes.

If there is one thing people find harder to hand over than their possessions it is their money, and Cervantes, with his long experience of supply collection in the south, can have harbored no illusions about the nature of his new job. If the compulsory purchase of provisions was a thorn in the fertile side of Andalusia, taxation was a running sore in the body of Castile as a whole. As the purchasing power of Spanish money had declined and the cost of maintaining Spain's military enterprises risen, the state's demands upon the country had grown; and Castile, as the crown's principal bulwark, had to bear the principal burden of taxation. The large number of people exempt from taxation on account of their social rank made life even harder for the poor. The financial situation in general was fast becoming an intolerable one, and in two years' time, the realm would be declared bankrupt. The fact that Cervantes's function was as much that of debt collector as of tax collector — since the taxes he was commissioned to collect were long overdue — must have counted in his favor. Any man capable of coping with the hostility and tantrums of Écija was presumably, in Cetina's eyes, eminently capable of extracting overdue taxes with maximum efficiency and minimum fuss.

His new duties took Cervantes back to Andalusia. Before setting out for Granada, where he was to start work, Cervantes had to provide the usual guarantor. He used a rather disreputable character called Don Francisco Suárez Gasco. In 1591, Don Francisco had been suspected of attempting to murder his wife, and he was shortly to be sentenced to exile for his unruly conduct. But perhaps Cervantes knew no one else prepared to stand surety for the very large sum of money involved: the taxes for collection amounted to well over six thousand ducats, and Suárez Gasco guaranteed four thousand ducats of it. His credit was obviously suspect, for Cervantes had to provide the Exchequer with proof of Suárez Gasco's financial standing and reliability. All this took time. But eventually, after both Cervantes and Catalina — no doubt summoned to Madrid for the purpose — had themselves underwritten the appointment with everything they possessed or were ever likely to possess, Cervantes's commission was handed him on 23 August. Soon afterward, armed with judicial powers, which included the right to confiscate and sell debtors' worldly goods, he set off on his first tour of duty.

As far as his salary was concerned, the Spanish Exchequer never changed its spots: although somewhat higher than before, now that his responsibilities were to the Exchequer directly, the salary was to take the form of a levy upon the towns whose overdue taxes made the whole recovery operation necessary. This levy Cervantes himself had to impose and collect. One's first reaction is that it would be difficult to conceive of a more distasteful complication to a tax collector's already unpleasant task. But the new appointment, as a more responsible and better paid post higher up the administrative ladder, was a promotion, and if Cervantes was by now wedded to the idea of a career in government service, as seems likely, then he clearly could not allow himself to be put off by the less agreeable aspects of his new appointment.

By 7 September, Cervantes had started on his rounds and was in Guadix. Two days later, in Baza, where the accounts were in disorder owing to the town's having no treasurer that year, there had to be an adjustment of the tax estimate. There was also a slight fracas over Cervantes's salary, for the town was made to pay for its inefficiency by meeting his salary during the days he had spent on the journey from Madrid; but with firm handling on his part, the matter was quickly settled. His progress was necessarily brisk since his schedule was strictly laid down: he was supposed to travel at the rate of eight Spanish leagues (thirty-three and a half miles) per day. But although he stayed in Baza only for a day or two, he could hardly have failed to hear about the scandal involving his old enemy in Algiers, Juan Blanco de Paz. Blanco had for a short time recently been prebendary of the church in Baza, but his misdemeanors had eventually caught up with him and he was now on the run both from the church, for misrepresentation, and from the law, for debt. Even someone as magnanimous as Cervantes must have felt some satisfaction that the wretched man was at last revealed to the world in his true colors.

In Granada things did not go so well: the town treasurer claimed (rightly, as it was subsequently revealed) that the taxes due had already been paid. So too did the outlying towns of Motril, Salobreña, and Almuñécar. And, of course, no taxes meant no salary. Fortunately the next two towns proved more cooperative, and by the beginning of October Cervantes was back in Granada. On 8 October, he wrote a report to the King, recommending that the four claims of paid-up taxes be checked and requesting that his time be extended to allow him to complete his tour of duty. When the reply was slow in coming, Cervantes went on anyway to Vélez Málaga near the south coast. Here the taxes could not be met, and Cervantes had to be content with a money order, cashable in Seville, for slightly less than half the amount owing. From Málaga, not on his rounds but on his way to Ronda, his last port of call, Cervantes wrote again to the King on 17 November with an account of his progress, asking for permission to proceed to Ronda. Twelve days later this request was granted in a letter from the King, which insisted that the Almuñécar, Motril, and Salobreña taxes be collected on pain of serious consequences to the three towns. By 9 December Cervantes was in Ronda where most, though not all, the taxes were paid (the town claiming that the Exchequer had its figures wrong) and on 15 December he was back in Seville cashing the money order made out to him in Vélez Málaga the month before.

With this, his business in the south should have been over, but there were still the debts in Almuñécar, Salobreña, and Motril, which the King had ordered him to collect. Presumably before making his way back to Madrid he called at these places, displaying the royal letter with its threats of confiscation and punishment, and obtained the money without too much trouble, for we hear no more about it.

Cervantes must have been reasonably content with his first experience of financial administration. The greater part of the taxes due had been collected and the money dispatched to Madrid; there had been relatively few complications, and by way of bonus he had visited interesting places that were entirely new to him. Deciding that it would not be safe to make the long journey back to Madrid with what taxes remained in his possession, he handed over the money, together with some of his own, to a Sevillian merchant for safety. The merchant, Simón Freire de Lima, gave him in return a money order payable in Madrid. Cervantes then set off for Madrid, blissfully unaware of what disastrous seeds he had sown for the future.

He arrived in Madrid to discover that family history, sadly, was repeating itself. His niece, Costanza de Figueroa (Andrea's daughter) was involved in a breach of promise affair with Don Pedro de Lanuza y de Perellós, an Aragonese aristocrat who, like the other young bucks with whom the Cervantes women managed to become involved, moved through society strewing debts and broken hearts in his wake. Marriage between such a high-ranking noble and a woman of Costanza's social background was, of course, well nigh inconceivable. On 5 July 1595, Lanuza, whose lands had been confiscated by the Crown after the Aragonese uprising in Zaragoza in 1590, promised to pay Costanza fourteen hundred ducats (quite a large sum, so clearly the affair was one of some moment) as soon as his fortunes improved. Before long they did, for in February 1596 Lanuza received a commandership in one of the military orders, and on 3 December 1596 he authorized Costanza, who had been pressing for payment, to collect her money in twice yearly installments of one hundred ducats over seven years. In her document of receipt, signed on 8 December and witnessed by Andrea, Costanza swore she was under twenty-five years of age: she was in fact almost thirty, her mother's daughter in more ways than one.

While this little saga unfolded, and while the Exchequer's officials sat on his accounts, Cervantes turned his attention once more to poetry. And to some avail. On 7 May 1595 he was declared a prize winner in a poetical joust organized by the Dominican order in Zaragoza to celebrate the canonization of Saint Hyacinth, the "Apostle of Poland." Cervantes had entered the second competition, which required a gloss on a given stanza about the new saint, and was awarded the first prize of three silver spoons. Judging by Cervantes's winning entry, the standard of the competition was not very high. It is unlikely that Cervantes was in Zaragoza in person for the joust, for on 18 May he was in Toledo acting as legal witness for the ordination of Catalina's brother Francisco.

Pleased as Cervantes was by his small triumph in Zaragoza, it could not have done much to alleviate his growing unease over his business affairs. There was no sign in Madrid of either Simón Freire de Lima or the money Cervantes had banked with him, and eventually Cervantes wrote to Seville. An anxious month later, a letter came back instructing Cervantes to seek payment from an agent in Madrid, Gabriel Rodríguez. But when Cervantes presented the order, Rodríguez could not honor it. Another letter to Seville then elicited the calamitous news that Freire de Lima had gone bankrupt for the huge sum of sixty thousand ducats and absconded.

Cervantes must have felt as if the heavens had crashed down around his head. Where could he possibly find five hundred and fifty ducats to reimburse the Crown? All he could do after a futile visit to Seville, where many of Freire's creditors had already gathered, was to petition that the money he owed the Exchequer be collected from the bankrupt's estate and to hand in to his superiors a sworn statement containing the facts of the matter. On 7 August 1595, the King accordingly wrote to Doctor Bernardo de Olmedilla, Judge of the High Court in Seville, ordering that the money be confiscated from Freire's estate, in satisfaction of the debt if there were no prior claims on the estate, pending further inquiries if there were any. In either case Philip II made it abundantly clear that his orders in no way absolved Cervantes from responsibility for the missing money or for any expenses incurred in its recovery.

Cervantes himself bore the instructions to Seville and waited there while Freire's affairs were looked into and the King's orders carried out. Had he known what an interminably long time it was going to take he would certainly have despaired: the money would not reach the Treasury until 21 January 1597, almost eighteen months later. Soon after he left the capital, his sister Magdalena paid into the Exchequer on his behalf the first of two sums of money — presumably borrowed — with which it looks as if Cervantes was attempting to protect himself against the total failure of his mission to Seville. Even this prudent act rebounded on him. For when all the money Cervantes had entrusted to Freire was eventually recovered from the latter's estate, Cervantes's personal share of it, and these two sums deposited by Magdalena, were retained by the Exchequer, as we shall see, to offset other putative debts. Since Cervantes was never paid his full salary for his months as tax collector in the south —

not to mention the time and money he expended on
trying to salvage the situation after Freire's departure —
the whole Granada venture proved an out-and-out financial disaster for him. His life, it must have seemed, was
destined to be one long succession of failures and disappointments. As the Priest in *Don Quixote* was to say pith-
ily a few years later: "I have been acquainted with this
man Cervantes for many years and I know that he is better versed in misfortunes than in verses." Cervantes's wry
self-knowledge rarely failed him.

Whatever Cervantes's ambitions for a career in administration had previously been, his long and eventful flirta-
tion with public service was now at an end. Either his
superiors decided — as they might well have done — that
he was more trouble than he was worth or he himself had
become totally disillusioned both with the work itself and
with his ability to cope with it. In the past the need for
employment had time and again sent him back for more,
regardless of difficulties, but it would be hardly surprising
if in the light of recent events he decided that he could
simply not afford any longer a job that swallowed money
instead of making it. In all probability he and the Exchequer parted by mutual consent, the realization having
grown on them both that he was neither a very practical
nor a very lucky man, and that for such a person there
was no safe place in the world of government finance.

Cervantes was, once again, unemployed. At home in
Esquivias the family's finances had improved somewhat
owing to the death in May of that year of Catalina's prosperous uncle, the priest Juan de Palacios. Catalina was
better off by two plots of land planted with olive trees
and a share of her uncle's humble household effects — two
French hangings, a bed and some bedclothes, and a
bucket. Her brothers too had profited and rather more
substantially. The elder boy, Francisco — now a student

priest in Toledo University — received some land, several houses, and all his uncle's Latin books; the younger, Fernando, two vineyards and a few other plots of land. Catalina's elder sister, María, with whom the old priest lived, received the lion's share of his estate, but the will, even so, went a little way toward making life easier for Catalina. When, in February 1597, she was short of money, she was able to sell a small parcel of land to raise some.

Cervantes seems to have stayed on in Seville during this period, supporting himself by setting up, on the strength of his many contacts in the city, as a free-lance man of affairs, a role he had briefly occupied once before in the mid-1580s. In 1596 with the publication of Cristóbal Mosquera de Figueroa's treatise on military discipline, his sonnet on the Marquis of Santa Cruz saw the light of day at last. Ironically enough, that same year afforded him the opportunity to write a sonnet of a very different sort on Santa Cruz's successor as commander in chief of the Armada, the Duke of Medina Sidonia.

A disgusted Spanish people, in their search for an explanation of the defeat of God's great design, had cast the Duke in the inglorious role of chief culprit and scapegoat. In his own home territory in Andalusia, where wit still trips easily from the tongue, he had been nicknamed "the god of the tunnyfish" since he was Admiral of the Fleet and the tunnyfish was traditionally regarded as timid. At the beginning of July, with the Spanish militia and navy in a state of total unpreparation and disarray, the English, this time under the Earl of Essex, made another daring raid on Cadiz, by now the richest city in Spain. They sacked it (one single house, so the story goes, yielded eighty thousand ducats), razed its defenses to the ground, and scuttled or burnt every one of the sixty-five ships in the harbor, destroying at a blow a major part of Spain's naval strength. Spain was scandalized and, like many of his countrymen, Cervantes attributed the disaster to the by now legendary cowardice of the Duke, who wrote pathetically to the King: "Nothing is left, neither ships, nor fleet, nor Armada, nor Cadiz itself." In his sonnet, read aloud no doubt in some Sevillian academy, Cervantes describes the Spanish militia, all plumes and bombast, as more frightening to the locals than to the English. While the enemy sacks the city, they scurry round in preparation for the fray, threatening, bleating, and blustering; then, "finally, when the Count had already departed scot-free, into Cadiz with duly measured step came the great Duke of Medina in triumph." The irony does not succeed in concealing the anguish he felt at this proof that the glorious days of the famous Spanish infantry, to which he had once belonged, were over.

This sonnet, incidental as it might seem, is in a way a small milestone in Cervantes's literary career, for with it a new note enters Cervantes's writing. The "straight" Cervantes, solemnly patriotic, respectful, earnest in the wooing of his poetic muse and highminded in the pursuit of a human ideal, while far from dead, assumes a more fractured existence, becoming merely one part of a changed, multifaceted and complex response to the literary possibilities of human experience. This Cervantes still achieves prominence, from time to time, particularly toward the end of his life, but never, for us, with the conviction and strength of the inspiration born directly of his disillusion. And even when he does relapse into the conventional he does so deliberately, for new purposes of his own. It is now, in 1596, with the scathing sonnet to Medina Sidonia, that we see that the scales have fallen from his eyes. His exposure to life as a government employee in Andalusia had accomplished what his years as a soldier and as a slave, susceptible even in the midst of danger and hardship of a heroic interpretation, had failed to do. It had stripped life of its enchantment. It had added a clarity to his vision and an edge to his pen which, while never pitiless or cruel and rarely mocking, will remain steadfast and uncompromising, transforming his writing from something ephemeral and exclusively of its time into something of lasting value. Much of the time that clarity and that edge will be shaped and maintained by an ironic amusement at the absurdity and perversity of man, but the amusement will never be free of a deep compassion for these very follies. It is this sense of humor, often wry, often deflating but never sardonic, which saved his artistic vision from pessimism and, we feel, his own life from despair. Cervantes was one of those rare human beings who, far from being spiritually impoverished by failure and misfortune, feed and flourish upon them. While often understandably bitter, he never became embittered.

In all probability this period in Seville marked the start of his really productive years as a writer, and it is now in my view that he began to acquire that close familiarity with the works of the literary theorists of his day which is so apparent in *Don Quixote* yet scarcely figures in *The Galatea*. Most of his publications are clustered together in the last eleven years of his life, from 1605 to 1616, but some of them, and certainly parts of some of them — poems and interpolated stories, for example — must belong to an earlier period. They may even of course be of very much earlier date and no doubt some of his ideas germinated as he traveled the roads of Andalusia, as he sat dreaming of freedom in Algiers or in between battles in Italy: it seems highly likely, for example, that "The Captive's Tale" in *Don Quixote* and his exemplary tale *The Generous Lover* were written not long after he returned from captivity to Spain. But the amount of time he actually spent writing was of necessity very limited during the earlier years, and it is only after he gave up regular employment that he can have had enough consistent free time to devote to his pen.

The problem of dating Cervantes's works is in any event a complicated one and probably incapable of final resolution. Some have ascribed his more idealized fiction to an earlier stage in his productive years than the more obviously realistic works; it is suggested, for instance, that the "romantic" exemplary tales are earlier than those where the social criticism is strong, with those which depict an idealized love in a pseudorealistic setting coming in between. But although the stories certainly span a number of years, Cervantes did not think in terms of realism and idealism in the way we do, and certainly did not regard them as value judgments, so that other dating criteria must be pursued. If there were a steady transition from romantic idealism to social and psychological realism, then he would not have died writing *The Trials of Persiles and Sigismunda,* which is far closer to the first of these modes than to the second, and still promising the appearance of a second part of *The Galatea,* in spite of Berganza's assertion in *The Dogs' Colloquy* that "all those books are gracefully written, dreamed-up things for the entertainment of the idle and contain no truth whatsoever."

There is not even, as one might expect on the evidence of his life, a complete shift from optimism to disillusion, at least not in a way which is reflected directly in literary mood or tone. A new note enters his writing in 1596, productive of the work for which we most value him, but by no means does he thereafter play a single tune. Perhaps because our illusions are shaped by our time in a way our disillusion is not, we make the mistake of thinking that disillusion necessarily leads to realism; it is as conducive to escapism, at worst, or constructive fantasy, at best, as it is to confrontation. Cervantes's literary disillusion is never cruel and is usually good humored; and in his work as a whole he balances his exposure of the folly of man with an affirmation of right values and right behavior — just as in *Don Quixote* his parody of the literature of knight errantry is underpinned by his assertions of what literature ought to be: responsible, congruous, and truthful.

As far as Cervantes's day-to-day life in Seville is concerned in the period after he left the government's employ, we are completely in the dark. His very reasons for staying in the south are obscure, unless he wished to keep an eye on the fortunes of Freire de Luna's bankrupt estate or had formed some attachment to keep him there. The only way we remain in touch with him is, alas, through the dismal and protracted financial repercussions of his brief stint as a tax collector. In January 1597, as we saw, the money he had entrusted to Freire de Luna was recovered from the latter's estate. Cervantes must have thought that the whole dreadful episode was now over. However, in August 1597 the Exchequer, having eventually got around to checking his 1594 accounts, asked Cervantes's sureties in Madrid, Francisco Suárez Gasco and Catalina, to account for discrepancies in the taxes he had collected in 1594; it will be remembered that in Vélez Málaga he had been able to collect rather less than half the amount owing. The Exchequer was now holding him responsible for the balance, which, taking into account the proportion of the Freire de Luna money which was Cervantes's own as well as the two sums Magdalena had paid into the Exchequer, still amounted according to the Exchequer's calculations to some 79,804 maravedíes, over 200 ducats (in reality it amounted to considerably more, but the auditors had their arithmetic wrong). Evidently Cervantes had not set out the facts with sufficient clarity when he submitted his accounts and, since he was in Seville, he was not on hand to offer an explanation. Suárez Gasco, terrified that the Exchequer would come down on him for the money, applied to the King for a subpoena compelling Cervantes to come to Madrid. A royal order was duly sent to the Judge of the High Court at Seville instructing him to obtain from Cervantes sureties guaranteeing his appearance in Madrid within twenty days and payment of the money he was judged to owe the Exchequer. If the sureties were not supplied, he was to be arrested and sent to Madrid's jail.

Unfortunately the order, in setting out the circumstances of the affair, made no mention of the fact that only a small part of Cervantes's total commission was at issue; the only sum mentioned was the full six thousand ducats that Cervantes had set out to collect in back taxes. Stupidly, the judge, a man of little judgment and doubtful honesty, took the letter's wording at face value and ordered Cervantes to guarantee the whole sum. Not surprisingly, no one could be found in Seville to underwrite such an amount, and the Judge accordingly arrested Cervantes and committed him to the royal prison in Seville.

It was Cervantes's second experience of jail, but this time there was to be no speedy release. It is not difficult to imagine his angry protestations, his indignant attempts at explanation; and the scars were to remain, as we see from *The Trials of Persiles and Sigismunda* years later, where he says that no one who fell into the hands of the legal authorities ever left them again "with the same lustre." The words are a revealing insight into the effect on his self-respect of the seven months he spent languishing in jail, surrounded by pickpockets, confidence tricksters, prostitutes, and murderers: a splendid source of information about the Sevillian underworld, which Cervantes was to make full use of in *Rinconete and Cortadillo* and *The Dogs' Colloquy*, but degrading for all that. The nature of justice and the relationship between crime and punishment will be a recurring theme in *Don Quixote*.

It has been claimed that it was here in prison in Seville that Cervantes, at the age of fifty, started writing *Don Quixote*. Part I of the book would not be published until 1605 and certainly eight years would seem a long gestation period for a work even of that length by an author with apparently little else to do. He himself claimed that his hero, "dried-up, wizened, fanciful, and abounding with thoughts never imagined by anyone else," was "conceived in prison, where every discomfort has its being and every pitiful noise its existence." But how much time elapsed between conception and parturition we cannot know. The prison he referred to might even have been that at Castro del Río in 1592, for none of the books mentioned in *Don Quixote* as belonging to the Knight's library was published after 1591, although, since Cervantes was in prison in Castro del Río for only a few days, it seems unlikely that he actually started writing there. There is every likelihood, however, that the work was initially planned as a short story — perhaps another exemplary tale — corresponding in length to what became the first five chapters or so of the extended narrative, which are relatively self-contained, and it might well have been this short parody that took shape between prison walls. Perhaps it was now, with months of enforced inactivity at his disposal, that he immersed himself in the romances of chivalry and that the notion of writing a parody slowly crystallized in his mind. Certainly Cervantes's spirits must have been at a very low ebb in prison in Seville and it is entirely plausible, psychologically, that he took refuge during the long hours of tedium in an interiorized world of artistic creation. More specifically, it would seem entirely consistent with events if it were indeed now that his imagination fathered upon his pen the idea of a country squire so bewitched by the narrative power of the romances of chivalry that he thinks he can recreate in his own time the fantasy world they portray. Alonso de Fuentes, in a digest of natural philosophy published in Seville in 1547, had denounced the romances of chivalry on the grounds that reading them had driven a Sevillian mad, and the story might well have been common gossip still in Cervantes's days in Seville. But a very special balance between disillusion and optimism was necessary to spawn the idea of a man who tries to impose his borrowed ideals upon an inimical reality and in the process — for such is the uncompromising nature of the real world — comes to comic grief, and the wretched limbo of an innocent imprisonment, perhaps, helped establish this delicate equilibrium.

Cervantes had no intention of accepting this detention lying down. From prison he sent a letter to the King pointing out that since he was in prison and away from home he could neither attend a hearing at Madrid nor find the necessary guarantors; he requested that the judge in Seville be instructed to release him subject to his providing sureties simply for whatever sum he was deemed to owe to the Exchequer. Convinced, as indeed he ought to have been, by the reasonableness of this argument, the King sent the judge new instructions, this time spelling out the extent of Cervantes's financial responsibilities. Cervantes was to be released provided he supplied "satisfactory" sureties for the sum owing and undertook to be in Madrid within thirty days. What happened next is very vague. Either Cervantes could not find the necessary sureties in Seville (his old friend and benefactor, Tomás Gutiérrez, had long since disappeared from Cervantes's financial life — perhaps he, too, had fallen on hard times) or the judge proved difficult to satisfy. Certainly Cervantes had no money to bribe him with. Whatever the reason, Cervantes was not released. Once again, his hopes had come to nothing, and success, so nearly in his grasp, receded.

The full effect of his continuing imprisonment is incalculable. Was it a period of spiritual crisis from which he emerged ready to countenance a renewed life of literary activity, to contemplate a reaffirmation of the lasting values in life? Was it now that optimism learned to triumph over pessimism, that humor learned to dispel despair? It is hard to see how these months of frustration and deprivation could have failed to have a profound and lasting influence on both man and writer.

At the end of March 1598, Cervantes, still in jail, must have thought it the last straw when he was required by Treasury accountants to make a signed statement concerning commissions he had carried out for Pedro de Isunza in 1591 and 1592, including particulars of the incident involving Nicolás Benito's seizures of grain at Teba. However, he was quick to grasp the possibilities of the situation. He assured the Exchequer that if he were soon released he would recover all his papers relating to that period from Málaga where he had left them, and supply the statement required. He was, after all, he reminded them, well known for his punctuality in submitting his accounts. It being patently clear that Cervantes could not do anything without his accounts to hand, his point was taken: the slow, confused working of the government's auditing machinery had come to his rescue. Toward the end of April he was released from prison; the Exchequer had not hesitated to go over the Sevillian judge's head in its relentless application of that mainspring of its operational philosophy — accountability. One wonders how long Cervantes would have been left to stew in prison had this spur to government action not materialized: on the evidence of this very incident his Granada tax commission accounts might well have been left in cold storage for years. As it was, on 28 April, Cervantes signed the deposition that had proved his salvation.

If the Exchequer expected Cervantes, now that he was free, to appear in Madrid as he had earlier been instructed, it was doomed to disappointment. Perhaps he despaired of proving his innocence, considering it pointless to precipitate disaster if disaster were on its way. Anyway, he stayed in Seville. How easily he picked up the threads of his life there again we can only guess. That his circumstances were fairly wretched is clear, for later in the year we find him purchasing some yards of cloth and a consignment of biscuits on credit. Obviously he had resumed, on a rather humble scale, his career as a free-lance man of affairs, which is how his sister Andrea somewhat later described him. For although this cannot have been easy in view of his recent history, Seville, as a thriving center of commercial activity, was rich enough and anonymous enough to allow many a man the opportunity to keep body and soul together by small-scale trafficking in goods and bills. Remembering this later on when he came to write *The Dogs' Colloquy,* he pronounced the city he knew and loved so well "a shelter for the poor and a refuge for the outcast." In Lope de Vega's pastoral romance, *Arcadia,* published that year, Cervantes's effigy appears alongside those of many other contemporary poets in the Palace of Poetry, but in the autumn of 1598 he must have felt himself nonetheless to be both poor and rejected.

We can safely assume that during this period Cervantes spent some, perhaps even much, of his time writing. What he wrote, however — poems, short stories, fragments of *Don Quixote* — is a matter of conjecture, although the evidence that he produced some time around now the early version of *Rinconete and Cortadillo,* which deals with Sevillian low life, is, albeit tenuous, fairly persuasive. If this is the case, the story, with its naturalistic dialogue, must have been one of his earliest experiments in Spain's sixteenth-century tradition of comic realism. *Rinconete and Cortadillo* reads like the introduction to a longer narrative. It tells how two boys meet on the road, continue together to Seville, there join a gang of thieves organized by a Fagin figure, Monipodio, and get to know the gang's members and rules. At the end of the story the gang disperses to meet again the following Sunday, and Rinconete muses and passes judgment on what he has seen. Disapproving as he is, we are told that he and Cortadillo remained with the gang for several months and that their adventures will be told on some future occasion: the conclusion thus smacks of something intended to be longer and hastily rounded off. The story, though unequivocal at the end in its condemnation of the thieves' dishonesty and hypocrisy (they carefully carry out their religious devotions) has a lightness of touch in its wonderfully vivid and lifelike detail, its humor, its irony, and its satirical innuendo, which might well have come from the pen of a man himself in or fresh from prison; a man disenchanted with the processes of law and order and familiar with the humor and drama, as well as with the sordidness, of the lives led by cutpurses, bullyboys and gangsters' molls. In fact the state of Sevillian justice comes in, not surprisingly, for direct and scathing comment.

That he was not writing plays we can be fairly sure, for there was no incentive for him to do so. In November 1597, after the death (on 6 November) of Philip II's daughter, Princess Catherine, Duchess of Savoy, the Madrid theaters were closed for a period of mourning. During the previous ten years or so, as the theater-going craze had grown, so too had the surge of protests from the theater's opponents, mainly churchmen, all of whom were convinced that both the drama itself and the theatrical world it supported were undermining public morals. The songs and dances which accompanied performances of plays were considered at best indecorous, at worst licentious; the actresses, often provocatively clad for their roles in doublet and hose, were regarded as little better than prostitutes; the plots themselves were considered to be an incitement to frivolous values and attitudes. The Spanish theater's career throughout most of the seventeenth century would be accompanied by a similar chorus of complaints, and time and again the authorities would make feeble efforts to introduce legislation controlling the activities of players and their performances. Already in 1596 a decree had been promulgated forbidding women to appear at all on the stage — without the slightest effect. The Duchess's death a year later, with its compulsory period of public mourning, was thus a heaven-sent opportunity for the theater's opponents, an opportunity which they did not fail to exploit. In response to their request that the theaters remain closed, the King referred the matter to a council of three theologians. As a result of their deliberations, a royal decree was issued on 2 May 1598, stating that no plays should for the time being be performed in Spain. It was judged that they encouraged idleness and pleasure-seeking, made men effeminate and unfit for the hardships of war and distracted them from warlike pursuits. The theater was sabotaging Spain's political health and military strength and playing right into the hands of the Turk and the English. (Had they known much about it, the critics might have derived some small comfort from the comparable popularity enjoyed by the

Shakespearean theater in the heart of enemy territory.) In other words the theater was made a scapegoat for the growing disenchantment of Spaniards with Spain's accelerating inability to cope with the consequences of its self-appointed role as defender of Europe's Catholic conscience.

Owing to Philip's own death in September 1598, the theaters remained closed until April 1599 when the town council of Madrid, anxious about the loss of charitable revenue to the city's hospitals, prevailed upon the King, by now Philip III, to reinstate the public theaters, ostensibly so that his betrothal to the Archduchess Margaret of Austria might be properly celebrated. In the event the concession was not implemented for almost another year.

In spite of the lavish celebrations that accompanied the accession of the new King, all was not well with Spain. Two years earlier the realm had been declared bankrupt. That same year, 1597, had seen the arrival in the north of the plague, which, slowly moving southward, reached epidemic proportions between 1599 and 1600, ravaging towns and villages and wiping out fifteen percent of the population. In the last years of the century too the harvests failed at home; while abroad, Spanish armies and expeditions met with the first of a series of military reversals and failures. The country was in the throes of an economic, military, political, and, above all, psychological crisis of grave proportions; and the new King, a young man of twenty, was not, as his father had foreseen, the monarch to cope with it. Philip III was a very different monarch indeed, weak where his father had been strong, pleasure-loving where his father had been austere, and more than content to hand over effective power to a second in command. The period of royal favorites and of the ascendancy of the aristocracy had begun. The court,

sober, restrained, and decorous under its previous, more
parsimonious monarch, now exploded into a frenetic
round of extravagance and self-indulgence, bearing society as a whole, particularly Madrid society, along with it
on its lemminglike rush down the slope toward spiritual
bankruptcy and exhaustion. Under the next King, Philip
IV, the entire process would only accelerate. As the rich
grew richer and the poor became destitute, Castilian society, seeking escape from a truth too hard to bear, became increasingly a society of outward display, of purchased honors and meaningless posturing, of hollow
values with little relevance to reality. It was a society in
which religious orthodoxy and intellectual containment
marched hand in hand with social hypocrisy and laxity of
manners; where self-delusion rubbed shoulders with insecurity, disillusion, fatalism, and cynicism; where, in the
face of a starving population, the cult of racial purity
became the source of idleness and an excuse for inaction.
Cervantes, his eyes already opened by failure and disappointment to the ways of his world, would no longer have
to infer corruption or intuit defeat: both would be there
for all who wished to see. Under Philip III, the carapace
of restraint imposed through example and control by
Philip II was shattered, the confidence in a Spanish destiny dispersed, and Castilians, clinging to their only life-
line — their illusion of superiority — proceeded to gather
what rosebuds they could while they still had the chance.

For all this, perhaps indeed because of this — for the
realism of disillusion arguably inspires greater and more
lasting literary artifacts than the idealism of hope — the
seventeenth century in Spain is a period of intense cultural activity of outstanding quality. In their different
ways Mateo Alemán, Lope de Vega, Tirso de Molina,
Góngora, Quevedo, and Calderón will, like Velázquez,
feed off the realities of the society that produced them,

each transmuting them into an artistic vision that is personal and distinct, all identifiably of their time yet at the same time transcending it. Ostensibly writing from within the intellectual parameters of their age — a matter in which there was little choice — and all in the last analysis committed to the prevailing ideology that saw in faith, order, and structure the necessary conditions for a stable, successful society, these authors all surpass the limitations of the intellectual climate in which they lived to write works that are not only aesthetically exciting but have a timeless human relevance as well. If it is the business of the artist, as T. S. Eliot held it to be the business of the poet, to express the greatest emotional intensity of his time, based on what that time happens to think, then these writers are indeed great artists.

In many ways Cervantes, the greatest of them all, is one of them. Indeed he is more overtly and consistently moralist than most of them — in spite of the fact that many critics over the years have chosen to believe, because it better suits their image of Cervantes, the universal genius, that his moralizing claims are a smokescreen to confuse the Inquisition's censors. For, undeniably eager as he is to give pleasure with his work, there is very little in it which may be construed as inconsistent with a deeply moral and responsible attitude to life in the truest Christian sense. He is neither a spiritual nor a social revolutionary and he takes for granted — or at least does not concern himself with — the great metaphysical issues of life. At the same time his is arguably the freest spirit of Spain's great seventeenth-century writers, the most genuinely experimental, imaginatively and technically, and the least tied in his writings — either in acceptance or in opposition — to the psychosocial, religious patterns that are definably of his own time. The least successful in the world's terms, the most harassed by life's misfortunes, his troubled, penurious life — for all that his very real ambition as a writer persisted when his ambitions in other directions had withered away — seems to have been an artistic and spiritual liberation, a conquest of freedom and detachment that led to a spontaneous reaffirmation of the most lasting human values.

Like other royal deaths, that of Philip II elicited a response from Cervantes. For him, as for many Spaniards, the passing of the monarch who had embodied the faith militant and set his face successfully against the Turk, only to live to see his dream of religious victory and unity begin to crumble around him, must have vividly symbolized the end of an era. What fixed his poet's eye, however, were the grotesquely ornate and pompous obsequies which followed — another symbol, this time of the vain strutting of a nation that was retreating from defeat and disillusion into a hectically stimulated display of glory and grandeur. In Seville cathedral a huge catafalque that took the city's architects, painters, and sculptors fifty-two days to construct commemorated the dead monarch. Sculpted scenes from the battle of Lepanto adorned its great bulk, inscriptions and epitaphs contributed by local wits and held on with pins festooned its sides. Cervantes's poem was one of these. It is suitably reverent, yet lighter in tone than we would expect had we no knowledge of Cervantes's personal reasons for ambiguity toward the sovereign who had certainly done him no favors, and laced toward the end with gentle digs at Spain's bankruptcy and the extravagance of the memorial. The fact that the service of dedication of the completed catafalque, initiated on 24 November, had to be suspended until the end of December owing to a stand-up row over precedence and procedure during the service between the Inquisition's representatives and those of the High Court, clearly caused Cervantes as much disgusted mirth as it did the town as a whole. For when he recited his second offering, the famous sonnet variation *On Philip II's Catafalque in Seville,* in the cathedral on 29 December, he did not pull any punches. What he says is unexceptionable; it is in the exaggerated tone of his awe that the send-up lies:

> I vow to God that the grandeur of it terrifies me and I would give a doubloon to be able to describe it. For who does this celebrated construction, this splendor, not astonish and amaze? By the body of the living Christ, each piece of it is worth a million or more, and what a shame it is that all this will not last a century, oh great Seville, a Rome triumphant in your spirit and nobility. I'll wager that the soul of the deceased to enjoy this place has today left the paradise where it spends eternity. All this a braggart overheard, who said: "All you say is right, Sir Soldier, and whoso'er denies it lies." And then, without more ado, he jammed on his hat, adjusted his sword, gave a sideways glance, departed — and then there was nothing.

The parody was too powerful to mistake, and the sonnet rapidly acquired a *succès de scandale* of which Cervantes was singularly proud, though he cannot have been serious when, in *Journey to Parnassus* (published in 1614), he described it as the most distinguished of his works. It is undeniably one of the best known and most often quoted sonnets in the Spanish language.

By now, however, Cervantes had more pressing, personal matters on his mind. On 12 May 1598, Ana de Villafranca, Cervantes's former mistress, who had been for some years a widow, had died in Madrid, leaving their daughter Isabel, now in her early teens, an official orphan. Magdalena could have lost no time in sending her brother the disturbing news, for clearly some provision for Isabel's future would have to be made; Ana's mother, Luisa de Rojas, was unable to look after her two grand-daughters — Isabel and her half sister Ana — indefinitely. The problem was what to do for the best. Even if Catalina knew of Cervantes's earlier affair it is unlikely, barren as her own marriage was, that she would want to take in her husband's illegitimate daughter by another woman. Somehow a solution had to be found for Isabel which would combine suitable support with discretion. Money, of course, was a further and permanent problem, although the recovery of a debt of ninety ducats from a Juan de Cervantes, probably a cousin, in Seville in February 1599 went a little way to alleviating the situation. Cervantes always had been and always would be an easy touch, hard-up though he was.

It is very likely that the ninety ducats in his pocket decided him to go to Madrid. In the same month he was summoned to appear in the capital within thirty days to present his accounts, on pain of a fine and increased liability; but it looks as though the summons might have passed him on the way. Even without it, with the plague now beginning to make inroads into Seville and with his daughter's future pressing for attention, he had strong motives for the journey. The excitement being generated in Madrid by the glamor and expansionism of the new King's court and by the lavish preparations being made for his triumphal entry into the capital with his new bride, was an added attraction, especially for a man who years before seems to have been swept away from Esquivias to Toledo in the wake of a religious procession, and then departed directly for Seville to seek his fortune. Patient and long-suffering as Cervantes was, his character had its impulsive side.

Whether he intervened in person or whether he conferred by letter with his sister Magdalena, by August a solution had been found for Isabel. On 11 August, Isabel entered her aunt Magdalena's household officially but incognito as an apprentice maid; Magdalena undertook to lodge and feed her, to teach her housework and sewing, and to pay her a total of twenty ducats for the two-year contract. The requirements of both duty and decency were thus neatly met, with Isabel lodged as close to her father as she could be without causing scandal or disturbing Catalina's peace of mind. Cervantes's other sister Andrea also lived in Madrid at the time, but apart from having a lawsuit on her hands over the rates of a house she rented, she had a daughter of her own and had in any case never been as close to her brother as Magdalena. Magdalena was, therefore, the obvious person to come to Isabel's rescue, and given that she had since her mother's death lived alone, she probably welcomed the idea of having a young companion about the house. No doubt, on 24 October they went together to join the great throng of people lining the especially widened streets under the triumphal arches to welcome their new young Queen to her capital. Glittering with jewels and seated on a golden throne set round with fifteen ladies-in-waiting on silver chairs, she could not have disappointed them. But as far as we know, this great public occasion did not stimulate Cervantes into verse. If he had indeed spent the summer in Madrid, he soon afterward returned to Seville. He certainly did not attend any examination of his accounts, and it might well have been the thought of doing so that drove him south.

❧

SEVEN

The Flowering of Genius

CERVANTES'S MOTIVES IN REMAINING in Seville during the years immediately after he left the government's employ are difficult to fathom. If it was cultural activity he sought, there was plenty in Madrid. His family was there and his wife was not far away and the capital was the obvious place for him to settle to work and write, particularly after the natural break provided by his unpleasant stay in jail. The conclusion one is driven to is that he was happier in Seville. It had, after all, been the urban focus of his life during his years of government service; most of his friends and acquaintances were based there, and the climate was kinder. And he must have found it congenial to be able to find intellectual stimulus and admiration in the same place; for he was better known in Seville, and his stock as a writer there was undoubtedly higher than it would have been in Madrid where the pool of talent was more liberally stocked with fish. After the appearance of his famous sonnet on Philip II's catafalque, he had become something of a celebrity in the city. There is also, of course, the possibility that he felt safer in Seville. Long as the arm of the Exchequer was, its headquarters were in Madrid, and absence was the only convincing excuse for not attending an examination of his accounts. Cervantes's reluctance to have the matter of his outstanding debt cleared up suggests that he was not in a position to prove his innocence and that he had decided in the circumstances that evasiveness was the better part of integrity. Whatever his reasons, one thing is clear: his feelings for his wife were not powerful enough to overcome them. Cervantes's behavior during this period looks like nothing so much as a deliberate evasion of domesticity; and whether or not he and Catalina were in any real sense temporarily estranged, life with her certainly did not offer whatever form of fulfillment he was seeking.

During these years he somehow made enough money to manage on. He had remained in touch with Agustín de Cetina, the Royal Paymaster — on 2 May 1600 he gave evidence in support of a petition submitted to the Seville city council by Cetina — and it is more than likely that Cetina was able to put some work his way.

His connections in Seville by this time were in any case extensive. Literary reunions were frequently held in the houses of artists and *littérateurs* and in the great palaces of noble patrons with which the city was so richly endowed, and Cervantes must have had access to many of them. Here he and his fellow writers undoubtedly discussed the merits of a new best-seller, Mateo Alemán's picaresque novel *Guzmán de Alfarache*. A strangely dualistic work which counters the comedy of its narrative of delinquency and low life with long, sermonlike interludes of profoundly serious moralizing, the book initiated the vogue for the picaresque in Spain. For all its black outlook on life — its author had spent some time as a government inspector looking into the horrifying working conditions in the mercury mines of Almadén — the book became a runaway success immediately after publication in March 1599, running into four editions in that first year and no fewer than seven in 1600. The spirit of idealism and escapism that had fostered the chivalric and pastoral romances had been usurped by a new-found relish for the amusing, the realistic, and the downright sordid that better reflected the prevailing mood of materialism and disillusion. It is interesting to speculate whether Cervantes's own writing was in any way influenced by the appearance of Alemán's long, complex, but nonetheless hugely successful novel. If Cervantes needed any encouragement to expand his *novela* about a mad hidalgo and try to produce a best-seller which would at the same time offer him unlimited scope to explore a fascinating idea and to exploit the rich layers of experience and observation that had been laid down in the course of a varied and eventful career, then *Guzmán de Alfarache* certainly fitted the bill. On the other hand, if the idea of a full-length work had already taken root, the *Guzmán*'s appearance must have convinced him there was little mileage to be extracted from a continuation of his embryonic picaresque story, *Rinconete and Cortadillo*, and that he should seek a different manner of hero. Ambitious and endlessly experimental writer as he was, it is difficult to believe that an enormously successful, complex work of the stature of Alemán's could have left him indifferent. He must have made Alemán's acquaintance in Seville, and the fact that Alemán himself was a Treasury official could not have failed to give him food for thought.

In February 1600, the theaters were allowed to reopen, and the theatrical world, restricted during the ban to religious performances, began once more to flourish. In theory the secular repertoire was to be confined to historical plays, but the companies did not allow this to inhibit their activities for very long. There was, in addition, more exciting news from Madrid. It was rumored that the court would soon be transferred to Valladolid, which would consequently become the capital of Spain. The Duke of Lerma, Philip III's favorite and effective ruler of Spain (his income was soon to reach two hundred thousand ducats a year), wished to remove the young King from the sphere of influence of his grandmother, the Empress María. Since the death of her husband, Maximilian II of Austria, in 1576, the Empress had lived as a nun in a Carmelite convent in Madrid and had become an implacable enemy of Lerma's.

Seville itself was by now in the full throes of the plague epidemic, which raged so violently there — eight thousand victims died in the space of two months — that the city began visibly to decline as the flow of travelers, merchants, and visitors petered out. During 1600, Lope de Vega lived in the city with his mistress, Micaela de Luján, but for most people without such commitments to keep them there, life was becoming far less attractive. When exactly Cervantes left is not at all clear. It has been assumed that he returned to Castile in July to be present at the legal preliminaries in Toledo in August to his younger brother-in-law's entry as a novitiate into the Franciscan monastery there. Fernando de Palacios certainly willed half his worldly goods to Doña Catalina and made Cervantes one of his executors — they had up to now been joint administrators of his estate, such as it was — but there is no evidence that Cervantes himself was in Toledo for the start of the young man's new life, though Doña Catalina, we can be sure, made the effort to attend.

As the year drew to its close, the Cervantes family received the tragic news that their soldier brother, Rodrigo, had been killed on 2 July at the battle of Nieuport, during which the Archduke Albert of Austria had been defeated by Maurice of Nassau. The successes of Rodrigo's earlier career as a soldier had not led to further promotion and he was still an ensign, or second lieutenant, when he died. It is no surprise to learn that at the time of his death he was owed a considerable amount of money in back pay by the Crown. Later on, in 1605, the Cervantes family started to take measures to recover the money, but the Exchequer, while recognizing the debt, intent as ever on husbanding its dwindling resources paid it in installments and at long intervals. Rodrigo's heirs were still receiving sums as late as the 1640s and 1650s and even so the full amount was never paid. A king's ransom might have been at stake rather than a soldier's wages.

That Cervantes was now based in Toledo, where, it will be remembered, his wife's family rented out a house they had inherited from her father, is often inferred from his description in *Don Quixote* of how he came to continue the narrative after Chapter VIII:

> When I was in Alcaná street in Toledo one day a boy came along to sell various portfolios and old papers to a draper and since I am an avid reader, even of torn scraps of paper from the street, I was driven by this natural tendency of mine to take one of the portfolios the boy had for sale and I saw that it contained letters I knew to be arabic.

The narrator has the boy translate something which is making him laugh and discovers that it is about Dulcinea del Toboso, Don Quixote's imaginary lady. He continues:

> When I heard him say "Dulcinea del Toboso," I was astonished and amazed because it then dawned on me that those portfolios contained the story of Don Quixote. . . . I bade him make haste to read the beginning and this doing, rapidly translating the Arabic into Spanish, he said that it read "The History of Don Quixote of La

Mancha written by Cide Hamete Benengeli, Arab historian."

However, this passage furnishes us with no sound reason for believing that Cervantes was actually in Toledo when he started expanding *Don Quixote* any more than for believing that the book was indeed the translation of a work in Arabic by Cide Hamete Benengeli. The latter claim was one of a standard type adopted by writers of chivalric romances to lend an air of authority and historical authenticity to their narratives. The truth is that we lose sight completely of Cervantes during this period of his life, and for all we know he remained living in Seville.

On 10 January 1601 it was indeed decreed that the capital and court should remove to Valladolid, to the apprehensive delight of that ancient city, one of Castile's historic capitals, and to the chagrin of Madrid, which saw torn out of its grasp its major source of revenue and employment. After expanding to meet the needs of the court established there almost forty years before, the specially created capital now faced the specter, not merely of unfashionability and neglect, but of depopulation and ruin. And its worst fears were realized. Within a few months, houses stood empty and streets that had formerly thronged with people were virtually deserted. Meanwhile, in Valladolid, facilities were strained to bursting point and shoddily built tenements mushroomed to accommodate the overflow. This overflow, almost certainly, did not include Cervantes. If the court could not draw him while it was at Madrid, so much nearer to Esquivias, then Valladolid's attractions were no greater.

On the other hand the theory that he was once more leading a fairly peripatetic life during this time when he was in all likelihood writing Part I of *Don Quixote,* or was otherwise distracted from continuous creativity, has a certain credibility. Part I with its small contradictions and occasionally clumsy linkages does perhaps suggest an author writing at different times and in different places under conditions which made complete concentration impossible. But whether this fractured life was centered on Seville or on some other city it is impossible to say. Since our last authentic sighting of him during this period was in Seville, then we probably ought to leave him there.

Wherever he was, the Exchequer had not forgotten him. On 14 September 1601, a Treasury memorandum issued in Valladolid, where the Exchequer had removed along with all the other departments of state, charged that the tax receiver in Vélez Málaga be required to report and that Cervantes be called to account for any discrepancy in the taxes he had collected. Two things are clear from the wording of these documents: first, that the Exchequer itself was not absolutely clear whether the affair had been settled or not and, second, that either Cervantes had foolishly never filed a statement concerning the money he had been unable to collect in Vélez Málaga (although there were records of what he had failed to collect elsewhere) or it had been lost. There is no evidence, however, that Cervantes was summoned at this point — perhaps like ourselves the auditors could not discover his whereabouts. Earlier that year, in March, Catalina's elder brother Francisco was ordained in Toledo (thus enabling him to take up the hereditary chaplaincy of Esquivias), but there is no reason to suppose that Cervantes attended this ceremony any more than there is to suppose that he had been in Toledo for Fernando's metamorphosis into Franciscan monk the year before. That he was still absent from Esquivias on 15 January 1602 is made explicit in a deed of sale signed by Catalina and

Francisco who were forced to sell a parcel of land in order
to pay off some of their late father's debts.

However, on 27 January, Cervantes, after a silence of
one and a half years, does at last materialize — in Esquivias, as godfather at a village christening. While this
documented event is no help in establishing where he
had been up to then, it does help to lay an old ghost.
Some Treasury documents of 1603 suggest that Cervantes
might have spent a second period in prison in Seville in
1602 and many have accepted that he did so, concluding
that this was the stay that witnessed the birth of *Don
Quixote*. But the wording of the documents is imprecise
and could well refer to his imprisonment in 1597. My
view is that it does. Since Cervantes would certainly not
have made the journey from Seville for a christening, and
since we know of no other event which could have
brought him temporarily to Castile, we can probably assume that he had by now left Seville for good.

It is during this period that Cervantes's relationship
with the great dramatist Lope de Vega — interpreted as
friendship by many commentators but largely consisting
up to now of a standard exchange of professional com-
pliments — developed very briefly into something closer.
The contrast between them could scarcely have been
greater: Lope, still a young man, reveling in fame and
success (despite the criticisms leveled at his work by the
theorists and the growing envy of his literary colleagues)
and flamboyantly leading his double life with second wife
and beautiful actress mistress; Cervantes, an aging ref-
ugee from failure and disappointment, struggling to turn
his modest literary reputation into something that would
guarantee him a permanent foothold on Mount Parnassus. Yet we know that Lope admired Cervantes's talent,
such as it had so far displayed itself. And when preparing,
for publication late in 1602, a compendium of poetry

under the general title *The Beauty of Angélica,* he either sought or accepted, earlier that year or during the previous one, a complimentary sonnet from Cervantes for inclusion at the beginning of Lope's narrative poem on Sir Francis Drake. How pleased Lope was by the sonnet is another matter, for it is noticeably mild in its praise and two lines,

> Modest Venus there* augments and nourishes
> The holy multitude of loves

may readily be construed as a mischievous allusion to something other than Lope's literary activities.

By the time *Angélica* and Cervantes's sonnet saw the light of day in November 1602, the amicable politeness between the two writers was disintegrating into a barely concealed animosity that was to last both their lifetimes. Which of them started it, and why, has never been satisfactorily established, but it is difficult to see what Lope could possibly have found in Cervantes or his work to provoke spontaneous disapproval or resentment. Cervantes, on the other hand, had every good reason to resent Lope, whose genius was widely recognized, who had powerful and rich patrons, whose pastoral novel *Arcadia* had superseded Cervantes's *Galatea,* and whose plays had driven Cervantes's off the stage. Perhaps it was around this time that Cervantes first tried seriously to reestablish himself as a playwright, only to discover that his services were not required now that Lope and his followers were there to supply the theaters with what they needed. If we add to Cervantes's genuine disapproval of Lope's anti-classicist drama the natural, human envy of the unsuccessful man, convinced of his own worth, for the wildly

---

* On the fertile *vega,* or plain, of Lope's inspiration.

successful writer whose talents he considers to be suspect, then we have motive enough for the blossoming of Cervantes's hostility, especially at a time when his fortunes and very probably his spirits too were at a very low ebb.

The opening salvo would seem to have been fired in Seville during a visit Lope paid to the city some time in 1602. There in the Ochoa Academy, a literary salon to which it is assumed that Cervantes belonged, although there is no evidence that he did, Lope's arrival was greeted by three satirical sonnets ranging from the mildly satirical to the insulting. One or more of these Lope was convinced came from Cervantes's pen. Now that it is known that Cervantes was in Esquivias early in that year, however, it seems less likely that he was in Seville when Lope arrived there. Furthermore, the sonnet of the three for which Cervantes is most often considered to have been responsible is quite unlike the sly satirizing to which Cervantes subjected Lope elsewhere; it is crude, unfunny, and absurdly dismissive. It is admittedly very reminiscent in tone and even in phrasing of the sonnet Cervantes had written in 1598 sending up Philip II's memorial in Seville — perhaps too reminiscent to be convincing:

–They say Lope was here. –It is not possible. –I swear to God that he passed by the very place I am at. –By Christ, I cannot believe it. –I do not lie to you. –Shut up, it is impossible.

God's death, you are the limit. I am convinced it is all a joke. –I swear to Christ he passed through the Macarena. –Who saw him? –I did. –That cannot be, for he is invisible.

Invisible, Martin? That is a lie, for Lope de Vega is a man, a man like you or me or John Doe.

Is he tall? –Yes, about my height. –If he be not as lofty as his name, I shit on you, on him and on his poetry.

The literary academies of the day were notorious for the way in which members attacked one another's, and other writers', personal and professional foibles; even physical defects were considered fair game, and in theory all was supposed to be taken in good part. A contemporary writer remarked that in them members "learned to make fun without causing bitterness and to sting without giving distress." But in fact the element of malice in all this verbal horseplay was often very pronounced, and my guess is that since Cervantes's disapproval of Lope's drama must have been well known in Seville, the sonnet was written at the academy, perhaps as a combined effort, in such a style as deliberately to cast suspicion on Cervantes (now probably safely departed) and thereby hugely increase the joke.

The battle continued with two sonnets of uncertain date, though most commentators ascribe them to the mid-1600s. The first, which was attributed to the great poet Góngora in early manuscripts, is a satirical piece with the incomplete line endings to which Cervantes was partial; it refers disparagingly to Lope's *Arcadia* and to his theater, both sore points for Cervantes. Whether Cervantes wrote it or not, Lope was clearly convinced that he had, and he retaliated with a sonnet which referred among other things to "your trashy Don Quixote," and to Cervantes's damaged hand. The victim of vicious personal attacks himself, Lope had no inhibitions about hitting below the belt.

His virulent dismissal of Cervantes's new work points fairly firmly to his having made its acquaintance in its published form rather than through hearsay. *Don Quixote* appeared in January 1605 and in it Cervantes, as we say, was unequivocal in his championship of the Aristotelian dramatic precepts and his praise of the neoclassical playwrights who, like himself, had fought Lope and lost. But his animosity to Lope in the work does not end there. In the Prologue, which would have been written shortly before publication, he makes surreptitious fun of Lope's attempts to hide his limited education under an inappropriate display of pedantry and ostentatious erudition, whatever the nature of the work in question, and also of his habit of prefixing to his works a whole series of complimentary poems from famous people. In one of the preliminary poems that Cervantes declares himself obliged to provide for his own book — unworthy as he is of the spontaneous attentions of others and too lazy as he is to seek them out — he aims a dart at Lope's social pretensions and at the spurious coat of arms he had placed at the front of *Arcadia* in 1598. With the publication of *Don Quixote,* therefore, the battle was out in the open. It has even been suggested that the false continuation of *Don Quixote* by Avellaneda in 1614 was written partly as a reply to these criticisms of Lope and his theater. That Lope resented *Don Quixote*'s success is obvious from the fact that he never missed an opportunity to run it down. In a letter written to a friend in the winter of 1605 he remarks, "Of poets, I say nothing! what an age we live in . . . but there is not one as bad as Cervantes, nor so stupid as to praise *Don Quixote*," going on to make it clear that he knew his plays were "odious" to Cervantes.

How deep the rift was, it is impossible to say. In Cervantes's interlude, *The Anxious Guard,* assigned to 1611, one of the characters satirizes the widespread popular use of the phrase "es de Lope" (it is Lope's=it is Lopean) as a term of consummate praise, as follows: "I know little about verses; but these sounded so well to me that they must be Lope's, as indeed everything is that is good — or seems to be." In the following year, 1612, however, they were frequenting the same academy; Lope on one occasion even borrowed Cervantes's reading glasses, as he told his patron, the Duke of Sessa, in a letter on 2 March:

> The academies are wild; at the last meeting two licentiates threw their bonnets at each other. I read out some poetry with some spectacles belonging to Cervantes which looked like badly fried eggs.

It looks as though some sort of armed truce had been declared, and, thereafter, they appear to have entertained for each other a mild dislike tempered by reluctant admiration. In his *Journey to Parnassus* of 1614 Cervantes said of Lope that "nobody surpasses nor even approaches him," though he has some ironic words later in the poem for Lope's theater; that grudge never really died. In 1615, in the prologue to his published plays, he concedes defeat on the dramatic front, yet in Part II of *Don Quixote*, also published that year, he refers to the accusations of Lope-persecution leveled against him in the spurious *Don Quixote* with sly innuendo about Lope's scandalous private life. By this time they lived near each other in Madrid, and Cervantes was fully aware of how Lope, now a priest, was living:

> ... I would not persecute any priest, particularly not one who was also a familiar of the Holy Office [the Inquisition] and if he [Avellaneda] spoke on behalf of the person he seems to have been speaking for, he was completely mistaken; for I worship the wit, and I admire the works and the unceasing virtuous activities, of that man.

As for Lope, he continued long after Cervantes's death in 1616 to damn him with faint praise, describing him in one of his short stories as being "not devoid of elegance and style." He was obviously not able to forgive the barbs in *Don Quixote,* for in his play *To Love Without Knowing Whom* he describes the work as an "extravagant" romance and calls on God to forgive Cervantes for having written it. It is unnecessary, however, I feel, to interpret his brief tribute to Cervantes in his *Laurel of Apollo* to either hypocrisy or remorse, as many have done.

There can be little doubt that Cervantes for all his envy and hostility recognized in Lope de Vega a remarkable man, a "monster of nature." By the standards of his day, the satire he is definitely known to have directed against him is restrained, if often unambiguous. As far as we can judge, its beginnings coincided with the years in which he was wrestling with Part I of *Don Quixote,* an undertaking that must have brought home keenly to him, as he traced his hero's collisions with reality, the extent of his own failed hopes and disappointed dreams. It is a period of self-appraisal and self-confrontation, perhaps even self-mockery, a period of severe disenchantment with the world, for all that his sense of humor and proportion lie never far below the surface of his life. To it, or just after it, the most uncompromising of the *Exemplary Tales* have for this reason been convincingly assigned.

Cervantes called these tales *novelas, novela* being the word used at the time to designate story and *historia,* ironically, that used to designate an extended narrative, what we would now call a romance or a novel. Twelve in all, they were published by Cervantes in 1613 but written over an extended period of time before that. Earlier versions of two of them, *Rinconete and Cortadillo* and *The Jealous Extremaduran,* circulated in manuscript in the mid-1600s.

The ones we now most value are the "realistic" ones, those which, while subjecting reality to the transforming processes of an artistic vision, never betray it. If any of his works ring with the tones of undiluted disillusion with the world and its ways, they are *The Jealous Extremaduran, The Deceitful Marriage, The Dogs' Colloquy* (the second being the framework of the third), and *The Licentiate of Glass.*

From *The Jealous Extremaduran* nobody emerges with credit. It is the story of an old man so pathologically jealous that he shuts his child-bride up in a house which no male animal is allowed to enter, and from which she herself sallies forth only to go to mass in the early hours of the morning. The false, disloyal servants who pursue their own pleasure, the gullible, drunken porter, the malicious, unscrupulous gallant who sees the wife's heavily guarded chastity as a personal challenge, the naive wife herself, so easily led astray — all contribute to the tragedy created by the foolish old Carrizales who puts all his faith in externals. It is significant that where in the first version of the tale, events run remorselessly to their logical and psychologically convincing conclusion with the seduction of the wife, Isabela, in the revised version published by Cervantes in 1613, Leonora (as she is now called) resists her seducer, although the old man does not discover this until he is on his deathbed. This definitive version, illustrating more satisfactorily as it does Cervantes's contention (elaborated in different fashion in *The Little Gypsy Girl* and *The Illustrious Kitchen Maid*) that true virtue thrives on freedom (a view that owes much to the Erasmian ideal of enlightened good), not only marks the triumph of artistic shaping over psychological probability, of a purer sense of tragedy, but also the reimposition of a more benign, more hopeful authorial mood, and a reaffirmation of belief in the principles of literary decency. The story is one of the most memorable he wrote, its atmosphere laden with expectant sensuality, its development rich in psychological exploration, and the whole carried out with masterly narrative control.

The black view of human nature and human society in *The Dogs' Colloquy* and its frame story, *The Deceitful Marriage*, was not susceptible of change, for its pessimism is generalized and open ended. *The Deceitful Marriage* tells a "biter bit" tale of an unscrupulous couple who deceive each other into marriage with a reciprocal display of false wealth. While the soldier, Campuzano, is recovering in hospital in Valladolid from the unpleasant physical aftereffects of this relationship, he overhears through the mists of his fever a conversation between the two hospital guard dogs, Cipión and Berganza — who have discovered they have the gift of reason and speech — as the latter tells his story and both comment upon the world of men which this story depicts. The dialogue, in its suppleness, its distinctiveness of characterization, its psychological accuracy, its pathos and its humor, is quite brilliant, and we have little sense, as we read, of its being a conversation penned almost four hundred years ago. But there is a great deal of Cervantes in this dialogue and of Cervantes at a particular stage in his life. In its pessimistic presentation of mankind as being at best hypocritical, dishonest, and selfish, at worst murderous and evil (the Jesuit fathers of Seville alone escape unscathed), it gives the strong impression of a man at odds with the world and deeply imbued with a conviction of its rottenness, of a man languishing neglected in poverty, bereft of favor and protection, while others, less deserving, flourish. The diatribe against those who lay claim to a learning they do not possess and who constantly bewail misfortunes of which they know little, links up with the sentiments expressed in the Prologue and preliminaries to *Don Quixote* and with the burgeoning animosity between Cervantes and Lope de Vega. Yet those Cervantine saving graces, humor and irony, are never absent for long. It is a story soaked in bitter, aggrieved disillusion, but not in despair, and here lies its lasting attraction. We end the story feeling in some strange, irrational way that as long as there are dogs like Cipión and Berganza in the world, all is not lost. The declared message of Berganza's tale, it must be said, is not hopeful. The witch Cañizares who adopts him, convinced as she is that he is one of twin sons born to a fellow witch who were turned into dogs by a rival, prophesies their return to human life as follows: "They will regain their true form when they see the proud and exalted brought low and the humble and downcast raised up." When this will be, Cervantes allows us to draw our own conclusions.

Conceptually, this story within a story, with its splitting of the narrative perspective into two — into author (Berganza) and reader/critic (Cipión) — exploring as it does the limits of imaginative literature, is a highly original creation. This is another reason for ascribing it to these years around the appearance of *Don Quixote* when Cervantes was at the very summit of his creative powers. That Cervantes was perfectly aware of the daring of his technique is clear from the discussion that takes place between Campuzano and the incredulous Licentiate to whom he relates his bizarre experience about the feasibility of what he claims to have overheard. Cervantes anticipates objection by bringing out into the open the clash between this very extreme manifestation of the "marvelous" and verisimilitude, both proper objectives of every writer at that time.

These were years, too, when Cervantes was fascinated by the workings of the imagination and the way in which fantasy can impose itself upon the shape of external reality, either in the form of madness, as in *The Licentiate of Glass* and in *Don Quixote* itself, or as here in the form of delirium, of dream-life at its most frenetic. As the witch, Cañizares, observes in *The Dogs' Colloquy,* "What happens to us in our fantasies is so intense as to be indistinguishable from what we really and truly experience." Evidently Cervantes was skeptical about the powers claimed by and for witchcraft. Campuzano in his fever, Don Quixote (increasingly), and Tomás Rodaja in their madness, all receive new manifestations of reality through the shifting forms of their imaginings. While Don Quixote's personal vision is distorted into untruth by its aggressive egotism, however, Tomás Rodaja's and Campuzano's are on different levels a passive revelation of truth; phobia and dogs respectively act as the objectivizing, externalizing devices which enable the protagonists, and hence Cervantes, to assume the position of dispassionate, uncorrupted, even innocent, commentators on the human condition. Once Tomás Rodaja is cured of his belief that he is made of glass, no one wishes to hear what he has to say, for the truth is tolerable only from the mouths of those who can be dismissed as incompetent to pronounce. *The Licentiate of Glass* — with its curious aphoristic form and abrupt changes of direction only a very partial success as an experiment in narrative — is in its way as damning a comment on human nature as *The Dogs' Colloquy,* although its strange, mad prophet-hero fails to move us in the same way as the two dogs.

Cervantes seems to have spent most of 1602 and much of 1603 in Esquivias and Madrid. His family too still lived in Madrid, with Andrea now a seamstress of some repute. In 1603 the Exchequer in Valladolid was still nibbling away at Cervantes's 1594 tax accounts. It was the Baza receipts, which had had to be adjusted on Cervantes's arrival there, which were now worrying them, but Cervantes himself does not appear to have been contacted. No doubt he was deliberately lying low and this prudent policy ultimately paid off. The 1603 Treasury documents are the last we hear of his financial problems for five years.

By this stage Part I of *Don Quixote* must have been very well on. In the previous year, 1602, another chivalric novel — the last to be published in Spain — had appeared: *Don Policisne de Boecia,* by Juan de Silva y Toledo. Cervantes read, digested, and possibly even used bits of it, as he forged ahead with his self-appointed task of deflating for once and for all the entire fictional world of knight errantry. The completed manuscript was probably handed over to the publisher, Francisco de Robles, son of the Robles who had published Cervantes's first novel, *The Galatea,* many years before, during the summer of 1604. The various prepublication references to the work have given rise to the suggestion that it was actually published in 1604; but not only is there no trace of such an edition, it is not even necessary to infer that there was one. News of the manuscript, parts of which Cervantes would have read to friends, must have spread like wildfire in the gossipy, competitive atmosphere of the literary gatherings of the day, especially in view of its criticism of Lope and his theater.

While Robles, who was based at the court in Valladolid, set about obtaining the necessary publication licenses for the book, Cervantes was sufficiently encouraged by the sum Robles had paid him for the manuscript (although, if his remarks about publishers later on are anything to go by, it was not very much) to move to the court himself. No doubt, had he been able to afford it, he would have gone before, but Valladolid, since its elevation to capital, was both wildly expensive and severely short of accommodation. Spaniards and foreigners flocked there to take part in the endless round of bull fights, tournaments, and celebrations, and building speculators had been unable to keep up with the demand for housing. By the beginning of the autumn, however, Cervantes and his whole family — wife, sisters, daughter, and niece — were settled in a modest second-floor apartment over a tavern in a newly built row of houses on the edge of the city near the river, between the cattle market and the Hospital of the Resurrection where Campuzano overhears the guard dogs' midnight dialogue. The life they lived together was certainly not a prosperous one, for Magdalena was at this time described as "poor" by a neighbor.

In the last months of 1604, the manuscript of *Don Quixote* was safely in the hands of the printer in Madrid, Juan de la Cuesta, with probably only the Prologue, the dedication, and the preliminary poems remaining to be completed. Cervantes must have felt that things were at last beginning to go well for him. Not only did he have a major work awaiting publication, but for the first time since his marriage twenty years before he was master in his own house with his family comfortingly gathered round him. At the age of fifty-seven, "with all my years on my back" as he says in the Prologue to *Don Quixote*, he was settled at last, or so it seemed, and in Spain's new center of cultural activity. Perhaps he entertained hopes of finding a rich patron there among the nobles at court. Certainly he dedicated his new work to the young Duke of Béjar, who was beginning to acquire the reputation of being a supporter of the arts, and with whom Cervantes up to then had had, as far as we know, little or no contact. The Duke's tastes in fact lay more in the direction of hunting than of literature, and the line that Cervantes hopefully cast in his direction landed nothing.

The Ingenious Hidalgo Don Quixote of La Mancha was published in January 1605 and was a huge and immediate success, not the most successful Spanish best-seller of the age (*The Celestina, The Diana,* and *Guzmán de Alfarache* went into more editions) but certainly one of them. Within weeks, large consignments of copies were sailing with the treasure fleet to the Indies. Within months, pirate editions were appearing in Portugal and Aragon, forcing Robles to apply for publication licenses for those kingdoms, too, as well as for Castile. Since these could not appear before the second edition, already under way, was published (in the event in May or June), which would be too late to stop the pirate editions, Cervantes empowered Robles to take any action necessary to put a stop to the piracy or, alternatively, to print and sell the book himself in the kingdoms of Portugal, Aragon, Valencia, and Catalonia. From the wording of the documents, it is clear that Cervantes had already sold the entire Spanish copyright of his work to Robles. Whatever the terms of the bargain, there seems no doubt that Cervantes's lack of business acumen had once more betrayed him. As for the Madrid edition, it went through six printings before the end of the year. Within Cervantes's own lifetime, the book was translated into French and English (Thomas Shelton's justifiably famous translation); and since then there has scarcely been a language into which the exploits of the famous knight have not been transposed, as one of the book's own characters, indeed, prophesied: "My guess is that there is not a nation or a language into which it will not be translated." Imagine Cervantes's delight had he been able to foresee the accuracy of that proud but essentially throwaway remark.

Cervantes was keenly aware of the long, unproductive years (at least in terms of published work) since *The Galatea* of 1585: he refers in the Prologue to *Don Quixote* to the many years he has lain asleep "in the silence of oblivion." The success of his new work must have come to him as a vindication beyond his wildest dreams of his literary ambitions and of his belief in himself as a writer. He had proved that it was possible to produce a profane work that would both delight and instruct, that earned the approval of public and theoreticians alike. He had also proved, too late perhaps, that he was capable of becoming one of the small new band of professional writers for whom Lope de Vega himself had acted as trailblazer.

EIGHT

"The Noblest Novel in the World"

Don Quixote is one of a handful of world masterpieces that have generated so much critical, imaginative, and speculative literature of their own that studies of the secondary literature itself are now necessary to keep the huge, sprawling network of influence, reaction, and counter-reaction under some vestige of control. Such titles as "Don Quixote in Sweden," "Cervantes in Russia," "Don Quixote and Moby Dick," and "Cervantes in the Work of Mark Twain" offer only the merest flavor of the extent and range of the inexhaustibly probing tentacles of Cervantes criticism. Every conceivable aspect (or so one is driven to believe — though no doubt scholarly ingenuity and endeavor will prove one wrong) of Cervantes the man and writer has, as the result of this, his greatest work, been explored: his philosophy of life, his theory of knowledge, his erudition, his literary theories, his language, his political, social, and historical views, his religious beliefs, his attitude to contemporary drama, his knowledge (expert, of course) of music and theology, his command of geography, his familiarity with things nautical, and so on and on, down the scale of relevance and up the ladder of conjecture. The process is an inevitable one, for great men, especially those whose lives remain par-

tially undocumented, attract mythmakers and storyspin-
ners as surely as light attracts insects. A Shakespeare
scholar was able recently to write a mighty tome charting
the creation of the bard's many different lives, and what
is the difference between Cervantes the theologian or
Cervantes the sailor and Shakespeare the Toper or Shakespeare the Deer-Poacher but the difference between the
way Spaniards view their past and the way the English
view theirs?

Cervantes has been held to be a free-thinking skeptic of
such originality that he seems, in his response to the
human condition and in his perception of the protean
nature of reality and its relationship to literature, to all
intents and purposes a modern man. At the same time, he
has also been held to be a conventional thinker firmly
embedded in his own sociohistorical context. *Don
Quixote* itself has been interpreted variously as a spiritual
biography, as a political fable on the state of the nation,
as a satire of the Spanish aristocracy, as a specific lampoon-
ing of the Duke of Lerma, as an investigation of the
nature of human knowledge, as a celebration of the transfiguring power of the human imagination, faith and will
— again the list is almost endless. At one stage, the view
was even held in Spain that Cervantes with his *Don
Quixote* had so undermined the chivalric values of Spain's
ruling class that he actually precipitated the collapse of
morals and ideals that supposedly led to the country's decline. Outside Spain, Lord Byron in his poem on that
other famous myth figure, Don Juan, presented *Don
Quixote* as the herald of a tragic disillusion:

> Of all tales 'tis the saddest — and more sad
> Because it makes us smile: his hero's right,
> And still pursues the right — to curb the bad
> His only object and 'gainst odds to fight

His guerdon: 'tis his virtue makes him mad.
But his adventures form a sorry sight;
A sorrier still is the great moral taught
By that real epic unto all who have thought.
                    (*Don Juan*, Canto XII, stanza 9)

For John Ruskin, Cervantes, as the great perverter of romantic feelings, was a crucial figure in the development of modern sensibilities:

> He, of all men, most helped forward the terrible change in the soldiers of Europe, from the spirit of Boyard to the spirit of Bonaparte, helped to change loyalty into license, protection into plunder, truth into treachery, chivalry into selfishness; and since his time, the purest impulses and the noblest purposes have perhaps been oftener stayed by the devil, under the name of Quixotism, than under any other base name or false allegation.
> (*Lectures on Architecture and Painting*, II)

In fact, of course, Cervantes was perfectly aware that there was as little chivalry about real-life Spanish society in the seventeenth century as there had been about real life in the Middle Ages. The whole point of *Don Quixote* — as we see if we heed the text and Cervantes's own comments on it — is that the chivalric ideal takes no cognizance of reality. If there is a historical relevance to the work — and some surely there must be — then the disillusion of *Don Quixote* is the effect, not the cause, of the crisis in Spanish confidence at the turn of the century.

The fascinating thing about this essentially ludicrous charge of Ruskin's, of course, is that it accords to *Don Quixote,* and hence to literature in general, the power and influence that Cervantes himself, along with many commentators of the time, suspected and feared fiction might have. The problem, familiar now though with the

arrival of the intrusive television set more pertinent than
ever, was at the time a relatively new one, created by the
invention of the printing press in the fifteenth century
and the consequent growth of literacy during the sixteenth century. The romances of chivalry proliferated in
direct response to these new conditions, forming the first
body of fiction written specifically for a mass audience.
The inevitable concomitant of the firmly held Renaissance belief that literature could be morally instructive
was that it could also, if permitted, be morally harmful.
The nature of the literary matter being digested by this
new and growing reading public was thus a question of
intense concern to Renaissance humanists themselves in
Spain, and even more so to the thinkers and theorists of
the Spain of the Counter-Reformation, doubly suspicious
as they were of the whole concept of a secular literature
of entertainment. The dissemination toward the end of
the century of Aristotelian views on the superiority of
poetry (that is, of creative writing in general) over history, of fiction over fact, merely served to complicate the
issue, not least because Aristotle had thoughtlessly made
no provision in his discussion for the emerging genre —
prose fiction — that was causing the greatest concern.
Firmly established (at least in the eyes of its practitioners) as the authoritative, superior form of literary truth,
poetry (fiction) thereby acquired serious responsibilities
that could not be evaded. Cervantes's quarrel with the
romances of chivalry was that in their exaltation of a
world so fashioned by fantasy that all idea of credibility
went by the board, they were not merely aesthetically
absurd but so untruthful to life — as it was, could be,
or ought to be — as to be morally harmful. This is a
fear that escapist entertainment has always inspired. In
Cervantes's day it was exacerbated by a general feeling
of insecurity as to where the dividing line between history

and legend, myth and fable, really was, an insecurity that was only just beginning to yield before the tentative new advances in scientific and scholarly method. How many people even now are absolutely certain whether King Arthur and his Knights of the Round Table were fact or fantasy?

For all that posterity has seen in the author of *Don Quixote* what it wanted to see — social satirist, progressive thinker, romantic ironist, perspectivist, skeptic, subversive or marxist existentialist — Cervantes himself was unequivocal about his intentions. His Prologue to Part I contains that elusive mixture of seriousness and humorous irony that characterizes the work as a whole, but there can be no mistake about the burden of the words of the "friend" with whom he discusses the book's presentation (this splitting of the narrative perspective was a favorite device of his):

> . . . the whole work is a diatribe against the romances of chivalry . . . [it] is concerned only with undermining the authority and influence exerted over the world and populace by the romances of chivalry. . . . You must seek also to ensure that, when they read your tale, the melancholic is moved to laughter, the merry man's smile grows wider, the simpleton is not bored, the discerning reader is amazed by its inventiveness, the solemn reader does not despise it, and the prudent reader does not fail to praise it. In short you must aim at demolishing the ill-founded edifice of those chivalric romances, abominated by so many and praised by so many more; and if you achieve all this you will have achieved not a little.

At the end of Part II his final words are,

> my wish has been none other than to render loathsome to men the fictional and absurd stories of the romances

of chivalry, which through the deeds of my authentic
Don Quixote are already tottering and will without
doubt collapse altogether.

These sentiments, insisted upon out of a genuine concern
for the effects of his own writings, we overlook at our
peril. Even if the reader chooses to move beyond them,
he can neither ignore them nor dismiss them as a smokescreen for some mysterious, undeclared purpose.

Clearly, reading a book is as dynamic an act as playing a piece of music. Each time the book is read it is
re-created; indeed, its author once dead, it lives only
through the eyes and mind of its readers, for marks on a
printed page between covers on a shelf have in themselves no autonomy, no meaning. And each act of re-creation is for its perpetrator a perfectly meaningful and
legitimate act. The difficulty arises when the interpreter/
re-creator assumes the mantle of the author/creator and
identifies his act of creation with the author's own, obliv-
ious to whatever textual evidence there is to the contrary.
The reader must therefore remain as self-aware as Cervantes insisted the writer himself should be, never losing
sight of his subjective role. The very least we can do in
our homage to the great writer is to allow him his inde-
pendence of mind and to try to establish *his* intentions
before we bury them under the pall of our own sensibilities and preoccupations. To discard or dismiss those parts
of a work that do not fit conveniently with our interpretation of the author's "real" or subconscious intentions —
Don Quixote's grateful recovery of his sanity at the end
of Part II is a case in point — is the worst form of critical
arrogance. The first duty of the reader, and particularly
the critic, is to the text and its historical context. The
validity of what the critic does thereafter will depend on

his persuasiveness and his credibility within the ideological climate of his age. It can never be definitive.

That said, it would be idle to pretend that any writer totally enclosed within his own world is going to survive to be called great by ages other than his own. There can be no greatness without relevance or the potential for it, and a work retains its vitality only in so far as it remains relevant to human experience, even if that relevance changes with the shifts of time. There is no doubt that Cervantes would have been both amazed and amused at some of the anachronistic interpretations to which his masterpiece has given rise; no doubt in others, if presented to him in the moral and philosophical language of his time, he would have seen some truth. But there can be no doubt either that the work itself has qualities that encourage speculation and exploration, that its dimensions are grand enough, its workings complex enough, and its detail rich enough to sustain, at least in part, a variety of approaches; that the whole conception of the madman-hero and his crazy, self-justifying enterprise as it evolves and deepens in the course of the book has an elemental boldness of appeal which tempts the reader away from declared authorial intentions into projected fantasies of his own. A myth-figure becomes a myth-figure because it embodies or acts out human needs, behavior patterns, or beliefs. In becoming a myth-figure, Don Quixote has severed the umbilical cord linking him to his creator and acquired a creative life of his own. Rostand's Cyrano de Bergerac, Melville's Captain Ahab, and Dostoevsky's Idiot are only three of the heroes Don Quixote is known or thought to have inspired. No doubt somebody soon will make the same claim for Robert M. Pirsig's Phaedrus. He has even undergone a process of re-creation, with Spanish writers inventing sequels to various episodes in the book, or excising and then elaborating upon those aspects that take their interest and serve their purpose. Nothing will alter this, and it is an indisputable indication of the inspired nature of Cervantes's creation. But what we must remember is that the Don Quixote of the nineteenth-century romantics, of the twentieth-century existentialists, is not, could not be, the Don Quixote of Cervantes.

For Cervantes, as for most of the book's readers in the seventeenth and eighteenth centuries, *Don Quixote* was a hilariously funny burlesque; a parody of the romances of chivalry — and hence much funnier to those intimately acquainted with the "victims" than to us — and a richly inventive and hugely amusing description of contemporary life and manners. Its predominant tone is one of mischievous, tongue-in-cheek irony, of which its comments on the damsels of chivalric romance are a trenchant example. Don Quixote is described as the first who

> . . . in these calamitous times addressed himself to . . . righting wrongs, succoring widows, and rescuing damsels of the sort who wandered with their whips and their palfreys and burdened down with their virginity from hill to hill and from valley to valley; for in times gone by there were maidens who, unless some good-for-nothing, some low peasant or some fearsome giant ravished them, after eighty years during which they had not spent a single night indoors, went to their graves as intact as the mothers who had given them birth.

As the narrator remarks in Part I, "The age is in need of merry entertainment." In his *Journey to Parnassus* Cervantes would describe his famous work as an "eternal antidote to melancholy." And while the book certainly finished off the already moribund vogue for the literature of knight errantry — in the process producing the most famous exemplar of them all, as the critics never tire of pointing out — there is, predictably, not a jot of evidence that it had any effect at all on life and manners at the time. How could it? It was a funny book, praised in Cervantes's own day for its inventiveness, its decency and decorum, its language and its fun, but regarded with none of the awed reverence of later times.

The great change in attitudes to *Don Quixote* came in the nineteenth century, when it began to attract attention on a scale hitherto unknown. Samuel Taylor Coleridge, William Lamb, and William Hazlitt admired it, Byron, Wordsworth, Hugo, Flaubert, Stendhal, Gautier, and Vigny all praised it. In Spain the work had already come to be regarded as the great masterpiece of Spanish literature, but it was with the Romantics that Don Quixote on his sorry old nag Rocinante galloped out of the realm of satire and burlesque into the rarified atmosphere of noble and heroic idealism. The emaciated figure of fun with his addled wits and his pathetic dignity, gratefully restored on his deathbed to sanity and normality, becomes an admirable, even sublime, figure, a martyr to idealism and a victim of sordid reality, not clinically mad so much as out-of-joint with his time. His becomes the true vision, "sanity" distorts.

The attractions of such an interpretation for a new industrial age hankering after the values and ideals of a Middle Ages re-created by the nineteenth century in the image of its own wish-fulfillment fantasies, is easy to understand. Don Quixote becomes a latter-day Canute, fighting to keep at bay the incoming tide of materialism, a visionary willing a noble ideal into existence and dying rather than accept defeat. He is the heroic victim of the conflict of two worlds, the old and the new, of two distinct ethoses, the ideal and the real. He is the eternal symbol of the irrepressible idealism and optimism that informs the human spirit, the very embodiment of man's imperative dimension, of his will to impose himself on his world. And whatever the drift of individual interpretations, this is essentially what he has remained for the world down to the present, in his comedy and in his tragedy the very synthesis of the dualism of man's existence. For Spain itself, Don Quixote has come to personify its own spiritual ethos and historical identity, to embody the national characteristics of its people. His confrontation with reality is that of Spain with its own destiny.

In spite of recent attempts to move thinking about *Don Quixote* back toward a truer appreciation of the text and its historical context, the Knight of the Sorrowful Countenance (a title with less of pathos and more of ridicule in it for the Spaniards of Cervantes's day) will remain what he has become: a peg for every age to hang its own metaphysical preoccupations and perceptions upon. And arguably, a work of literature deserves to be judged on its own merits, for perhaps the measure of genius is the extent to which the artist in his creation does surpass his own intentions. The completely unacceptable aspect of this process of magnification, however, is the tendency to identify the author completely with his creation so that the two become one and the same. Thus, Cervantes's words at the end of Part II: "For me alone was Don Quixote born and I for him; he knew how to act and I how to write; we and we alone are one," intended as a final affirmation, in the face of Avellaneda's *Don Quixote*, of the indissoluble bond between himself and the creation that was his alone, have been interpreted instead as a statement of complete spiritual affinity. And hence the apocryphal story related by Alfred de Vigny (in his *Journal d'un poète*, entry for February/March 1840) that when Cervantes on his deathbed was asked whom he had intended to portray in *Don Quixote*, he replied, "Myself . . . he represents the sorry fate of imagination and enthusiasm out of place in a vulgar and materialistic society." But Cervantes's Don Quixote was not Cervantes, however dear the creation became to the creator, and posterity's Don Quixote is certainly not. The novel is probably the most layered, complex, and diversified that has ever been written, but however closely it seems therefore to correspond to the relativism of modern thought, there is not the shadow of doubt that Cervantes *knew* what reality, truth, and morality were, humane as he was and capable as he was of seeing more than one side of a situation or predicament. We marvel at the ingenuity of his endless playing with the overlapping worlds of literature and life, particularly in Part II of the work where Don Quixote and Sancho Panza not only meet people who are already familiar with them as literary figures from Part I, but encounter a character out of Avellaneda's continuation to Part I who acknowledges them to be the real Don Quixote and Sancho Panza, not the false imitations masquerading as them. But we are never in doubt as to what is ultimately truth and what is illusion. The aim of the endlessly receding mirror images is to amuse, not to confuse or disconcert. They serve also, of course, and quite brilliantly, to illustrate the possible range and power of literary manipulation, dangerously abused by the writers of romance who failed to make any distinction between the world of fiction and the real world. Their lack of artistic self-awareness was for Cervantes one of their greatest faults.

Clearly *Don Quixote* must be in large measure a distillation of Cervantes's experience of life, not merely a compendium of insights, longings, and perceptions. We cannot ignore the ending of the novel (Don Quixote's return to sanity) and its declared aims just because they seem too prosaic for our interpretation of the novel's mood. If Cervantes is anybody in the work he is Alonso

Quijano the Good, Don Quixote's sane other self, emerging from his failure to impose his distorted vision on the world a wiser man, a man who has learned through bitter experience how to live in the real world and is all the better for it. If we choose to regard *Don Quixote* as a work of disillusion we must remember that in the seventeenth century disillusion was an essential characteristic of rational, discerning man. If we wish to see it as the symbol as well as the product of its place in Spanish history, we must not forget that the flight from reality was one of the gravest symptoms of the nation's ills.

The real danger is that in using the work to echo and confirm our own strivings and anxieties, we do less than justice to Cervantes's own achievement, that in applauding it we applaud ourselves. Do we really see it for what it is? More pertinently, do we read it? Or are we so satisfied with the world's Don Quixote that we do not even feel the need to read *Don Quixote*. How many people now who blithely deploy the adjective "quixotic" or hold an image of Don Quixote in their mind's eye have ever bothered to open the pages of Cervantes's book? Very few, and this is unfortunate, for the rewards are enormous and they are not the rewards we necessarily expect to find. The difficulty, of course, lies in coming to the work with an open mind and an unjaded palate, a mind receptive to what we read and a palate unaffected by what others have told us.

In outline, the plot is a simple one. Alonso Quijano, an impoverished, elderly hidalgo living with his niece and his housekeeper in an unnamed village of La Mancha (the hidalgo, because of his social and psychological pretensions, was a common figure of fun) is so addicted to reading romances of chivalry that he ceases to be able to distinguish between their world and his own. Thereafter, all his perceptions and his experiences are translated into

chivalric terms as he seeks to create the appropriate context for his attempts to win fame for himself as a valiant
and chivalric knight. The narrative traces his determined
search for adventures and the equally determined efforts
of his family and friends to get him home. The clash
between the two provides many of the incidents and
much of the humor in the book. For his second sortie,
Don Quixote acquires a squire, a local country bumpkin
called Sancho Panza who, with his proverb-ridden speech
and very basic attitude to life, provides a perfect foil to
the learned and rarified ravings of the knight. For his
lady, an essential prerequisite for any knight errant, Don
Quixote metamorphosizes Aldonza Lorenzo, a buxom
wench he knows of but has rarely seen, into the beautiful
Dulcinea del Toboso, who dominates the poor man's
imaginings and pervades the whole book, yet never actually appears. How can she? She does not exist. Eventually,
after a series of ridiculous adventures and humiliating
encounters, interspersed in Part I with self-contained episodes and stories during which Don Quixote and Sancho
Panza retire into the wings as spectators, the deluded old
man is brought home, regains his sanity, and dies.

The story in essence depicts a situation where the hero
through madness is out of harmony with his world, and
where dislocation through the assertion of that madness
becomes collision. The resulting fracture and disillusion
may reasonably be seen as functioning on two levels: that
of literature, since the book depicts reality exploding into
the middle of one of the ideal fantasy worlds of Renaissance literature; and that of history, since the book reflects the way in which the mood of optimism which created and nourished these fantasy worlds gave way to the
realities of European political life. It stands, in a very real
sense, at a crossroads in the development of European

sensibilities, even though its dualism, which is more apparent than real, points forward rather than backward.

Don Quixote's madness is in itself an inspired device, allowing Cervantes to re-create a fictional world and the real world simultaneously. Thus, while the novel is a parody, it has none of the limitations of parody, for the discrepancy between the two worlds is perceived not merely externally by the reader but internally by the other characters as well. The parody is not only formal but organic. Its rich complexity largely lies in the interaction between Don Quixote and the other, sane, characters who people the novel. It lies too, however, in the conception of the madman himself: it has been said of Dostoevsky that his acute psychological insight was accompanied by the much rarer gift of psychological imagination, and this certainly applies to Cervantes. In accordance with the ideas current at the time, Cervantes presents Don Quixote's madness as being accompanied by lucid insights; the traditional association of genius with mental imbalance and of simplemindedness with wisdom is clearly related to this view of insanity as being at once ridiculous and revealing (and here, of course, dwell the seeds of the Romantics' interpretation of the knight). Lucid intervals or not, for Cervantes and his contemporaries, Don Quixote, whose "deeds" — that is, interference in the lives of others — do more harm than good, remained a ridiculous lunatic. At the same time, these lucid intervals allow Cervantes the opportunity not only to put some serious words into the knight's mouth, on the Golden Age of Man, on Arms and Letters, on Poetry, but also to create a fully rounded and developing character. The depth and the nature of Don Quixote's insanity are modified by his experiences and encounters, not least by his relationship with another wise fool, the practical Sancho, as he strives to accommodate his illusions to an intrusive reality. Even at the start, when his first makeshift helmet breaks, he carefully refrains from putting the second to the test. In Part II, Don Quixote's will begins to prove no more successful than his imagination in holding reality at bay, as the dream sequence in the Cave of Montesinos indicates.

Reality is not all his lunacy has to contend with, however. The common reaction to a madman is to humor him into compliance and not unnaturally Don Quixote's friends try the same ploy. Hence, when they wall up his library after his first sortie, to keep him from further harm, they arrange to offer him the explanation they know he will accept: an enchanter has done it. The Barber and the Priest masquerade as a damsel in distress and her squire in order to entice him home. When Sansón Carrasco in his turn sets out in Part II to bring him home, he dresses up as a knight errant himself and challenges Don Quixote to a duel, so that after defeating him he may command his obedience. Their motives are irreproachable. Nevertheless, they are confirming Don Quixote in his madness (and here, of course, lie the seeds of the view that Don Quixote is successful in imposing his vision on reality). The reader himself does not know what is happening in the episode of the duel until Sansón's helmet comes off to reveal his identity, and Sancho, who by this time does not know whether he is coming or going, is perfectly prepared to accept his master's theory that an enchanter has again been at work. In Part II, however, the characters' motives are often less generous. Having read Part I, the Duke and Duchess and their court humor Sancho's ambition (he wants to be the governor of an island) and Don Quixote's fantasy with a succession of practical jokes involving talking heads, enchanted ships, flying horses, princesses, and enchanters, which constitute deliberate deception, all for their own amusement. Sancho, too, is guilty of a deliberate and important falsification of reality, in his case to save his own skin. Having claimed in Part I to have delivered a message from Don Quixote to Dulcinea, in Part II when his master insists on going to Toboso to see her, Sancho has somehow to produce her. Relying on Don Quixote's madness, he tries to pass off three peasant girls mounted on donkeys as Dulcinea and her maidens. When Don Quixote in a moment of dazzling lucidity counters, "All I see, Sancho, are three peasant girls on three donkeys," Sancho is driven into a complete reversal of roles, insisting that what he sees are maidens and palfreys. Only too eager to believe him, Don Quixote once again takes refuge in the idea of enchantment.

As the behavior of those around him becomes less dignified, Don Quixote himself grows in pathos, dignity, and moral stature. As they sink into deception, he rises to the surface of his madness, relying increasingly for the preservation of his fantasy upon the fabrications of others rather than upon the strength of his own imagination. As Tomé Cecial observes, when Sansón Carrasco, disguised as the Knight of the Mirrors, challenges Don Quixote to a duel and to his consternation is defeated, "Now tell us, who is the madder of the two: he who is mad because he cannot help it or he who is mad by design?" And when, as Don Quixote lies dying, his sorrowing friends try to jolly him into recovery with talk of the disenchantment of Dulcinea and of his plans for a new future as a love-sick shepherd, he firmly rejects the fantasies they offer him out of love, preferring to embrace his real identity along with his sanity: "At times like this a man does not trifle with his soul." The moment is the most deeply moving in the whole book.

Since we no longer laugh at and ridicule the insane, it

is almost impossible to discuss *Don Quixote* now without being drawn into a mood where amusement seems distasteful. But as we actually read the text itself, its comedy, happily, still predominates. Sancho's deception of Don Quixote over Dulcinea, for all its implications, is extremely funny. So too is the network of fabricated fantasy in which the Knight is deliberately involved by other people, whatever their motives. The work's humor is as complex and varied as the work itself, operating all the time on a series of different levels and within a series of different moods. It ranges from hilarious slapstick through linguistic and literary parody and situational comedy to sophisticated conjuring tricks with the entire concept of fiction. It employs the whole range of humor's weaponry, including irony, satire, and burlesque. It involves knight errantry and contemporary reality; countryside and city; court life and roadside inns; convicts, puppeteers, and kitchen maids as well as licentiates, aristocrats, and clerics. It is inherent in the way in which Don Quixote's fantasy interacts with reality, in the insidious manner in which his vision and Sancho's become entangled and modified. It is central to the entire inspired idea of a protagonist so creative that he sets out to write his own biography using actions in place of words.

While humor is the predominant mood of the book, however, to deduce from it that life for Cervantes was simply "merry play" is as misleading as to claim for it the status of a metaphysical pronouncement. No man who had lived the life Cervantes had lived, resilient as he was, sees life as merry play. The humor has its pathos, the irony its serious undertones, the literary parody and manipulation its genuine concern. Comedy itself is for him an instrument of criticism, though no one would deny that as a creative writer he possessed an originality to which he never aspired as a literary critic.

Toward the end of Part II, Cervantes states that the name of Don Quixote's home village was not revealed so that all the towns and villages of La Mancha could vie for the privilege. By now, of course, after the gratifying success of Part I, he speaks with the wisdom of hindsight. Even so, justifiably proud of his achievement as he was, he can have had no idea of the significance his work would eventually acquire. The hindsight of centuries is necessary to know that it would be *Don Quixote,* the destroyer of false romance, and not *The Trials of Persiles and Sigismunda,* the attempt at a true romance, which would become not only the creator, very largely, of a new genre of prose fiction — the novel — but its unsurpassed and most influential exemplar.

The creation of Europe's first novel proper, in other words, with its psychological complexity and dynamism and its literary realism, was in a sense a literary accident. It would be ridiculous to see *Don Quixote* as a work of unconscious genius. Yet it remains true that it was anti-romance, not romance, which in the event proved to be the way forward for prose fiction; and this Cervantes could at most have only half intuited. Unsure whether romance was a legitimate literary form in any case (the lack of classical precedents was to ensure that the novel, and literary realism along with it, would not receive the accolade of recognition as art until the nineteenth century), theorists and writers at the time saw the form of imaginative prose's future as being a sort of prose epic. This ideal romance is described by the Canon in *Don Quixote.* In addition to the thematic scope and variety of incident, mood, and style of existing romance, it should possess a controlled appropriateness of style and an inventiveness shaped always by truth. These conditions *Don Quixote* fulfills absolutely. In Cervantes's eyes, *The Trials of Persiles and Sigismunda* fulfilled them also. The crucial difference is that the two are shaped by different concepts of truth, and while Cervantes in *Persiles and Sigismunda* celebrates what for him seems to have been the superior form of truth — poetic truth or idealism — posterity in the shape of the novel intuitively settled for *Don Quixote* and historic truth, that is, realism. The Aristotelian exaltation of poetry as the celebration of life as it could be, or as it ought to be, had never provided a satisfactory answer to the problem of how these two states (not at all identical, as Don Quixote himself painfully discovered) could be reconciled, and the imaginative exploitation of life as it was somehow slipped in unnoticed to fill the gap.

What makes *Don Quixote* the outstanding achievement it is, what makes it tower above the progeny its realism helped spawn, however, is that it can be seen as a perfect synthesis of both forms of literary truth. It explores the worlds of both the imagination and real life in its depiction of the clash between the two. Even if we see *The Trials of Persiles and Sigismunda* as a final reaffirmation of Cervantes's intellectual commitment to the purist world of poetry, it is the hybrid *Don Quixote* that marks his moments of highest creativity and originality. The book may celebrate the triumph of reality and sanity, but without this dual perspective it would lose both its fascination and its profundity.

Apart from its humor, perhaps its most enduring appeal, however, irrespective of changes in critical fashion and philosophical preoccupation, lies in its literary self-consciousness. And it is this self-consciousness that gives it its strongly modern flavor. Whichever Cervantes we see to be dominant in his work, the controlling literary magus or the irrepressible imaginative genius, his interest in literature, in its function and its power, is unquestionably an inalienable aspect of his creativity. *Don Quixote,*

after all, started out as a book about literature before it
became a book about life, and literature becomes part of
the book's very fabric and texture. Don Quixote enacts
literature because he is mad, and many of the other characters do the same although they are sane. Most of the
people he encounters are themselves addicts of the old
ballads and romances and not a few would be hard put
to it to pronounce on their truthfulness. As the tangible
cause of Don Quixote's lunacy, his library, before it is
burnt, is discussed at length by the Priest and the Barber.
The Priest and the Canon are more than ready to air
their views on literature in general and the romances and
the drama in particular. Don Quixote and Sancho are
rarely slow either in commenting upon the tales that
other characters have to tell. Yet criticism is present not
only as criticism but in the entire parodic shaping of all
the hero is, says, and does. Part I is encrusted with stories
within the story, at once self-contained and woven into
the main narrative. In Part II, Don Quixote, always con-
fident that his exploits will be recorded, discovers the
existence not only of Part I but of Avellaneda's *Don
Quixote,* not merely a false biography but a false biography of a false Don Quixote. And in order to give the
spurious biography the lie, he sets out not for Zaragoza,
where Avellaneda takes him, but to Barcelona instead.

Throughout the book, Don Quixote functions both
from within and from without his heroic conception of
himself, and the book itself is not written by Cervantes
but translated from the mysterious chronicler, Cide
Hamete Benengeli, for Don Quixote's exploits, after all,
are history not fiction. Not only is the book as intricately
layered as an onion in its exploitation of the very notion
of fiction, however. At the same time it is a glorious
hamper crammed full with every conceivable literary
mood, style, and genre. It is in turn heroic, romantic and

academic, epic, lyric and dramatic. It contains satire, parody, burlesque, irony, and farce. It encloses fable, proverb, and thinly concealed autobiography. It dallies with the pastoral, the picaresque, and romance. It has a strongly defined narrative trajectory, yet pauses in entertaining byways and lingers over its own multidimensional structural complexity. In other words it is a true hybrid with all a hybrid's vigor and genetic potential. By pointing in no single direction, it allowed the emerging novel form, groping as it was for shape and identity, to obey the imperative dictated by Europe's psychological and philosophical mood, while at the same time displaying an inimitable literary character of its own. Too complex and distinct for direct imitation, its immediate influence on the prose literature of Spain was not nearly as great as that exerted by the *Exemplary Tales*. Its long-term significance for the development of European prose fiction is incalculable.

NINE

Hostages to Fortune

AT THE END of Part I of *Don Quixote,* Cervantes, while not actually promising a second part, leaves the way open for one. We are told that although tradition in La Mancha has it that Don Quixote made a third expedition, to Zaragoza, the author of his history has been unable to find any authentic record of it. In hopeful anticipation that a manuscript might one day come to light, therefore, he ends his history with Don Quixote's epitaph and some poems in praise of Rocinante, Dulcinea, and Sancho Panza, all found, he claims, in a lead box in an old hermitage during renovations. Thus, until the very last line, Cervantes's intention seems to be to whet his reader's appetite for more. He then ends, however, with a line from Ariosto's *Orlando Furioso,* "Another, perhaps, will sing with a finer plectrum," which seems to imply that he did not at this stage really envisage spending any more time in Don Quixote's company. Indeed the line, in retrospect, seems almost an open invitation to the world to regard Don Quixote as its own property, a historical figure whose deeds and descendants might be charted by a succession of biographers in the way the chivalric cycles of the Middle Ages had been built up, although Cervantes can hardly have meant the invitation to be taken seriously.

It was the book's success, almost certainly, which decided him to write its sequel. But although it was well under way when Avellaneda's continuation appeared in 1614, how soon he began it we do not know. The years from 1604 to his death in 1616 constitute the most productive period of his life, as if, conscious of his advancing years, he suddenly felt the urgent need to make up for the lost years of creative inactivity spent in the service of his country. This sense of urgency reached a climax in the last three years of his life, as we shall see, when the fruits of this productive period came tumbling in hectic succession from the press. And the reception accorded to *Don Quixote* must have played a significant part in the unlocking of the flood gates. As Don Quixote says later, in Part II,

> One of the things that must give the greatest pleasure to a virtuous and distinguished man is, while still alive, to see himself in print and at the press, his good name constantly on people's lips.

In the mid-1600s, two of Cervantes's exemplary tales, *Rinconete and Cortadillo* (mentioned in *Don Quixote*) and *The Jealous Extremaduran,* were also attracting attention, circulating in manuscript in Seville. They were subsequently included, unattributed, in a manuscript collection of miscellanea compiled by a cleric, Francisco de Porras de la Cámara, for the delectation of his superior, the Archbishop of Seville. Porras could not have known the identity of their author: he is scrupulous in attributing other pieces to their authors and would certainly have been more than willing to commend the stories to his master by presenting them as the work of that famous new writer, Cervantes. This sudden success as a prose writer must have gone a long way toward compensating him for his continuing failure as a dramatist; the interludes and most of the later plays in their final form date from this last period of his life, and that he persevered with the theater at all says a great deal about his resilience of character and his ambitions as a professional writer. More important, however, with the publication of *Don Quixote,* any misgivings that Cervantes had harbored about his ability to achieve recognition as a creative artist were largely exorcised. Rich, popular, and feted he would never be, but well known from now on he certainly was.

His view of himself as a man dogged by misfortune, however, did not change, and soon afterward he received incontrovertible proof, if proof were needed, in support of this view. It is difficult not to arrive at the conclusion, though, that his misfortunes, serious as they were for him, lack the fine edge of tragedy. It would be no easy task to weave into a tale of pathos and grandeur the calamitous details of his life — the unusable left hand, the five years of insubordinate slavery, the excommunications, the mismanaged accounts, the absconding of his banker, the misjudged legal punctiliousness that led to his imprisonment, the setbacks and problems of his life in the south — all have a touch of the ludicrous about them which would convert too readily into farce. And it is this painfully acquired awareness of the proximity of the calamitous to the absurd which quite consciously shapes and informs *Don Quixote.* While Cervantes would be — and indeed was — the first to reject Don Quixote's madness and the distorting fantasizing to which it gives rise, he would not deny that he knew what it felt like to charge at giants that turned into windmills. But by the time he came to write *Don Quixote* he had achieved a degree of ironic detachment great enough to translate disappointment and disillusion into brilliant comic vision.

The incident that occurred a few months after the book's appearance was of a similar nature — somewhat sordid, very unpleasant, potentially extremely serious, yet in the event not disastrous. By now Don Quixote, Dulcinea del Toboso, and Sancho Panza were becoming household names, and soon scarcely a public celebration would take place in the Spanish-speaking world without one or other of their distinctive figures appearing to delight the onlookers. In Valladolid, however, Cervantes was just one more celebrity, and a poor one at that, in a city teeming with the rich, the powerful, and the famous. He was still dabbling in business affairs, and in June he was employed by Simón Méndez, a friend and Treasury official then in prison for debt, to collect tithes for him in the province of Toledo. In the same month he appears to have earned some extra money by writing a commissioned account, now lost, of the lavish celebrations held on and around 29 May to mark the christening of Philip III's newborn heir, who was to ascend the throne sixteen years later as Philip IV. The tender and loyal poem he wrote describing the Queen's glittering procession to mass after the Prince's birth he included in his exemplary tale *The Little Gypsy Girl.*

The excitement and splendor of these days of rejoicing were greatly enhanced by the presence at court of a large English retinue led by Lord Charles Howard, Earl of Nottingham, in Valladolid to cement the peace treaty signed by the two countries the year before. Being both English and Protestant, the visitors seemed little less alarming to the Spaniards than the Devil himself, and an order was proclaimed forbidding women on pain of severe punishment to go abroad without male escort after dark, for fear of contamination by the heretics. In the event the English comported themselves with such dignity and discretion that they were suspected of being secret Catholics (which is by no means unlikely — Howard himself was), although the anonymous author of one satirical sonnet clearly did not subscribe to this view:

> The Queen gave birth; the Lutherans arrived
> With six hundred heretics and heresies;
> We spent a million in a fortnight
> Giving them jewels, hospitality and wine.

Cervantes would have had trouble obeying the decree, for in his new second-floor apartment he lived surrounded by women: his wife Doña Catalina, his sisters Andrea and Magdalena (the latter now devoting herself to religion and good works), his daughter Isabel (by this time known to be so not only by Catalina herself, who appears to have accepted the situation without fuss, but by the neighbors as well), his niece Costanza, and a maid. The whole house, in fact, was full of women. Across the stairs from the Cervantes family lived Doña Luisa de Montoya, the widow of a well-known chronicler and probably a distant relative of Cervantes. She had previously lived in Toledo and had rented her house there to Micaela de Luján, Lope de Vega's mistress, when she moved to Valladolid the previous autumn. On the floor above Doña Luisa lived Doña Juana Gaitán, widow of the poet Pedro Laínez and a friend of Cervantes from their days both in Esquivias, where she still owned property, and in Madrid. After the death of her second husband, in spite of being fairly comfortably off, she had taken three lodgers — a couple and another woman — along with their maids, to live with her, her sister, and her niece. Above Cervantes lived a widow, Doña Mariana Ramírez, with her mother and two small daughters; Doña

Mariana and a visitor of hers, Don Diego de Miranda, a friend of her late husband's and a married man, had not long before been charged by the civil authorities with concubinage — not, it must be said, on very reliable evidence — and ordered not to see each other again. Finally, in the attic at the very top of the house lived Isabel de Ayala, a widowed old gossip who kept an envious and eagle eye on all that went on, although as a *beata*, or lay sister, she ought to have busied herself instead with practicing the charity she preached. All these people were to be swept up into the unfortunate events which now followed.

Around eleven o'clock on the night of Monday, 27 June 1605, not too late an hour for decent folk to be still abroad returning from church through the cool night air, or for maids to be fetching water from the fountain, one of Doña Luisa's sons heard shouting in the street outside. Opening the window he saw someone at the door below crying for help. Hurrying down with his brother he let in a badly wounded man dressed in black and carrying a drawn sword and a shield. Cervantes, who had already retired, was roused and the three helped the man upstairs to Doña Luisa's room. A priest and a surgeon were called, and shortly afterward two justices and a magistrate, Cristóbal de Villarroel, arrived.

The wounded man was Don Gaspar de Ezpeleta, Knight of the Order of Santiago and down-at-heel hanger-on at court, immortalized by the poet Góngora in a poem satirizing Ezpeleta's ignominious fall from his horse during the bull feast held recently in honor of the English visitors. When questioned, Ezpeleta would say only that after dining with his friend, the Marquis of Falces, captain of the Royal Archers, he had been walking along the street when he was confronted by a figure who ordered him out of the way. Angry words were exchanged, Ezpe-

leta drew his sword, they fought, and after wounding him
his assailant ran away. But quite clearly the story was a
cover-up. Ezpeleta, it emerged, was involved with a married woman, Inés Hernández, wife of the royal notary
Melchor Gaván, whose house he frequented, and there
had lately been some trouble over a pair of rings in Ezpeleta's possession which had been given by Gaván to his
wife; these rings were actually found on the wounded
Ezpeleta by the magistrate. Had Ezpeleta been going in-
nocently about his business that night, he would scarcely
have dismissed his servants and gone out equipped not
only with a sword but with a shield as well. Three times
as he lay dying on Doña Luisa's bed he was pressed for
the truth and three times he gave the same answer: the
duel had been an honorable one, he had been the first
to draw his sword, and his assailant was unknown to him.
He died on the morning of 29 June without changing his
story.

Ezpeleta's page communicated in confidence to Villarroel, the magistrate, the name and address of the woman
his master had been seeing and all but accused her husband, or a relative, of being Ezpeleta's assailant. Two
days later, after Ezpeleta had died, a veiled woman —
presumably Inés Hernández in search of her rings — was
discovered by the magistrate's runners in Ezpeleta's lodgings and interviewed in private by the magistrate. She
revealed her identity but claimed to have entered the
house on a charitable impulse after seeing the last sacrament being taken in — Ezpeleta's landlady was indeed by
then seriously ill.

The page's testimony put the magistrate, Villarroel, in
something of a quandary. Duelling was forbidden by law
in Spain; duelling at court was a particularly serious
offense subject to severe penalties, the standard one being,
as we know, the amputation of one hand. So the Ezpe-

leta affair would have to be investigated. On the other hand the wounded man himself had refused to implicate anybody, and any interrogation of his mistress's husband and relations, well-connected as Gaván was, could have embarrassing consequences for Villarroel. Indeed, it is not at all improbable that Villarroel knew Gaván and decided to cover for him by ignoring the lead given by the page. Ezpeleta was a disreputable figure in Valladolid, and public opinion in any case would probably consider him to have received no more than his just deserts for philandering with another man's wife. Villarroel's solution was to concentrate his attention instead upon the hapless occupants of the house where Ezpeleta had taken refuge. Even if nothing came of it, the magistrate would at least be seen to have done his duty.

Accordingly, throughout the night of 27 June and the following day, Cervantes and his family (with the exception of Doña Catalina who appears not to have been at home at the time), along with most of the other occupants of the house and the adjacent houses, were required to make statements. Each was interrogated not only about what had happened that night, but also about the private lives of the other tenants, in the hope, obviously, that some link could be established between Ezpeleta and someone in the immediate neighborhood. In the meantime, the zealous magistrate dispatched runners to all the churches and monasteries to discover whether anyone had taken sanctuary that night and to all the surgeons who might have treated a man with sword wounds.

Early on in the inquiry it became Villarroel's explicit intention, in the officious execution of his duty, to make this a morals as well as a murder investigation. The district was not a very reputable one, and rumor had it that gentlemen callers came to the house "day and night." He therefore determined to "establish just how freely the women who lodge there, who have no visible means of support in the court, live." Ezpeleta, it seems, had several times visited Doña Juana Gaitán's apartment; so too had the Duke of Pastrana and the Count of Concentaina. The Cervantes household had recently been visited by several men, among them a Genoese contractor who was an acquaintance from Cervantes's Seville days, Simón Méndez, with whom, as we saw, Cervantes had business dealings, and a friend of Méndez's, the Count of Higares, former Ambassador to Venice and France. As for Doña Mariana, the whole neighborhood knew of her supposed relationship with Don Diego de Miranda. It seems clear that most of these comings and goings were relatively innocent, certainly of anything that might lead to murder. The Duke and the Count had visited Doña Juana twice, ostensibly to discuss the dedication of two of her late husband's works, though since the books were never published, Doña Juana's real intentions in inviting the two young aristocrats to her house might well have been social rather than professional. Of Cervantes's visitors, the Genoese and Méndez were certainly in his house on business and so, too, in all likelihood was Higares, for whom Andrea sometimes did some sewing. He knew Ezpeleta, and one of his "visits" to the Cervantes household was in fact a visit to the wounded man: the sick room had been so crowded with visitors that Higares had retreated to the Cervanteses' apartment. As for Ezpeleta's visits to Doña Juana's home, their acquaintance apparently dated back more than twelve years, and they had recently met again in Valladolid; the visits in any case amounted only to two.

It seems equally clear that the eyes and ears that transmuted these comings and goings into evidence of scandal-

ous living were those of Isabel de Ayala in her attic,
spying without really seeing, listening but never properly
hearing, forever willfully misconstruing the evidence of
her eyes and ears. Her testimony was damaging. Doña
Luisa, she had to admit, led a blameless life, but none of
the other inhabitants escape her malicious tongue. Isabel
de Saavedra, referred to by the other witnesses as Cervantes's "natural daughter," she describes unequivocally as a
"bastard." In Spanish the phrase "natural daughter" is
less genteel and the word "bastard" stronger than in English, and among the mealy-mouthed notary's clichés,
Isabel de Ayala's "bastard" rings out with special force.
In the Cervanteses' flat she had heard people talking,
gentlemen went in and out night and day, causing scandal and gossip (no other witness makes this claim). It was
public knowledge, she claimed, that Simón Méndez, a
married man, was living in sin with Isabel — she herself
had often scolded him about it; and she knew for certain,
"since everybody said so," that he had given Cervantes's
daughter a skirt costing more than two hundred ducats —
a tall story if ever there was one. She proceeded to tell
the magistrate of Doña Mariana's previous trouble with
the law and to impugn the reputations of Doña Juana
Gaitán and her companions.

None of this connected any of the people mentioned
with the duel that was to lead to Ezpeleta's death. Villarroel, however, was convinced, or pretended to be convinced, that he had uncovered a nest of impropriety and
loose living. The situation was not helped by the fact that
Ezpeleta in his will embarrassingly left a silk dress to
Magdalena "for the love he bore her." As the magistrate
observed, why would he leave a silk dress to a woman who
wore the rough habit of a lay sister? He clearly suspected
that the gown was intended for one of Magdalena's nieces,
although the witnesses all agreed that it must have been

a token of Ezpeleta's gratitude to Magdalena for remaining at his side and helping him to "die well."

Indeed, Isabel de Ayala's testimony apart, the witnesses' statements are remarkably consistent, and unless there was some vast conspiracy of silence over the events of the night of 27 June — which seems highly improbable — then the evidence indicates that the Cervantes and Gaitán households were innocent, certainly of involvement in the Ezpeleta affair, and probably of all Isabel de Ayala's accusations. Both Cervantes and Doña Juana had numerous literary and business connections, some of them in common; and it is not surprising that they enjoyed a greater degree of social intercourse than was usual in the back streets of Valladolid; as the widow of a former gentleman-in-waiting to Philip II's unfortunate son Carlos, Doña Juana was certainly accustomed to a rather more sophisticated existence than the one she now led. The sewing activities of the Cervantes women, too, must have generated visitors.

Villarroel, however, willfully chose to follow up the suspicions aroused by his star informant rather than the quite different lead given him by Ezpeleta's page and, on 29 June, without one scrap of evidence to link any of them with the crime, Cervantes, Andrea, Isabel, Costanza, Doña Juana Gaitán and her companions, Doña Mariana and Don Diego de Miranda (who had not even been in the house on the night of the crime) were all arrested and ignominiously carried off to prison. Magdalena seems to have been spared out of respect for her lay habit. Simón Méndez, as we saw, was already in jail, but he too was implicated by the magistrate. By now Cervantes was only too familiar with the shortcomings of Spanish justice, but this further indignity, made so much worse by the involvement not only of his womenfolk but of a business acquaintance as well, was deeply wounding.

His recently acquired fame, now a guarantee that the shaming episode would soon become public knowledge, must have turned to ashes in his mouth.

In prison, the suspects stuck to their stories; the Cervanteses were all adamant that the visitors to their home came on respectable missions. It soon became obvious to the four magistrates who heard the case that there was no evidence against them and, accordingly, on 1 July they were released from custody. Their humiliation, however, was not over. A legal advisor was appointed to act for Cervantes's daughter and Doña Juana's sister and niece, all under twenty-five, indicating that the possibility of further legal action had not been ruled out. Then they and all the other women were placed under house arrest. Cervantes was simply released on bail. Diego de Miranda was ordered to leave the court within a fortnight and forbidden to see Doña Mariana again (they had both in fact denied seeing each other since the last ruling to this effect). Simón Méndez — and this must have been the hardest cut of all since the evidence of immorality was based on no more than an old woman's envious gossip — was charged never to set foot in Cervantes's home again or ever to speak to Isabel. The women appealed immediately against their confinement, but thereafter the records are silent.

In May or June, the second Madrid edition of *Don Quixote* had appeared. But Cervantes's elation at its success could not have survived intact this lamentable episode in which eleven people went to jail just because a dying man had come to their door for help. As Cervantes feelingly remarks in *The Illustrious Kitchen Maid,* a visit from the police upsets and terrifies even the innocent. Not only had three of his womenfolk suffered, but the clear implication of the magistrates' stricture upon Simón Méndez was that Cervantes's supervision of his daughter was not all that it ought to have been. The fact that there was probably no truth whatsoever in the implied accusation would have done nothing to save Isabel's reputation — up to now intact or we would have heard of it from Isabel de Ayala — from the local gossips. It certainly did nothing to save her from the speculations of posterity. Isabel's name has been often linked by commentators with those of both Ezpeleta and Méndez, and many Cervantes specialists have only added fuel to the flames by attempting unnecessarily to draw a discreet veil over the whole affair.

The truth of the matter is that once again Cervantes had fallen victim to the ill luck that dogged him, although it has to be conceded that so much misfortune does begin to look a little like carelessness. If in his management of his family he had betrayed once more the lack of caution that had sometimes characterized his behavior in the past, it was a testimony more to ingenuousness than to irresponsibility. He had spent a great deal of time away from his family and had assumed his parental responsibilities when his daughter was already on the threshold of womanhood. As a result, not only had he forfeited much of his authority, but he had lost sight of the unpleasant fact that the world in its assessment of a woman's character judged first and foremost by appearances.

His attitude, perhaps, owed more to principle than to prudence. The theme of freedom as the natural habitat, the only true habitat, of virtue and of love was one dear to his heart, which he explored in different ways, not only in the exemplary tales *The Jealous Extremaduran, The Little Gypsy Girl,* and *The Illustrious Kitchen Maid,* but in his plays *The Labyrinth of Love* and *The Gallant Spaniard.* Both plays dramatize the conflict between Nature and Society, between the individual's impulses and the efforts of the established order to protect itself by restraining them, depicting heroines who are driven by repressive male relations into unorthodox and dangerous behavior simply in order to marry the men they love. Personal desires and social demands are both ultimately gratified (as they are indeed in the short stories when Preciosa, the gypsy, and Costanza, the maid, are discovered to be of noble blood), but only after authority has been flouted. And, although the plays are lighthearted in tone and outcome, their serious undertones do not pass unnoticed. Preciosa and Costanza for all their exposure to a rough-and-tumble life succeed in imposing themselves upon their circumstances and environment and in winning the unconditional devotion of their young admirers long before their true origins are discovered; this discovery, by making marriage possible, rewards the young men for their willingness to forego their own social rank in the pursuit and conduct of their love. In the plays, however, Margarita, Julia, and Porcia are more perilously placed. They not only have a point to prove; they have to defy social and sexual convention in order to prove it, setting off in search of their lovers in male disguise. They assert, and are eventually granted, their right to fall in love and marry where they please. Not only is virtue, in other words, its own protector, but repression encourages not obedience but revolt. In Part I of *Don Quixote,* the shepherdess Marcela defends herself against the accusation of cruelty toward Grisóstomo, dead of a broken heart, with a devastating denunciation of the false logic of the literary lover, whose attitude she sums up as being "I love you for your beauty: therefore you must love me in spite of my ugliness." Her long speech indicates on Cervantes's part an acute awareness of the injustice of the traditional attitudes that governed relations between the sexes in literature as in life and is in essence a plea for freedom. In the context of Cervantes's writings taken as a whole, the Neoplatonic view of the uplifting nature of true love, which informs several of the exemplary tales, is seen to have possessed for him only a partial relevance to the complexities of human existence.

Surrounded by women as he was — and Andrea and Magdalena had had their adventures — it is not surprising that he saw and sympathized with their point of view. Repressive paterfamilias he certainly was not: his ability to empathize with the need of young men to spread their wings a little before settling into their allotted niches in life is a strong and attractive feature of the *Exemplary Tales*. That he gave careful thought to the whole problem of woman's freedom of behavior and choice is clear, and certainly some of his views must have crystallized as a result of his firsthand experience, through the Ezpeleta affair, of the traditional mentality in action: innocent visits misconstrued, acquaintances metamorphosized into lovers, eyes and ears always believing the worst, and wagging tongues gleefully transmitting it. All the result of a claustrophobic morality, rooted in fear and prejudice, which put its faith, like Carrizales in *The Jealous Extremaduran*, in externals. Cervantes's position on such matters, however, is always a realistic one. He was enough of a Renaissance man to be unequivocal in his championship of personal integrity as the only basis of true honor and nobility — as his story of the raped Leocadia in *The Force of Blood* amply illustrates. At the same time, he does not underestimate the power of social convention. Leocadia's loving parents unhesitatingly stand by their daughter in her hour of shame, but her baby is born in absolute secrecy and brought up elsewhere. And we need not, I think, interpret this as a sell-out to reactionary Counter-Reformation values. The literary ethos of the Counter-Reformation in Spain was, essentially, concerned with revealing the hollowness of a morality based on appearances, not with the propagation of such a morality. But like the other writers and thinkers of his day, Cervantes saw that society's unwritten laws, however misguided, have deep and powerful roots which cannot easily be pulled up. In *The Comedy of Entertainment* the heroine is reminded that "A woman must be good and, more importantly, appear so." There have been few societies down to the present day where this has not been the case. Unfortunately for Cervantes, a crowded tenement was no place to lead a life that could be readily seen as decorous, and in any case Isabel, as we shall see, had more of her two aunts in her than of those two spirited but irreproachable heroines, Preciosa and Costanza.

It was probably around this time that Cervantes received the insulting sonnet reliably attributed to Lope de Vega who, not content with reading it to his friends, actually had it delivered, carriage unpaid, to Cervantes's house. Years later Cervantes referred to the incident in his prose Postscript to *Journey to Parnassus:*

> While I was in Valladolid a letter was brought to my house for me with a carriage fee of one *real* to pay; a niece of mine [Costanza] accepted it and paid the carriage — would that she had not; but she explained that she had often heard me say that there were three things on which money was well spent: giving alms, paying competent doctors, and receiving letters, whether from friends or enemies; for those written by friends give information, and from those written by enemies some indication of their thoughts may be deduced. They gave me the letter and within it was a bad sonnet, dull and without style or wit, denigrating *Don Quixote*; what I minded most was the waste of the *real*.

It is difficult to believe that the poem did not annoy him, for in addition to denouncing *Don Quixote* as trashy it implied that Cervantes was a cuckold and impotent and that his behavior generally was unsuitable in a man of advanced years, though the exact meaning of this last accusation is unclear, unless it was intended to suggest that he was a dirty old man. There is not a shred of evidence that any of these things was true. All were standard forms of insult at the time, though by no means robbed by usage of their literal meanings. Yet it is not difficult to see how such thoughts might have suggested themselves to an enemy determined to be as offensive as possible. Catalina had spent years apart from her husband, their union was barren (Lope was probably unaware of Isabel's existence), and there had very recently been a scandal implying that Cervantes dwelt compliantly and complacently in a house full of women of easy virtue visited day and night by young men about town. Cervantes seems to have borne his years well — Avellaneda in the false *Quixote* describes him as a "soldier as old in years as he is young in spirit," though this, too, is certainly meant as some sort of insult — and clearly this did nothing to discourage speculation about his personal life. In light of such a deeply offensive attack, Cervantes's retaliation in subsequent years was, as we have already seen, remarkably self-controlled, never descending from the ironic and humorous to the crude and distasteful, as this sonnet undoubtedly does.

After the Ezpeleta affair, we lose sight of Cervantes for a time. Doña Luisa de Montoya, Doña Juana Gaitán, and Doña Mariana Ramírez all fled the house of scandal with their families, and the Cervantes family in all probability followed their wise example. His sisters were still resident in Valladolid in November of 1605, but Cervantes himself appears to have been elsewhere, possibly on business of some sort.

Toward the end of the year the rumor began to grow that the court would soon be moving back to Madrid. In the new year, the rumor proved to be correct: Madrid had managed to save itself from ruin by bribing the King to move the capital back to where it has remained ever since. And since the Empress María had gone to join her late husband, Lerma himself had no objection to accepting the generous bribes which Madrid was prudent enough to offer him as well. The Madrid council even undertook to pay the royal removal costs. The court itself welcomed the news. Valladolid was acquiring the reputation of being an unhealthy place to live. The royal family suffered from impetigo, and the previous year there had been a serious outbreak of measles and smallpox (which killed one of the princes of Savoy); since the medical dangers of overcrowding and lack of sanitation were then unknown, the Valladolid climate was blamed instead.

The news was made public on 24 January; the King and Queen reentered Madrid on 4 March, the Royal Seal made its exit from Valladolid on 15 April, and, thereafter, the hectic exodus began. Back they all trooped — the royal household, the government officials, the clerics, the merchants, the suppliers, and the thousands of hangers-on of every rank and calling, blocking the city gateways and the roads as they rushed to secure accommodation. And as Madrid, shabby and run down, slowly reinflated again to bursting point like some monstrous balloon, so Valladolid shrank pathetically back to its former size, its abandoned new buildings a mocking reminder of the five short, glorious years it had enjoyed as the center of Spain's vast empire. Within twelve months, according to one contemporary estimate, four thousand lodgings lay vacant, and special tax concessions had to be made to get the city on its feet again.

Since the Cervantes family had followed the court to Valladolid, it is reasonable to assume that they did not delay in following it back to Madrid. Certainly Andrea, Magdalena, and the two younger women, living as they did by their needles, would have had little alternative but to follow their wealthy customers. If they were wise, Cervantes and Doña Catalina would have retired to Esquivias to allow things in Madrid to calm down before making for the capital themselves; but by late 1606 they too were settled there in a lodging of their own. Soon afterward, Isabel de Saavedra, who had been living with her aunts and cousins in Madrid, married Diego Sanz del Águila. Sanz's identity is a complete mystery, but given Isabel's clouded origins and her lack of dowry he could have been a man of neither wealth nor social standing. But, humble or not, marriage was important to Isabel. It provided her with the social identity and respectability denied her by birth and with the freedom to live her own life; under cover of her marriage the matron enjoyed a degree of immunity from gossip unknown to the maid.

Respectability and immunity secured, Isabel proved no laggard in exploiting them. Early in 1607 she became the mistress of a middle-aged married man who was already a grandfather. Juan de Urbina was secretary to the House of Savoy at the Spanish court and deeply involved in a wide range of business affairs, including speculation in land and building; consequently, a wealthy and influential man. In the summer of 1606, Urbina's family had been ordered to Italy with the young Princes of Savoy, leaving him behind to look after the Savoy interests in Spain. In their absence, Urbina soon found companionship and consolation elsewhere, and by March 1607 Isabel was pregnant by him.

Cervantes's own life during the years that followed in Madrid remains a frustrating blank. We do not even know where he lived until 1609, when he and Catalina appear in the Calle de la Magdalena, living once more with Andrea, Magdalena, and Costanza. Cervantes was getting on in years — he was sixty in the autumn of 1607 — and his physical restlessness was now a thing of the past; he would remain in Madrid until he died. Much of his time, one imagines, was spent in conversation and debate, though since the principal literary gatherings were dominated by Lope de Vega, Cervantes probably preferred to stay away from these and frequent instead the bookshop run by *Don Quixote*'s publisher, Francisco de Robles, a well-known meeting place for writers which at some point doubled its attractions by becoming a public gaming house as well. Lope's animosity in any case must have made Cervantes persona non grata in many gatherings, and whether on account of this, or his poverty, or for some other reason, Cervantes never became an accepted member of the literary establishment, remaining always slightly on the fringe of fashionable literary activity.

A great deal of time was devoted to his pen. *The Illustrious Kitchen Maid, The Little Gypsy Girl,* and the play *The Grand Sultana* have been convincingly ascribed to the years immediately following the move to Madrid, and his publication rate later on testifies to more or less continuous literary activity during the last nine years of his life. The full-length plays and the interludes he wrote during this last period, after the Madrid theaters had started picking up again with the return of the court, were an attempt to earn a living, or part of one, by writing for the stage, and his failure to earn a single penny with them before they were finally published in 1613 was a profound disappointment to him, particularly in view of the concessions he made in the writing of these plays to Lope's new drama. He even wrote with specific players, and hence a specific theatrical manager, in mind, on occasion, but to no avail. And one is driven to wonder, given the undoubted merits and actability of these later plays — of the interludes above all — whether Lope's resentment toward Cervantes did not influence theater-company managers in their reluctance to perform his works. Lope was the great box office draw, and no company could afford to incur his displeasure. His judgment, in any case, carried great weight. The bookseller's assertion that it was common knowledge that little could be expected of Cervantes's verse clearly derived its authority from somewhere, and Lope, as we have seen, denounced Cervantes as the worst poet of the age, a grossly biased piece of malice. In the Postscript to his *Journey to Parnassus,* published in 1614, Cervantes would claim defensively that his plays were not performed "because the theater-company managers did not come looking for me and I did not go looking for them," explaining that since they had their milksop poets who suited them very well, they did not look for stronger fare. But Cervantes knew the form: no manager would seek out a poet who had not had a play performed since the 1580s, and it is impossible to believe that hard-up as he was, he did not try actively to interest managers in the plays he spent valuable time writing. And if some of the plays of this period are indeed the rewritings of early plays that they seem to be, then Cervantes quite obviously entertained hopes for their commercial success.

The income he and his wife had to live on was consequently a meager one, eked out by Doña Catalina's very modest income from her family property in Esquivias and by advances against later publications: Robles lent Cervantes some money in 1607, probably in anticipation of the publication of the *Exemplary Tales,* a project already under way. The couple were but two among the many at court without any very visible means of support — the magistrate's description, it will be remembered, of the female tenants of the house in Valladolid — yet there is a sad poignancy about the wretched situation of this man whose fame was already spreading in two hemispheres and whose book was giving pleasure to thousands of readers, yet who lived in poverty back home in the most lavish court in the world, ignored by Crown and noble patrons alike. And it was a poignancy that Cervantes himself did not miss, for his later writings are scattered with references to his poverty and neglect, and to the puny rewards received by writers for their labors. As for the court itself, Cervantes continued, as he always had done, to denounce its failure to patronize the right people:

> Oh court, that encourages the hopes of claimants who push themselves forward and cuts short those of the withdrawn and virtuous; that abundantly supports shameless rogues and starves to death the modest and discerning.
>
> (*The Licentiate of Glass*)

By 1609, Cervantes and Doña Catalina had decided they could manage only by once more sharing house with Cervantes's sisters.

The decision to write the half-promised sequel to *Don Quixote*, whenever it was taken, was undoubtedly influenced partly by Cervantes's need to write something which would guarantee him some money; and there is a suggestion at the beginning of Part II that the decision came fairly early on, with Cervantes making a start on the sequel in 1607, encouraged no doubt by Robles who would have been eager for another printing success. If this is indeed the case, then Part II took Cervantes over seven years to write, an indication, perhaps, of hardening arteries but certainly not of a faltering imagination. The truth was that, incomparable as *Don Quixote* appears to us, Cervantes had other literary dreams and ambitions to fulfill and all the evidence points to the fact that for a period of years, roughly 1608–1612, Cervantes was writing drama, poetry, and several different prose works simultaneously. It was as if the physical restlessness of his earlier years had perforce given way to an intellectual restlessness that expressed itself in endless experimentation. *Don Quixote,* therefore, had to take its turn with the rest, and indeed might never have been completed but for the appearance, to Cervantes's enormous chagrin and indignation, of Avellaneda's sequel. After that, completion became a point of honor, an essential and definitive assertion of authenticity and ownership, as the legitimate father laid claim to his brainchild.

This was something, of course, that Juan de Urbina could not do. He did, nonethelesss, go to some trouble to ensure that Isabel and her child, Isabel Sanz, born in or just before the new year of 1608, were well provided for. Sanz himself inconveniently died some months after his putative daughter was born, and on 24 June Urbina installed both Isabels in a house he owned near his own. Great care was taken to preserve appearances, the house being legally "rented" to Isabel de Saavedra by a friend and agent of Urbina's called Sebastián Granero, in whose name the property had originally been bought. If Cervantes had hitherto been unaware of the liaison, he must necessarily have discovered at this stage what was going on. Isabel and her daughter now had a roof over their heads, but they still needed support and, more precisely, whether the liaison was to continue or not, Isabel needed another husband. Accordingly, Urbina, with the aid of a large dowry, conjured up a new one: Luis de Molina, a banker's agent. In the marriage contract, signed on 28 August in Cervantes's presence (which judiciously but inaccurately describes Isabel as his "legitimate" daughter), some measure of decorum was preserved by presenting Urbina and Cervantes as being jointly responsible for the dowry of two thousand ducats, though Urbina clearly provided the whole sum, for he offered several houses, two windmills and some other property he owned as surety. The provisions of the contract granted Isabel and Molina the use of the house Isabel had been living in, rent free, until little Isabel married; if the latter died young, Isabel was to have the use of it during her lifetime and in the event of her death — whether there was issue of the marriage with Molina or not — Cervantes himself was to inherit the rent-free lease, with the right then to will it outright to whomever he pleased. In view of Cervantes's age, it was highly unlikely that this rather curious provision would ever be implemented, and it seems to have been included merely in order to protect his granddaughter by excluding Molina from any rights to the house. Subsequently, Cervantes — one assumes by prior agreement — signed a statement making over the house to Urbina in the event of his granddaughter's death, although he continued on occasion to refer to the house as his own. Not for nothing was Urbina an experienced man of affairs.

Any scruples we might have about the nature of these negotiations would be entirely anachronistic. Marriages of convenience were the order of the day and this was no more calculated an example than many others. Molina was as fully aware that he was being bought as the other side was that what it offered was an attractive commercial proposition. He was to prove no less capable of looking after his interests than Urbina. As for Cervantes, however distasteful he might have found his necessary collusion in the matter, since he himself could afford no alternative solution, he was scarcely in any position to stand in his daughter's, and more importantly, his granddaughter's way with pointless moralizing. Nothing was going to change Isabel, and Cervantes was in such matters nothing if not a realist. His predominant response to the marriage must have been that of any practical but impecunious seventeenth-century father — relief. Two months later his own financial situation was once more at issue when the Exchequer caught up with his case again, ordering him and his erstwhile guarantor, Francisco Suárez Gasco, to account for the discrepancies in his Granada accounts way back in 1594. Since this is the last we ever hear of the matter, it would seem that Cervantes was at long last able to satisfy the Exchequer, either with money or an explanation. Perhaps Urbina helped him out.

It was probably in the year or so that followed this solution to his daughter's future that Cervantes wrote what is arguably his best and certainly his most delightful play, *Pedro de Urdemalas*. An episodic mixture of pastoral, gypsy, and picaresque motifs, it contains some scintillating scenes — always the dramatic unit with which Cervantes was happiest — with excellent dialogue. Yet it is not difficult to see why a theater-company manager might have turned it down. More reminiscent of an extended interlude than a play proper, its plot lacks consistent direction, its pace is uneven, and its ending undecided. Most unsettling of all, perhaps, for the prospective buyer it is both self-conscious and provocative. The characters' world and the audience's at several points overlap (the Pedro of the title, a manipulating but lovable rascal who ends up becoming an actor, may have been based on a real-life theatrical figure whose colorful life ended in an apoplexy in 1610). The beautiful "gypsy" heroine is a

Preciosa, but without any of the inherent charm and virtue normally associated in Cervantes's characters with noble blood. The King, when we last see him, ominously rejects his newly discovered relationship with the gypsy girl (she is his wife's niece) as being sufficient to stop him pursuing her. While Pedro himself ends the play with a mocking denunciation of some of the standard ingredients of the Lope drama of the day: the play the audience will see on the morrow (for what they have been so far watching, of course, is "real") will not, for example, end in a happy-ever-after marriage. He is in fact referring to *Pedro de Urdemalas* itself, clearly.

The play's mood, therefore, is redolent of an amused but deliberate iconoclasm. If we detect a somewhat jaundiced view of human nature in his depiction of the selfish, ungrateful gypsy girl and the weak and lustful king, then in view of his recent experiences at home this would scarcely be surprising. But if Cervantes's sole aim had been to write a play which would be snapped up by the theater, then he had sadly misjudged his market. Since he patently knew that market inside out — his mocking references to the standard recipe show he was fully aware of what met with the public's approval — he clearly could not bring himself to sacrifice artistic integrity to commercialism. Even so, the play's loose structure suggests that his was not ultimately the sort of mind that could submit to the discipline imposed by the demands and constraints of the three-act play of his day. His great gifts were for narrative, characterization, and naturalistic dialogue, not one of which in itself, not even dialogue, equipped him for the action-packed but increasingly tightly structured *comedia*. Very much at his ease with the small dramatic unit, where dialogue could reign supreme, only narrative could successfully absorb the creative expansiveness of his imagination, and only extended

narrative could really do it justice. Some of his short
stories are very tightly constructed, but it is significant
that most of the best and most interesting — *The Licentiate of Glass, The Dogs' Colloquy,* and *Rinconete and
Cortadillo* — have, as we saw, a pronounced air of incom-
pletion. Never short of ideas, his major problem lay always in molding them into formal shape. The originality of his inspiration inevitably dictated the form of its
expression, which is why his greatest work is also his least
conventional. The fact that the conventions of the drama
were by now so powerfully controlled by the demands of
a highly commercialized theater meant that only original
minds able and content to work within the conventions —
Lope de Vega, Tirso de Molina, Calderón — could find
artistic fulfillment in the drama. In Cervantes, originality
was incompatible with these formal constraints, as *Pedro
de Urdemalas,* for all its strengths, shows.

That he had high hopes of selling *Pedro de Urdemalas*
— perhaps to the very Nicolás de los Ríos mentioned in
the play on whom Pedro was possibly based — is indicated
by the fact that he wrote an interlude to accompany it,
both intended for performance on Midsummer's Day.
Plays were always preceded and punctuated by such tid-
bits, and indeed they often constituted the main attraction; many audiences, we are told, yawned through the
principal business and were kept in their places only by
the prospect of the dances and farces to come. In *The
Jealous Old Man,* however, Cervantes produced a sketch
almost too hot to handle. A dramatization of the basic
plot of his story *The Jealous Extremaduran* (the old man
of the title is even given a similar name, Cañizares), it
depicts the revolt of a frustrated young bride against the
unnatural relationship with the old husband who,
through jealousy, keeps her isolated from the world. The
outcome and the message are the same in both versions,

but here tragedy has become comedy and the farce has all the outright bawdiness of an Italian *novela*. As the pathetic, hoodwinked Cañizares stands outside her door listening to Lorenza's cries of what he deems to be feigned delight, she vigorously frolics with the young stranger who has immediately before been infiltrated into the house by a neighbor for that specific purpose. It is by far the least restrained of all his brilliant, hard-hitting farces, and evidently Cervantes's conscience was as yet untroubled by that concern for the morality of his work that was to prey upon his mind when he came to publish the short stories a few years later. The cynicism the farce portrays is not unlike that revealed by the king and the gypsy girl in *Pedro de Urdemalas,* and it is perhaps not too fanciful to see it as in some sense the reflection of a mood of disillusionment created by his daughter Isabel's behavior. That sordid little story of a young woman's self-interest and a grandfather's philandering had unfolded too closely before his eyes to leave no mark.

Significantly, in another play written around this time or afterward, *The Comedy of Entertainment,* he puts uncharacteristically severe words on the subject of daughters in the mouth of one of his characters: "Sons are half one's soul; but daughters are the fuller half and their father must look to their honor like a lynx"; and, even more feelingly, "Oh disobedient daughters who put personal preference before the experience of age, may God destroy and Heaven curse you." The play has all the lightheartedness and amorality of tone of an extended interlude (there is even a rather meaningless and certainly unsinister incest motif clumsily deployed as a plot complication) ending, defiantly, without the conventional clutch of happy-ever-after marriages. Yet these exclamations, for all that they come from the sort of oppressive father of whom Cervantes disapproved, have here a heartfelt ring to them. The events of the last few years had brought sharply home to Cervantes an unpleasant truth: if the man with a wife and children has given hostages to fortune, as Francis Bacon so feelingly held, then in a society where appearances were all, the seventeenth-century Spaniard's womenfolk rendered him doubly vulnerable.

TEN

The Last Years

As THE FAME of Don Quixote and his creator spread at
home and abroad, Cervantes's own life for the most part
continued upon its now settled, uneventful course. Only
the frequency with which he and his family moved house
in Madrid during his last years — at least six times between 1609 and 1616 — betrays the stringency and discomfort of his domestic life. Relations between Cervantes
and Catalina, whatever they had been during the long
years of his absences, had settled into something like
companionable harmony; and when Molina and Isabel
were formally married in church in March 1609, both
Catalina and Cervantes acted as sponsors. This was a gesture of consideration for her husband rather than a sign
of affection toward Isabel, if the will she drew up in June
1610 is anything to go by; for there, while Cervantes's
niece Costanza is included, Isabel's name does not appear.

The fact that Doña Catalina's brother Francisco de
Palacios, rather than Cervantes himself, was the major
beneficiary of this will has no dark significance. Not only
was Cervantes nineteen years Catalina's senior and, therefore, unlikely to survive his wife, but since most of what
she possessed had come from her mother's side of the
family and since Francisco had undertaken payment of

the debts on the family estate, then it was clearly just that the family holdings should revert to him. We can be sure that she did not wish them to go to Isabel. Cervantes himself is left a few things "for the great love and good company we have had together," perhaps merely a legal platitude — her maid is referred to in similar words — perhaps not.

The atmosphere in the Cervantes household — temporarily settled in 1609 in modest quarters in the Calle de la Magdalena — was by now assuming a pronounced devout flavor. The year before, in 1608, Magdalena had received the habit of the Third Order of St. Francis, a lay order founded shortly before, and now lived the secluded life of a lay nun. On 8 June 1609, both Catalina and Andrea followed her example. On 17 April, Cervantes himself had joined a religious brotherhood, the Confraternity of Slaves of the Most Blessed Sacrament, founded the year before. Cervantes, perhaps, had decided that the time had come to give thought to his soul; as he observes in his Prologue to the *Exemplary Tales* a few years later, "I am no longer of an age to trifle with life beyond the grave." But the brotherhood, which met in the Calle del Olivar, certainly had other, more worldly attractions as well. It enjoyed illustrious patronage, including that of the King and his favorite, Lerma, and membership soon became very fashionable in court and literary circles. By late 1609 it was four hundred members strong, Quevedo and Lope de Vega among them. Possibly Cervantes hoped that membership would bring him into contact with a potential patron; possibly he merely welcomed the opportunity to mingle on equal terms with the great in a context where his poverty did not signify. He does not, however, appear to have aspired after any of the official positions in the brotherhood's organization and, it is fair to say, he was early rather than late in the rush to join. The step was a common one to take in the devout Spanish society of the day, a society in which religious life and secular life were in a significant sense indivisible. Nearly all the great Spanish literary figures of the seventeenth century had close connections with the Church, constituting as it did one of the few great career structures of the day — Tirso de Molina was a Mercedarian friar, Góngora and Calderón were ordained priests, and Gracián was a Jesuit. Even Lope de Vega, for long a familiar of the Inquisition, took Holy Orders in old age, not that that succeeded in curtailing his more worldly activities. As a member of the confraternity, Cervantes's duties included going to mass every day and to communion on the first day of every month, following a regime of prayer and self-discipline, and visiting the sick. There is no reason to suppose that he did not take these duties seriously, although it would be naive, of course, to believe that everybody did — like others of its kind, the brotherhood was as much a club as a charitable society. Membership also brought literary opportunities. Cervantes was commissioned to write laudatory verse for the brotherhood's sumptuous Corpus Christi celebrations that year, and again in 1612, as in 1609, actually emerged as one of the winners in the poetic jousts.

Four months after entering the Third Order of St. Francis — during which time the family had moved out of the Calle de la Magdalena and then back again to a different address — Andrea died and was given the humble burial that was all the family could afford. She was sixty-five. Personal tragedy, however, was soon eclipsed by a national event of consummate importance.

In the winter of 1609, the rising ground-swell of feeling against the continuing presence on Spanish soil of a large population of Moriscos (converted Moors) of suspect orthodoxy, and, therefore, patriotism, erupted in a series of decrees of expulsion. The hard-working, abstemious Moriscos — Spaniards of centuries' standing — represented Spain's major agricultural force, and their loss to the countryside and to the economy at large was to prove a crucial one. While some more perspicacious Spaniards doubted the wisdom of the move and feared its repercussions, the vast majority rejoiced, Cervantes among them. The picture he paints of the Moriscos in *The Dogs' Colloquy,* in *Don Quixote,* and in *The Trials of Persiles and Sigismunda* leaves us in no doubt that while he was keenly aware of what the expulsion cost in terms of human suffering, the popular conception of the Morisco as a treacherous, avaricious, unchaste, and un-Christian saboteur was his too. Ricote, the Morisco encountered by Sancho Panza in Part II of *Don Quixote,* is a sympathetic figure, but what commends him to Cervantes is his readiness to denounce the machinations of his fellow Moriscos and to recognize the "divine inspiration which moved his Majesty to put into effect such a noble resolution." Having failed to assimilate the Moriscos it had forced into Christianity, Spain was now punishing them for not making good Christians, and it would have taken a far more objective eye than Cervantes's, exslave of Islam as he was, to detect the tragic irony.

As the Moriscos' last hours on Spanish soil ticked away, the shadows in Cervantes's own life were beginning to lengthen. In February 1610, Magdalena, her novitiate year in the Third Order over, was fully professed. In June, Doña Catalina made her will and herself professed. Magdalena's health by now was failing. By October she was confined to bed where she too made a will which, in ghostly travesty of a vanished past, told of a large unpaid debt owed her from long ago by a married man. Like Catalina's, Magdalena's will ignored Isabel in favor of Costanza. Among her bequests to Costanza was her share of her brother Rodrigo's estate and her allowance from an erstwhile suitor, Enrique de Palafox. Since Magdalena had shown no lack of good will in taking Cervantes's daughter into her home years before, obviously Isabel had forfeited her family's affection through her subsequent behavior.

That the rift with the family extended to her father there is little doubt, for, in a deed signed by Cervantes on the very day Magdalena made her will, he signed over his own share in Rodrigo's estate to Costanza as well. This deliberate and evidently prearranged exclusion of Isabel from the family inheritance, such as it was, is a mute testimony to the depth of Cervantes's disappointment in his daughter.

It is also, sadly, one of several indications that little Isabel Sanz, Cervantes's granddaughter, was already dead, a complication to Isabel de Saavedra's position with regard to the ownership of the house she lived in that was to drag painfully and sordidly on for years. Among the provisions of the marriage contract, drawn up in words aimed at concealing the truth rather than clarifying it, passing reference had mysteriously been made to the child's existing ownership of the house which Urbina had arranged for Isabel de Saavedra to use during her lifetime. On the basis of this flimsy statement, Isabel, as her daughter's lawful heir, seized the chance to try and acquire the house outright. Urbina, for his part, his responsibility unexpectedly removed even before the promised dowry was due to be paid, seems to have considered his obligations cancelled. Certainly he was determined to retain legal ownership of the house, although he was quite prepared for Isabel and Molina to have the use of it. Cervantes's role in the struggle that followed is confused, but it is clear where his sympathies lay. In March 1610, he signed a statement claiming that the house had been paid for by him — a ruse obviously agreed upon with Urbina to secure ownership of the house, for Cervantes immediately afterward ceded ownership to Urbina and his heirs.

Little wonder that by October Cervantes, caught in the web of this unpleasant legal wrangle, had had enough of his daughter's opportunism and transferred his share in Rodrigo's estate in disgust to his niece. Isabel was not to acknowledge Urbina's ownership of the house until she made her will in 1652.

Perhaps it was the unpleasantness over this affair with his estranged daughter that turned Cervantes's thoughts so longingly to Italy, and possibly even to the son he had left there long ago. In the late spring of 1610, it became known that Pedro Fernández Ruiz de Castro y Osorio, seventh Count of Lemos and nephew and son-in-law of the powerful Duke of Lerma, had been appointed Viceroy of Naples, and that, as a generous and enthusiastic patron of the arts, he intended taking with him to Italy to grace his court a bevy of gifted literary men. They were to be chosen by his new secretary, the poet and historian Lupercio Leonardo de Argensola. Cervantes, who had met the Count, made it known that he would like to be included. But it was not to be. Flattering words were pronounced and promises were made, but in the event both Cervantes and the poet Góngora, for whom Cervantes entertained the greatest admiration and who had also applied to go, were omitted from the suite that embarked for Italy with the Count on 3 July. The reason for their omission is obscure. Since Argensola was an admirer of Lope's, perhaps professional partisanship was at the back of it: there was even less love lost between Lope and Góngora than between him and Cervantes. Perhaps Argensola simply preferred not to weight the scales of talent and renown too heavily against himself. Or perhaps, in

Cervantes's case, he was just too old and unglamorous. Whatever the motive, Cervantes was deeply hurt, as his feeling reference to the incident in his *Journey to Parnassus* shows:

> If I hoped for much, they promised much;
> But possibly preoccupations new
> Made them forget what they had said.

It was his last bid for tangible recognition.

By June 1610, the Cervantes family had moved to a house in the Calle de León. There, on 28 January 1611, Magdalena died, leaving Cervantes alone with his wife and niece. Since a codicil to her will had directed that she be buried in the neighboring Franciscan convent, her funeral expenses at least did not have to be met by her brother: on account of her poverty, the order itself undertook to bury her, and indeed the codicil was evidently added with this in mind.

Emotionally, the blow to Cervantes must have been severe. All his life Magdalena had been a close friend and confidante, and for years now they had thrown their lot in together and lived under the same roof. The bond of affection between them was deep, deeper perhaps than that between Cervantes and his wife, and Magdalena's death left a gaping void in his life which would not be filled. Estranged from his own daughter, his granddaughter dead, all the family he had left to comfort him in his declining years were a niece who was soon to leave to set up house on her own and a wife with whom he had shared neither children nor the greater part of his active life and whom he had but recently been prepared to leave once more. Little wonder that in *Journey to Par-*

nassus his thoughts turn touchingly to the son he was not to see but whose existence he there unequivocally, even defiantly, affirms.

Neither disappointment nor personal loss stopped him writing, however. Nothing now was to succeed in upsetting the psychological equilibrium he had achieved, and with little left to care or hope for and with nothing to leave behind him but his name, he had two clearly defined goals to which to dedicate his energies — keeping body and soul together in this life and carving out immortality for himself in the next. His priorities in the pursuit of these aims may seem somewhat curious. Seven years had passed since his last and most successful publication — Part I of *Don Quixote* — and the surest way of earning money would have been for him to get Part II finished as soon as possible. A large and ever-growing public awaited the continuation of the knight's exploits; the playwright Guillén de Castro had already transferred them to the stage. But a lot of work remained to be done on *Don Quixote,* and the rewards of publication were in any case not very great. And so instead, Cervantes kept trying for the quick returns the theater seemed to offer. If he managed to break into the commercial theater, the rewards promised to be prompt and recurring; authors, on the other hand, received no royalties and in the absence of an efficient copyright system no publisher could afford to pay huge sums, even for a book with a guaranteed market.

But Cervantes's persistence in writing plays indicates that his motives were not entirely financial. Having proved himself a master of prose narrative, and sated perhaps with the knight and his adventures, he still hankered after success in the theater — by now, indeed, the theater seems to have assumed the proportions of a personal challenge in his mind. He continued, therefore, to divert his energies from *Don Quixote* into writing plays and interludes to accompany them.

In early January 1611, he had obviously been engaged on one of these interludes, *The Sham Biscayan*, about a trick played on a gullible woman by two confidence tricksters with the help of an artificial gold chain. For mischievous mention is made in it of the decrees proclaimed at the beginning of that month in a vain attempt to curb the extravagance and immorality seen to be endemic in Spanish urban society. Henceforth, clothing and bedlinen were to be left naked of embroidery; gentlemen's collars were to be of simple design and plain linen; only the most modest jewelry was to be worn; women were not to sport heavy veiling and could enjoy the male company only of husbands, fathers, grandfathers, and sons when they traveled abroad in their coaches — notorious by now for the activities that habitually took place behind their lowered blinds. Cervantes was clearly as amused as everyone else by the fatuous impracticality of it all.

The interlude, which has the pace, wit, and sparkling realism of most of Cervantes's compositions in this genre, was possibly meant to accompany his one attempt at a play with a religious theme, *The Fortunate Ruffian*, which has been ascribed to this period when religious activities were very much to the fore in the Cervantes household. The play belongs to an already well-established tradition of religious drama for the secular theater, specifically to a group of plays designated "saints' plays," which, typically, dramatize the conversion of some historical figure from sinner to saint. Conscious no doubt of the Canon's denunciation in Part I of *Don Quixote* of the absurdities of much religious drama, Cervantes constantly stresses the veracity of the miraculous adventures that unfold in *The Fortunate Ruffian,* the plot of which he took straight from a contemporary history of the Dominican order in Mexico. This self-consciousness extends somewhat obtrusively to the play's unity — or rather lack of it — for like *Pedro de Urdemalas, The Fortunate Ruffian* has a geographical span, opening in Seville and ending in Mexico, which would have scandalized the Cervantes of years ago. Cervantes accordingly anticipates any accusation of inconsistency by introducing into the beginning of Act II two abstract characters, Curiosity and Drama, who discuss the matter, Drama claiming that times change and art with them. As an admission, however grudging, of the validity and legitimacy of the new drama, the scene is fascinating, but it is difficult to believe that an audience caught up in the excitement of the first act, with its racy, character-packed depiction of low life in Seville, would care one bit for the author's theoretical concerns. Once more Cervantes's concern for his artistic integrity had got the better of dramatic intuition. After this, the pace and interest of the play inevitably flag — sinners make better dramatic fodder than saints — but Cervantes's play is certainly as good as many others in the genre which reached the stage and were received with acclaim, and his sense of frustration at not finding a buyer for it must have been enormous.

Short of money for day-to-day living as he was — by the summer he had hopefully written another farce, *The Anxious Guard,* in which a soldier and a sacristan compete for the favors of a kitchen maid — his potential financial problems were even more serious. By 28 August 1611, Isabel's dowry of two thousand ducats, for which both he and Urbina had made themselves responsible, was due to be paid. In February, Urbina tried to secure Molina's good will, and possibly his absence, by employing him as his business agent for the lease and organization of an iron works he was negotiating for at Cañizares, near Cuenca. Molina and above all Isabel, however, were no fools, and when 28 August came and went without any sign of the dowry, Molina caused a warrant to be issued against his father-in-law and Urbina, citing the former as principal debtor. Fortunately for Cervantes, Urbina honored their gentleman's agreement — it would not have done his official career any good had he not — and paid up almost at once. Ultimately of course he had no choice, for he had stood surety for the whole dowry, and Cervantes had neither money to pay nor goods to confiscate.

Urbina by now must have been ruing the day he met Isabel, but she had not finished with him yet. Cervantes and Urbina had undertaken to pay the rates and ground rent of the house Isabel and Molina were given the use of, and in the May of the following year Molina sued Urbina, about to depart for Denia with his royal employer, for payment. Urbina was subsequently compelled to meet that undertaking as well. Thus far the couple, comfortably off as they were, were only demanding what was legally theirs, although Urbina, clearly, felt that his moral responsibilities had died with his daughter. But with their unwarranted claim to ownership of the house, and their subsequent legal persecution of Urbina and his heirs, they revealed themselves as an unsavory pair who thoroughly deserved each other. There is no doubt, however, that Isabel was by far the more grasping, unscrupulous one of the two. Molina maintained reasonably good relations with the Cervantes family before and after Cervantes's death, and the fact that he managed to dissipate a large part of his wife's dowry presumably looked like nothing so much as poetic justice later on to Doña Catalina.

By the autumn of 1611 it looks as though Cervantes had finally reconciled himself to the unpleasant truth that no one wanted his plays, and the closure of the theaters on the death of the Queen on 3 October must have settled the matter. He accordingly put the manuscripts away. With that avenue of income now closed and with Part II of *Don Quixote* nowhere near completion, he turned his attention to the short stories he had written over the years and set about revising and arranging them into a publishable collection. In October a French printer was spurred by his inability to discover a copy of *The Galatea* in the whole of Castile into publishing a third edition of the book in Paris, but while it would have gratified Cervantes enormously had he known about it, it served to put not one penny in his pocket. In England Beaumont had recently (and unsuccessfully) staged his dramatized imitation of *Don Quixote, The Knight of the Burning Pestle,* but at home in his own country the creator's genius, for all his fame, went unrewarded.

There is some evidence that Cervantes and his wife had spent part of 1611 in Esquivias, possibly in order to cut down on their living expenses. But by the end of January 1612 they were back in Madrid, in gloomy lodgings in the Calle de las Huertas. There on the 31st of that month, Doña Catalina signed over her life interest in the property she had inherited from her mother to her brother Francisco, in recognition of his payment of the debts on the Palacios family estate and possibly of more personal debts as well, since it would have been strange had Catalina not appealed to her more prosperous brother for help. This left her still in Francisco's debt and the two small plots of land she had willed to her husband were therefore mortgaged, with her husband's consent, to Francisco as well. Clearly Cervantes and his wife were having difficulty in keeping their heads above water, and the need to publish something was becoming pressing. He found time that spring, however, to fre-

quent at least one of the three literary academies then
functioning in Madrid, though which one is not certain,
and on 2 March there occurred the meeting during which
Lope de Vega, the breach partially healed at last, borrowed his battered spectacles.

For all the urgency of the projected publication, Cervantes devoted some considerable time to rewriting and
polishing his tales, some of which dated back twenty years
or more. Into at least two of them, *Rinconete and Cortadillo* and *The Jealous Extremaduran,* as the early Porras
de la Cámara texts show, he introduced considerable
changes; these were mainly stylistic, although in the case
of *The Jealous Extremaduran* there was a new, radically
different, dénouement as well. The other tale in the Porras de la Cámara manuscript which is often attributed to
Cervantes, *The Feigned Aunt,* he did not include, either
because not being his he knew nothing about it or because he judged it unsuitable for a collection of stories to
which he intended giving the title *Exemplary Tales.*
The story tells of a crude little incident in which three
rakes lay siege to the three-times mended virginity of a
young girl, brought up by her supposed aunt to sell herself to order. There is much explicit talk of broken maid-
enheads and their repair, all executed without any lightness of touch or one sympathetic character. If Cervantes
had written it years before, and on stylistic grounds this is
not implausible, it is easy to see why he decided to reject
it in old age — for all that the tale was included by Porras
in a collection destined for the entertainment of an archbishop.

The collection's exemplariness has over the years been
a subject of much debate. If we search for a specific,
carefully spelled-out moral in the tales we shall not find
one. Even in *Rinconete and Cortadillo,* where the narrator's explicit judgment on the life led by the criminal

gang is one of condemnation, there is nothing in the details of the plot nor, for all its irony, in its tone, to induce aversion in the reader. Yet that Cervantes was concerned about the moral impact of his stories is clear from his cutting of the seduction scene from *The Jealous Extremaduran* — although, as we saw, there was a strong aesthetic motive as well for this — and from his Prologue to the collection, where he is emphatic about his honorable intentions:

> I have given them the title *Exemplary* and if you look closely there is not one from which some beneficial example may not be drawn; if it would not prolong this matter I would perhaps show you the rich and honest fruit that could be gathered from the collection as a whole as well as from each story in itself.
>
> My intention has been to set out in the marketplace of our republic a billiard table where everybody may come to amuse himself without fear of coming to any harm from flying balls; I mean, without harm to either body or soul, for pleasant and honest entertainment is of greater good than harm.
>
> One cannot always be in church, one cannot always be at prayer, or engaged on business, however important; there are hours of recreation, when the afflicted spirit rests.
>
> It is for this reason that groves of trees are planted, that springs are sought, that hills are leveled and gardens eagerly cultivated. One thing I shall make bold enough to say to you: if I somehow discovered that reading these stories might incite people to some harmful desire or thought, rather than publish them I would cut off the hand with which I wrote them. I am no longer of an age to trifle with the life to come . . .

There is no reason to dismiss these protestations as mere window dressing. At the same time, Cervantes clearly felt somewhat vulnerable, and it is not difficult to imagine why. The *novela* was a genre imported from Italy, and it still retained the rather scurrilous associations of Boccaccio and his successors. Proud of the fact that he was the first to write original *novelle* in Castilian — those that had been doing the rounds in Spain were translations or imitations, as he points out in his Prologue — Cervantes patently wished to disassociate himself from a suspect tradition and establish the short story in Spain as an acceptable and worthwhile form of secular literature. If in the process he overstated his case a little with regard to the exemplariness of his own stories, written over a long span of years, and particularly with regard to the "message" of the collection as a whole, then this is hardly surprising at a time when the idea of a secular literature of entertainment was still not wholly approved of. And it is fair to say that the tales, for all their diversity, never fail to make clear, whether explicitly or implicitly, the distinction between what is right and what is wrong, how the world works and how it ought to work. The overriding impression they give of their author is that of a highly, though not narrowly, moral individual, and with a censor to please and with all his years and the experience of his disillusionment upon him, Cervantes now wished to make this morality unequivocal. That he should have entertained no such scruples about his dramatic works when he came to publish them, even about the blatant bawdiness of *The Jealous Old Man,* indicates only that different criteria altogether operated for the theater, for all the moralists' attacks on it. His collection of plays and interludes passed the censor without a murmur.

That Cervantes had not taken the step of publishing such a collection of stories before suggests that he did not have at his disposal, already written, the twelve pieces that made up the standard collection of published prose pieces or plays of the time. But which of the tales was (or were) the makeweight it is impossible to say, although *The English Spanishwoman,* the story of a Spanish girl captured by the English during the sack of Cadiz and brought up in London, has been proposed for the role. It certainly bears signs of having been hastily written, and there is internal evidence that could be taken as indicating that the tale was written as late as 1611 or 1612, when relations between the two countries were particularly close. More important, perhaps, *The English Spanishwoman,* with its highly sympathetic portrait of Elizabeth I, has the same sort of wonderfully improbable and romantic flavor as *The Two Damsels* and *The Lady Cornelia,* as well as *The Trials of Persiles and Sigismunda,* and it is very possible that all three short stories belong to this last period of Cervantes's life when the keen observer of human reality gives way to the storyteller, when the aging writer seeks an answer to a troubled world in beauty, virtue, and heroism. Part II of *Don Quixote* is anchored inevitably in the psychological and circumstantial realism of Part I, but even here the element of imaginative fantasy is much more pronounced and the espousal of life's eternal virtues less equivocal. Little wonder that at this stage he rejected *The Feigned Aunt,* if indeed it were his.

In the event the twelve stories submitted by the publisher, Francisco de Robles, to the censor for approval on 2 July 1612 were *The Little Gypsy Girl, The Generous Lover, Rinconete and Cortadillo, The English Spanishwoman, The Licentiate of Glass, The Force of Blood, The Jealous Extremaduran, The Illustrious Kitchen Maid, The Two Damsels, The Lady Cornelia, The Deceitful Marriage,* and *The Dogs' Colloquy.* The censor found them to be both irreproachable and exemplary in the way in which they exalted virtue and exposed vice. The order in which they were printed by Juan de la Cuesta later that year — the order given above — offers a digestible, fairly even distribution of the realistic and the romantic, but whether this was by Cervantes's own choice or Cuesta's is not known. How much Cervantes was paid for them is not known either. On 9 September, he sold Robles the book's ten-year license for 1,600 *reales,* but most of this he appears to have received already in the form of advances against the publication of the stories and probably of Part II of *Don Quixote* as well.

How soon Cervantes learned of the publication in England that year of Thomas Shelton's excellent *The History of the Valorous and Wittie Knight Errant Don Quixote of the Mancha,* the first full-length translation, is not recorded. But diplomatic relations between the two countries had improved dramatically since the death of Elizabeth and the news cannot have taken long to filter through. This international recognition offered an added incentive to forge ahead with Part II now that the *Exemplary Novels* were completed. Before it appeared, however, Cervantes's French admirer, César Oudin, would produce the first full-length French translation of Part I, in Paris in 1614. The work was a resounding success in both countries.

Cervantes, however, could still not bring himself to concentrate his energies on *Don Quixote* alone; even by July 1614 he had only got as far as Chapter 36 of Part II, out of an eventual total of seventy-four. This need for variety in his work would seem to have been very real. In Chapter 44 of Part II where he comments on the interpolated episodes in Part I, he counters the criticism that they are irrelevant to the narrative by claiming that concentrating on one subject and a handful of characters would have been "unbearable toil." He avoided this toil

in Part II, much more tightly structured than Part I, by
seeking diversification inside the framework of the main
storyline rather than outside it.

From his Prologue to the tales, written in the summer of 1613 just before publication, it is plain not only
that he considered the end of Part II to be in sight, but
that he had by then written his long poem *Journey to
Parnassus,* that *The Trials of Persiles and Sigismunda* was
under way, and that a further work, *Weeks in a Garden,*
never to materialize, was being planned.

This Prologue indeed is a mine of information, not
least because in it he gives the following description of
himself:

> . . . aquiline of face, with chestnut hair, smooth clear
> brow, merry eyes and hooked though well-proportioned
> nose, the whiskers now silver that not twenty years ago
> were gold; large mustachios, small mouth, with teeth
> neither small nor large since he has but six of them and
> these in bad condition and worse positioned, having no
> correspondence one with the other; the body between two
> extremes, being neither tall nor short; the complexion
> bright, pale rather than sallow; a little bent in the
> shoulder and not very nimble of foot.

He completes the description by indicating that the stutter he had mentioned years before in the letter written in
Algiers to Mateo Vázquez, was still with him. As for his
age, his memory erred on the kind side: he gives it as
sixty-four when he was in fact nearing his sixty-sixth
birthday. Immediately before this description of himself,
Cervantes makes a tantalizingly ambiguous allusion to
the contemporary poet-painter Juan de Jáuregui:

> . . . this friend [someone who had apparently encouraged
> him to publish the tales] might do well to have my

portrait engraved on the first page of this book, for the
famous Juan de Jáuregui would give him my picture.

This innocent remark, which could be taken to mean
either that Cervantes had been painted by Jáuregui or
that the painter could, if asked, produce such a portrait,
predictably sent posterity haring off on a wild goosechase
in an effort to discover the authentic likeness of the great
man. But alas, there is none, and the portrait most often
reproduced as being that of Cervantes, dated 1600, bearing the name Jáuregui and entitled Don Miguel de Cervantes, is not genuine. In 1600, Jáuregui was at most
seventeen, he never spelt his name Iaurigui, which is how
it appears on the painting, and at no time during his
lifetime was Cervantes ever awarded the gentleman's title
"Don";* Jáuregui, on the other hand, never failed to
include his "Don." The painting is almost certainly a
nineteenth-century fraud.

His teeth and a touch of arthritis apart, Cervantes, obviously, carried his years well, and it is a telling feature of
the self-description that after all his hardships and disappointment, and in the midst of near penury, Cervantes
could still pride himself on having a merry eye and untroubled brow. Even if the words were tinged with wishful thinking it is evident that for him resilience and good
cheer were qualities to be prized and cultivated. But
since he had never lacked either for long, perhaps the eye
and the brow had indeed remained unaffected by adversity. To be completing one major work and embark-
ing upon two more at the age of sixty-six in itself showed
no lack of either optimism or energy. And it must not be
forgotten that poor as he was, and only half-recognized
as he was by the literary establishment, he did now have

* The Cervantes women, as was common practice at the time, were always
accorded the courtesy title "Doña."

consolation of a kind dear to his heart. Of the success of his *Don Quixote* he had no doubt and his spreading fame was no secret to him — some of his characters had already made their first appearance on the Madrid stage. He still had his open detractors, for all that the rift with Lope de Vega had seemingly narrowed: Cristóbal Suárez de Figueroa in his *The Traveller* in 1617 would attack his claim to fame with undisguised viciousness. Yet his poetry, which he continued to write, was respected by the literary peers he contrived to mingle with from time to time, and, more important, he was becoming acknowledged as a master of Spanish prose (considered to be an inferior genre at the time, admittedly), then still in its infancy yet capable of throwing up a practitioner who remains unsurpassed. Setting his face against the growing fashion for brilliant linguistic pyrotechnics in literature, he continued to pursue the classical twin ideals of elegance and eloquence. Even the officials who licensed and approved the *Exemplary Tales* commented in their statements on his services to the Castilian language. As for the tales themselves, he knew them to be the first of their kind in Spanish, and, given the diversity and appeal of their subject matter, he must have had high hopes of their success. To cap it all, in October 1612, Diego de Haëdo's *History of Algiers* had appeared, in which Cervantes's exploits in captivity were described for all the world to read. Inadequate consolation certainly, but consolation nonetheless.

The tone of *Journey to Parnassus* is, as a consequence of this, much less astringent than it might have been. It was written in the course of the year that elapsed between the completion of the *Exemplary Tales* and their publication. Yet in the Prologue to the collection, he implies that he was already widely known to have written it: "This is the face (the physical description already given) of the author of *The Galatea, Don Quixote of la Mancha,* and he who made the *Journey to Parnassus* in imitation of César Caporal Perusino (Perusino's *Journey to Parnassus* had appeared in 1582)." Presumably he had been giving readings from it to his friends, many of whom, of course, are mentioned in it.

As well as being a survey of the literary figures of his day — a common enough enterprise at the time — the poem, written in tercets, is a combination of autobiography and credo, a catalogue of activities, successes and defeats, a statement of personal and literary identity. It is easy to envisage it as a form of therapy, enabling Cervantes to get off his chest the grudges and disappointments he had had to live with for so many years, though few of these, if any, are allowed to cloud his literary judgments, which tend to be benevolent in the extreme. His need to write it was evidently a very powerful one, for its 3,308 hendecasyllables must have been the product of quite intense activity in a writer more at home in prose, particularly at a time when Robles was pressing for Part II of *Don Quixote.* The verse is in fact among the best he ever wrote, and the poem as a whole, in conception and execution, is something of a triumph, for all that it received scarcely a mention when it was published.

It relates how Cervantes, setting out on a spiritual journey to the mountain of fame and immortality, is deputed by Mercury to be the judge of which poets should be chosen to help Apollo defend Parnassus against the unworthy host trying to scale it. It reaches its climax in an extraordinarily amusing dream sequence in which the good poets and the bad fight it out, hurling sonnets, odes, stories, and essays at one another. Its tone, when not humorous or ironic, is matter-of-fact and accepting rather than bitter. While littered with references to poverty — even hunger — disappointment and misfortune, and to the false flattery, envy, and spite to which he saw himself as having fallen victim, it is the testimony of a man who tells a truth he has learned to live with, of a man who is temperamentally an optimist although his experience pushes him toward pessimism.

Sure as he is of his worth as a writer: "I am he whose invention exceeds that of many," his poverty, however irksome, has become a source of pride, a guarantee of integrity and virtue, of a fame that owes nothing to influence, wealth, or favor. And thus he can truthfully say, "I content myself with little although I deserve much."

There are two very tangible explanations, however, for the comparative serenity and benevolence of Cervantes's last years. Some time before the publication of the *Exemplary Tales* in the July of 1613, Cervantes had at long last found a patron. How he reestablished contact with the Count of Lemos, still Viceroy of Naples, is not clear, but his reference to the Count in the tales' dedication to him as his "true lord and benefactor" is unequivocal, and, thereafter, until his death three years later, Cervantes received a financial subsidy of some sort from Lemos. His immense elation at this tangible recognition of his genius after the long years of struggle and neglect is vibrant in the almost pathetic expressions of his gratitude to the Count, made at every opportunity.

His other comfort in his old age was religion. The similar references to his concern for the life of the soul in the Prologue to the *Exemplary Tales* and at the end of Part II of *Don Quixote* — his own "I am not of an age to trifle with the life to come" and Don Quixote's "at times like this a man cannot trifle with his soul" — reveal that age had brought with it, predictably enough perhaps, a deepening of religious consciousness, a settling of priorities. This spiritual preparation assumed a practical form on 2 July 1613 when Cervantes, following in his wife's and his sisters' footsteps, received the habit of the Third Order of St. Francis, the Franciscan Tertiaries, at Alcalá de Henares.

When the *Exemplary Tales* appeared that same month — the publishing license for Castile had been obtained the previous November, but there had been a long delay over the Aragonese license — they were an immediate success, and before very long their plots and characters began, like those of *Don Quixote* itself, to find their way into the works of other writers, particularly in England where for a decade and a half after Cervantes's death his works, including even his plays, were assiduously mined for the ore of inspiration. Thomas Middleton and William Rowley's *The Spanish Gypsy*, for example, owes much to both *The Force of Blood* and *The Little Gypsy Girl*, while John Fletcher adapted or used at least seven of the stories for plays like *The Queen of Corinth, Love's Pilgrimage, The Fair Maid of the Inn, Rule a Wife and Have a Wife,* and others. Earlier that year (1613) in February, had Cervantes but known it, Shakespeare himself, in collaboration with Fletcher, had launched a play, now lost, called *The History of Cardenio*, based on Chapters 23–27 of Part I of *Don Quixote*. It was performed as part of the celebrations held to mark the marriage of Elizabeth Stuart, daughter of James I, to the Elector of Palatine. Shelton's translation had not taken long in bearing fruit, although Fletcher at least, along with some of the other Jacobean dramatists, was probably able to read the work in the original: the phrase "to fight with a windmill" was being used in England as early as 1607. When the royal couple subsequently made their entry into Heidelberg, there taking part in a comic tourney held to greet them were Don Quixote himself, with a bucket for helmet, and his faithful squire Sancho Panza.

In Spain, Cervantes's place among the literary celebrities of his day was gradually being conceded. When *Journey to Parnassus,* with its prose Postscript, written since the publication of the *Exemplary Novels,* appeared in late November of 1614, one of the censor's licenses, issued by a cleric who was himself a writer and poet of standing, José de Valdivielso, stated that the poem contained "many things that were equable and entertaining and entirely in keeping with those others by the same author which bring honor to the nation and are celebrated throughout the world." The adjective "equable" is a significant one. In a period when the literary world was a scene of intense personal rivalries and bitter, outspoken attacks, Cervantes, in his estimate of his fellow writers, was never less than measured and rarely overtly disparaging. The *Postscript to Parnassus,* dated 22 July 1614, is a humorous piece describing how Cervantes, a few days after his return from Parnassus, meets a rich young poet, smothered in a huge starched collar heavy enough for an Atlas, with cuffs up to his shoulders to match — a dig at the foppish extravagances the new laws had tried in vain to stamp out. The young man bears a letter to Cervantes from Apollo which contains the god's rules and instructions for Spain's poets, and from it it is painfully clear that for all the improvement in his fortunes and for all the humorous tone of the provisions of the letter, his poverty could still rankle.

> First that some poets be as well known for their shabby appearance as for the fame of their verse.
> Item, that if any poet say he be poor he be forthwith believed without any other oath or inquiry whatsoever.
> That it be decreed that all poets be of mild and even temperament and not pick holes, for all that they have them in their stockings.

Item, if any poet arrive at the house of a friend or
acquaintance who is eating, and invites him to join in,
although he swears that he has already eaten, that in no
way should he be believed but be made to eat by force,
for in the event little will be needed . . .

What a vivid picture of hardship and humiliation these
words conjure up. It is easy to denounce the pretentious
layabouts, like Quevedo's *picaro,* Pablos, in *The Life of a
Rogue,* who rather than work for a living sprinkled
crumbs on their chests to give the impression of having
eaten. It is a chastening discovery, however, that a Cervantes should be reduced to dining off pride alone.

Journey to Parnassus is dedicated not to Lemos, Cervantes's new patron, but to the young Don Rodrigo de
Tapia, son of a minister of state. Evidently Cervantes had
committed himself to this dedication earlier on, and the
delay in the publication of *Journey to Parnassus* —
already referred to in the Prologue to the *Exemplary
Tales* — was probably due to Cervantes's understand-
able anxiety to dedicate his next and much more important publication to his new benefactor, Lemos. From the
Tapia family Cervantes appears to have received no bene-
fits — other than, possibly, the printing costs of the poem
— and both Part II of *Don Quixote* and *The Trials of
Persiles and Sigismunda* would be dedicated to Lemos.

Some weeks before *Journey to Parnassus* appeared,
Spain had celebrated the beatification of one of her most
famous saints, Teresa of Ávila. Cervantes was one of the
forty-five poets who took part in the poetry joust that
accompanied the service of thanksgiving in the chapel of
the convent of the Barefoot Carmelites in Madrid on 25
September 1614, with a poem entitled "By Miguel de
Cervantes on the Ecstasies of our Blessed Mother Teresa
of Jesus." Whether he won a prize is not known. Since

Lope appears to have been one of the judges as well as a competitor, he very probably did not. One of the highlights of the Córdoban celebrations was a student masque depicting the imaginary betrothal of Don Quixote and Doña Dulcinea. The comic costumes — Don Quixote wore hollowed-out marrows on his feet, onions in his garters, and flower pots for stirrups — illustrate once more that for people everywhere at the time Cervantes's great hero was an irremediably ridiculous figure.

There is a hint in the *Postscript to Parnassus* that Cervantes's health was beginning to fail: Apollo's letter ends with the admonition that he pay attention to his health and look after himself. Rather than impeding the progress of his work, however, the warning signs seem to have served only to make him drive himself harder, and after sending *Journey to Parnassus* off to the printers, he forged ahead with *Don Quixote*. When he wrote the *Postscript* he had, two days before, reached Chapter 36 of Part II: Sancho Panza's letter to his wife in that chapter is dated 20 July 1614. By the time he heard of Alonso Fernández de Avellaneda's continuation he had finished Chapter 58. Exactly when this happened — Avellaneda's work was licensed on 4 July, though the license may not have been any more authentic than the book itself — we do not know, but its impact on Cervantes could have been nothing short of devastating.

Incredulity, indignation, fury, and resolve must swiftly have succeeded one another as he digested the implications of this terrible blow, and had *Journey to Parnassus* not already been at the printers we can be sure it would have recorded their passage. His reaction, when he actually read the offending work, must have been very mixed — scorn and relief at its obvious inferiority to his own creation (his declared verdict in Chapter 59 of his own Part II is that it was stupid and obscene), anger that his

beloved Don Quixote should be so traduced, outrage at
the gratuitous insults directed at himself in the work's
insolent preface. In fact Avellaneda's *Don Quixote,* for
all its coarse humor and its heavy dependency on the
characterization and narrative tone of Part I — whereas
Cervantes's characters grow and change, carrying the narrative with them — is not without skill and ingenuity.
But as has so often and so rightly been remarked, no man,
however equable, can easily tolerate being called a cack-
ling, bumptious, garrulous, cantankerous, envious,
friendless and one-handed old roué, or hearing his best
work denounced as tainted with the fretful, malicious,
restless, and bad-tempered tone of the prison in which it
was written (a reference to Cervantes's remark at the beginning of Part I). Coming as they did from a man who
had almost certainly never even met Cervantes (he refers
to his having only one hand), these judgments were as
grotesque as they were vicious. For example, his claim
that Cervantes was so friendless that he had had to write
his own preliminary poems for Part I was due to either a
very obtuse or a very malicious misconstruction of Cervantes's takeoff of Lope de Vega's habits in the preliminaries to the first part.

Avellaneda certainly knew that Cervantes was himself
writing a continuation to Part I: Cervantes had said as
much in his introduction to the *Exemplary Tales,*
which Avellaneda had clearly read. But not content with
stealing the inspiration of Cervantes's Part I and the
thunder of his Part II, delighting in the anticipation of
robbing him of his meager profits, he felt it necessary for
some reason to revile him as well. Many have suspected
that Avellaneda — whose real identity remains a mystery
for all the gallons of ink used up in proving that he was
this writer or that Aragonese cleric or even Cervantes
himself — was a disciple of Lope de Vega, and he cer-

tainly rises hotly to Lope's defense in his Prologue. But there must have been something more than mere literary rivalry behind his outrageous words, and, indeed, in his Prologue he claims that Cervantes had been offensive to him in Part I, though what slights, real or imagined, he refers to no one has ever been able to establish. It is always possible, of course, that he started out in good faith to write a continuation of *Don Quixote* — it would have been considered a perfectly respectable enterprise at the time — only to be driven onto the defensive and into anonymity by the news of Cervantes's own forthcoming sequel.

Whatever Avellaneda's motives, Cervantes was stung into retaliation, and could not resist denouncing Avellaneda's continuation in a scene in Chapter 59 in which Don Quixote comes face to face with his spurious biography, in terms which are curt but, for Cervantes, very strong. Then, to establish the authenticity of his own Don Quixote, he sends him off to Barcelona instead of Zaragoza, as Avellaneda, following the predictions of Part I, had done.

Cervantes then proceeded to complete Part II as fast as he was able, scattering disparaging references to Avellaneda as he wrote. By 27 February 1615, the work was in the hands of the official censor. He had written thirty-eight chapters — half of Part II — in seven months. By the time he came to write his Prologue, the text now safely completed, he had regained his equanimity, disdaining to repay his detractor in kind. He does, however, take the opportunity of replying with considerable dignity to some of Avellaneda's accusations, though he cannot resist making a dig at Lope's scandalous life or telling two amusing anecdotes at Avellaneda's expense. If he is old, he cannot help it; if he is maimed then at least he became so fighting for his country. As to the profits of his Part II, he does not need them when he has a benefactor as generous as the Count of Lemos; in any case, poverty is no bar to honor, nobility, or virtue. The Prologue is a triumph of dignity, humor, and restraint. Perhaps he foresaw that with the appearance of the authentic Part II, Avellaneda's sequel, licensed only for the diocese of Tarragona (if genuine license it was) would disappear from sight, not to be reprinted until 1732.

If Cervantes needed balm for his wounds, he very soon received it in the shape of an exceptionally warm and appreciative recommendation from one of the official censors, the Licentiate Márquez Torres. In the course of it, Márquez reports a conversation about Cervantes that had taken place on 25 February 1615 between himself and some gentlemen from the French Ambassador's suite, in Spain for discussions about the marriages already arranged between the future Philip IV and the King of France's sister, Isabella of Bourbon, and between the Dauphin (later Louis XIII) and Philip III's daughter, the Infanta Anne of Austria:

> Their praise [of his works] was such that I offered to take them to see their author, a suggestion they greeted with expressions of great eagerness. They asked me detailed questions about his age, his profession, quality and circumstances. I was obliged to say that he was old, a soldier, a gentleman and poor, to which one of them replied with these express words — "Is such a man not, then, richly treated in Spain and supported out of public funds?" At this another of the gentlemen acutely remarked, "If necessity obliges him to write, please God he never be wealthy so that through his works, although a poor man, he might enrich the world."

By now Cervantes already had reason to be grateful to Márquez's superior, Don Bernardo de Sandoval y Rojas,

Archbishop of Toledo; he had started to receive a small daily pension from the Archbishop and he mentions him with gratitude in the Prologue to Part II in the same breath as his glowing tribute to the Count of Lemos. But this story of Márquez's, so generously recounted, was doubtless as great a source of satisfaction to him now as any more tangible acknowledgment of his genius.

The whole year was to slip away before all the necessary formalities were completed. *The Second Part of the Ingenious Knight Don Quixote de la Mancha* — the publisher carefully added after Cervantes's name on the title page, "Author of the First Part," so that there should be no confusion — appeared in November, to become an immediate success. Taking no chances this time, Cervantes kills off his celebrated hero at the end of the book, determined that his second series of adventures should be his last. In the meantime, another work had been sent to the printers, though not to the one engaged upon Part II of *Don Quixote* and not under the auspices of Francisco de Robles; if his remarks about Madrid publishers in *The Trials of Persiles and Sigismunda* are anything to go by, Cervantes was thoroughly dissatisfied with what he had received both for the *Exemplary Tales* and Part II of *Don Quixote*. This work was his *Eight Plays and Eight Interludes.* Cervantes had decided that even if nobody wanted to perform his plays, at least the world should be given a chance to judge them for itself — a highly unusual step at the time, when publication invariably followed performance.

In the *Postscript to Parnassus,* Cervantes, after mentioning some of his early plays, had stated that he had six plays and six interludes then in stock — not enough to merit publication. Since it is highly unlikely that he could have written two new full-length plays as well as two interludes in the interim, the extra plays must have been revisions of earlier ones. Which ones these two are, however, is far from certain, although *The Labyrinth of Love* and *The House of Jealousy and Woods of Ardenia* are likely contenders for the honor. *The Labyrinth of Love*'s plot is confused enough to convince us that it might be a rewriting of *The Comedy of Confusion,* while *The House of Jealousy* — an extraordinary mixture of chivalric romance and elements from classical mythology — and medieval moralities — must surely date back to his early days as a dramatist; it does in fact bear signs of a hasty reduction of the number of acts to the by now standard three. As for the two farces, they were probably *The Cave of Salamanca,* another variation on the theme of the husband cuckolded and tricked by his wife, and *The Widowed Ruffian,* one of his only two interludes written in verse, which relies heavily for its characters and action on the much livelier and more charming *Rinconete and Cortadillo.*

In his Prologue to the published plays, Cervantes makes no mention of these revisions, and his tone is deliberately casual. The subject of his plays had arisen, it appears, during a conversation with the publisher Juan de Villarroel, who said he would have wanted to publish them long before had he not heard from a theater-company manager that Cervantes's verse was nothing like as good as his prose. Spurred into action by this, Cervantes had searched the pieces out. Judging them then worthy of exposure to the light of day but unwilling to bother anymore with managers and actors, he had sold them to Villarroel and pocketed his money without further ado. In fact it could not have happened quite as simply as he describes, and, indeed, at the end of the Prologue, Cervantes claims to be writing another play — old habits died hard. But clearly after the disappointments of the past, he wished to be seen to be investing no emotional capital in the venture, and it was just as well. The collection sank without stirring a ripple of interest, not to be printed again for over a hundred years. The Prologue, however, is of compelling interest for what it has to say about the early theater in Spain and about Cervantes's own fortunes as a dramatist, and for its expressions of now unadulterated admiration and praise for Lope de Vega. With his own particular genius gaining recognition, he could afford to be generous in his acceptance of Lope's. It was an honorable admission nonetheless.

Villarroel proved far more efficient in organizing the publication of the collected plays than did Robles with the sequel to *Don Quixote* and in the event the plays, probably not ready until the summer of 1615, appeared first, in October. Indeed, Villarroel's haste was such that the plays were initially printed without prologue and dedication, an oversight which Cervantes soon put right.

By now Cervantes, presumably on the strength of the money he had earned from them, had moved out of his gloomy quarters in the Calle de las Huertas and back to the Calle de León, which was a lively thoroughfare and actors' stamping-ground, to the recently renovated house round the corner from Lope de Vega's, which was to be his last home. In modern Madrid, number 7, on the corner of León and Cervantes, marks the spot, the commemorative plaque sitting somewhat misleadingly above the entrance from Cervantes, number 2. Here he and Catalina occupied a small apartment on the ground floor.

In the dedication to the plays, written in September 1615, Cervantes promises *The Trials of Persiles and Sigismunda, Weeks in a Garden,* and, "if my old shoulders can carry such a load," the second part of *The Galatea.* When he came to write the Prologue to Part II of *Don Quixote* a month or so afterward, he overlooked *Weeks in a Garden* (was it, perhaps, no more than an old man's dream?), mentioning only the other two. *Persiles and Sigismunda,* he claims, he was already in the process of completing; in his dedication he is more precise: he will finish within four months. He was not to survive to see it published.

The cost to his health of this feverish rate of productivity during the last few years of his life must have been severe. The move to pleasanter surroundings doubtless provided some relief, but in his October dedication of Part II of *Don Quixote* to the Count of Lemos, he describes himself as being very short of money (either because the help he was receiving by now from both Lemos and the Archbishop of Toledo was very limited or because his openhanded generosity to his friends had not flagged with the years), and in poor health. Both conditions, he says, will prevent his accepting an invitation from the Chinese Emperor to become director of the school of Castilian he proposes to establish in China, with *Don Quixote* as the only teaching text. In his combination of irony, humor, realism (will the Emperor pay his expenses?), and proper pride, the little piece is a moving cameo of its author. But as his health deteriorated, Cervantes drove himself even harder in his determination to complete *The Trials of Persiles and Sigismunda,* significantly described by him, both in *Journey to Parnassus* and in his dedication of the *Eight Plays and Eight Interludes,* as "the great Persiles." In his eyes it was to be his crowning achievement, and the friends he read it to, as it progressed, seem to have agreed with this judgment. He found time even so to supply two acquaintances with complimentary sonnets for their forthcoming publications.

The world in which he immersed himself as he wrote was the world of Shakespeare's last works. *The Trials of Persiles and Sigismunda, A Story of the North* is a fairy tale of high adventure that traces the fortunes of the young Periandro (Persiles) in his search for the girl he loves, Auristela (Sigismunda). As the narrative, floating free of geography, ranges from one disembodied country to another, from the icy mists of Greenland and Norway to the Mediterranean, capture, shipwreck, pirates, war, magic, treachery, and abduction follow one upon the other in a succession of improbable coincidences and miraculous escapes. Disguise and mystery are the work's common currency, and even the identities of Periandro and Auristela are not revealed until the end. In essence, of course, what the work describes is a pilgrimage, a pilgrimage in search of happiness, identity and truth, with Persiles and Sigismunda triumphing over overwhelming odds by dint of their nobility, courage, optimism, and strength. It is possible, I suppose, to see it as an old man's escape from reality into romance, from disappointment into dream; but Cervantes, I am sure, saw it as an affirmation of hope, a declaration of belief in the enduring vitality of the human spirit. The world through which Persiles and Sigismunda move is a country of the mind, light years away from that with which Don Quixote collides, but just as Alonso Quijano el Bueno's resolute embracement of his true identity marks the triumph of sanity and truth, so Persiles and Sigismunda are rewarded for their faithfulness to the eternal verities of life. If their story is heavy with coincidences, then "these bizarre changes fall within the power of what is commonly called Fortune, which is nothing other than Heaven's firm intervention." It is no accident that the pilgrimage ends in Rome.

For Cervantes himself the work was not a search, but rather a combination of manifesto and catharsis, a pouring out in the interstices of the narrative of accumulated judgments, opinions, and wisdom, ranging in explicit

fashion over a huge spectrum of concern — women and
marriage; love and beauty; childbirth and death; super-
stition, witchcraft, and astrology; dreams, mysteries, and
miracles; Jews and Moriscos; justice, honor, and ven-
geance; free will and God; kingship, war, and suicide;
virtue and fame: Cervantes has something to say about
them all and much more besides. Here too are his views
on history and fiction, literary harmony and discord, on
poetry and the drama, on literary truth and imagination.
It was as if he sensed that this was to be his last opportunity to commit himself to paper and to posterity. Out
of it all there emerges a consistent image; that of an eminently reasonable, sane, and compassionate man, a man
of independent judgment with a strong sense of moral
values and a profound faith in his God.

The work, therefore, makes fascinating reading, its
omantic solemnity laced with the wit and irony of his
passing comments and disquisitions. The narrative itself
is more sophisticated than it sounds in description, with
numerous complicated flashbacks and with Cervantes in-
tervening from time to time to explain his procedure, to
comment on what is happening, and to play with the
problem of fiction claiming, like this one, to be history.
How can it be known, he queries, what a person thinks
or says when alone? The self-consciousness is lighthearted
but pronounced, with characters becoming, as it were,
readers and voicing their likely reactions to what other
characters do or say — even Persiles himself is gently criti-
cized for his longwindedness in describing his adventures.
But all is done with a lightness of touch that compels
admiration. Undoubtedly the work is too rambling and
too long, without the structural strength of its third-
century model, Heliodorus's *Ethiopian History of the
Loves of Teagenes and Cariclea,* a work that had been
very popular in Spain since first translated into Spanish

in the mid-sixteenth century. Yet at its best, it has narrative pace (much more to my mind than Heliodorus) and is eminently readable, while even at its worst it is fascinating for what it reveals of Cervantes the writer and the man. What Cervantes himself thought it to be, sadly it is not. Integrity it has in abundance; greatness passes it by.

Cervantes's estimate of how long it would take him to complete the work was an accurate one. It was finished by the beginning of March 1616. That he was running out of energy is clear — Book IV of the work has only fourteen chapters, compared with Books I to III's twenty-three, twenty-two, and twenty-one chapters, respectively. By 26 March, when he wrote a letter of thanks to Don Bernardo de Sandoval y Rojas, Archbishop of Toledo, for his latest "favor," he was so ill that he felt he would not recover: "I think it will be the end of me." By 2 April, Easter Saturday, he was sure enough to want to emulate his wife and be fully professed as a Tertiary of St. Francis, thus sparing her the expenses of his burial. Since he was too unwell to leave the house, the ceremony was performed at home.

In the Prologue to *The Trials of Persiles and Sigismunda,* his complaint is diagnosed as dropsy; what he probably suffered from was diabetes, then an unknown complaint of which dropsy is a symptom. He relates how on the way back recently from Esquivias he had met a student who, after greeting him with enthusiasm as "the merry writer" and "the Muses' delight," titles which Cervantes firmly rejects as rubbish, proceeded to pronounce his illness to be dropsy and to advise him to drink less. Cervantes, however, is under no illusion as to the seriousness of his illness: "My life is coming to an end, and when my pulse's daily course is spent, which will be this Sunday at the latest, my life's race will be run. . . .

Goodby favors, goodby witticisms, goodby merry friends; for I am dying and hoping to see you soon happy in another life."

Since the journey, if indeed it took place and was not merely a convenient literary fiction, must have preceded his confinement to the house, Cervantes's end was not to be quite so swift as he anticipated. It was not, however, very far off. On 18 April, he received extreme unction, from the same priest who had ministered to his two sisters. The following day, he rallied sufficiently to write his dedication of *Persiles and Sigismunda* to the Count of Lemos, a task he was desperately concerned not to leave undone. In it he talks of writing, if a miracle should occur to save him, the sequel to *The Galatea, Weeks in a Garden,* and a hitherto unmentioned work, *The Famous Bernardo.* But the characters and ideas that crowded his imagination were now no more than the stuff that dreams are made of, and Cervantes knew that miracle there would not be:

I would wish that those ancient lines, famous in their day, which begin 'With foot already in the stirrup' were not quite so appropriate to this letter of mine, for with almost identical words I can begin them, saying,

> With foot already in the stirrup
> With the pangs of death upon me
> This letter, great lord, I write you.

Yesterday they gave me extreme unction and today I write this letter; time is short, the pain increases, hope wanes but my life is borne aloft by the desire I have to live and I would like to call a halt until I can kiss Your Excellency's feet; for the joy of seeing Your Excellency back in Spain and in good health might be enough to bring me back to life. But if it is written that I must lose it, may Heaven's will be done, and may Your Excellency at least know of my desire and that you had in me a servant so eager to serve you that he wished even to pass to the other side proclaiming this intention.

In *The Trials of Persiles and Sigismunda,* Cervantes had said of death that "in whatever guise it comes it is terrifying." This acknowledgment renders doubly impressive the dignity with which he met his own.

He died, almost certainly, three days later, on Friday, 22 April 1616, and not on 23 April as was traditionally thought on the basis of the burial certificate — thereby robbing history of what would have been one of its more satisfying coincidences, for on 23 April, in England, William Shakespeare too cast off his mortal coil. The day could never have been the same, for England still followed the Old Style Julian calendar, but coincidence of date was scarcely less pleasing and appropriate; now we have neither. On the following day, the 23rd, Cervantes's body, clothed in his Franciscan habit with face uncovered, was carried from his home in the Calle de León to the recently founded convent of the Discalced Trinitarians, the order that had redeemed him years ago from captivity, round the corner in the Calle de Cantarranas, where his remains and those of his wife, who joined him there ten years later, still lie.

The convent, much enlarged, is there today, a commemorative plaque on the wall outside, another inside the now richly ornate convent chapel, near the altar beneath which Cervantes is thought to be buried. Isabel too was at one time thought to be buried there, but now her name has been crudely erased from the plaque, the undisguised gap a mute testimony to her fall from her father's affections. The Calle de Cantarranas is now the Calle de Lope de Vega. The Calle de León still retains its original name, and it is the Calle de Francos, on the corner of which Cervantes had lived and died, which now goes as the Calle de Cervantes; halfway down it is the Lope de Vega museum that marks the spot where the great dramatist lived and died nineteen years later. And so Cervantes is buried in Lope de Vega and Lope died in Cervantes. Through a nineteenth-century municipal blunder, the onetime enemies in life have been inextricably intermingled in death. Cervantes at least would have appreciated the irony.

Five months after his death, Doña Catalina sold *The Trials of Persiles and Sigismunda* to Villarroel. The book appeared in early 1617, was reprinted five times within the year and was soon translated into French and English. No trace of any other manuscript has survived. Of Cervantes's will nothing is known except that he directed masses to be said for his soul. It matters little. Poor to the last, all he had to bequeath to his widow were the profits from *Persiles and Sigismunda,* and it looks as though the wily Villarroel might even have done her out of these. As for the riches Cervantes left to posterity, however, they placed him firmly where he had always wanted to belong — on the summit of Mount Parnassus. That too was an irony he would dearly have loved.

Works by Cervantes

❧

THE LIST BELOW gives Cervantes's major surviving works. The occasional poems and complimentary verse, which cover the period 1569 to 1616, are not listed. The two early plays apart, the dates given are dates of publication.

1585 *Primera parte de La Galatea* (Cervantes's pastoral romance *The Galatea*. No second part ever materialized.)

1580s *El cerco de Numancia (The Siege of Numancia)* ⎫
       El trato de Argel (The Traffic of Algiers) ⎬ Plays

1605 *El ingenioso hidalgo don Quijote de la Mancha*

1613 *Novelas ejemplares (Exemplary Tales):*
      La gitanilla (The Little Gypsy Girl)
      El amante liberal (The Generous Lover)
      Rinconete y Cortadillo (Rinconete and Cortadillo)
      La española inglesa (The English Spanishwoman)
      El licenciado Vidriera (The Licentiate of Glass)
      La fuerza de la sangre (The Force of Blood)
      El celoso extremeño (The Jealous Extremaduran)
      La ilustre fregona (The Illustrious Kitchen Maid)
      Las dos doncellas (The Two Damsels)
      La señora Cornelia (The Lady Cornelia)
      El casamiento engañoso (The Deceitful Marriage)
      El coloquio de los perros (The Dogs' Colloquy)

1614 *El viaje del Parnaso (Journey to Parnassus)*
      Adjunta al Parnaso (Postscript to Parnassus)

1615 *Ocho comedias y ocho entremeses (Eight Plays and Eight Interludes):*
      El gallardo español (The Gallant Spaniard)
      La casa de los celos y selvas de Ardenia (The House of Jealousy and Woods of Ardenia)
      Los baños de Argel (The Bagnios of Algiers)
      El rufián dichoso (The Fortunate Ruffian)
      La gran sultana (The Grand Sultana)

El laberinto de amor (The Labyrinth of Love)
La entretenida (The Comedy of Entertainment)
Pedro de Urdemalas (Pedro de Urdemalas)
El juez de los divorcios (The Divorce-Court Judge)
El rufián viudo (The Widowed Ruffian)
Elección de los alcaldes de Daganzo (The Election of the Sheriffs of Daganzo)
La guarda cuidadosa (The Anxious Guard)
El vizcaíno fingido (The Sham Biscayan)
El retablo de las maravillas (The Miracle Show)
La cueva de Salamanca (The Cave of Salamanca)
El viejo celoso (The Jealous Old Man)

1615 *Segunda parte del ingenioso caballero don Quijote de la Mancha*

1617 *Los trabajos de Persiles y Sigismunda (The Trials of Persiles and Sigismunda)*

Select Bibliography

❦

The BIBLIOGRAPHY for Cervantes's life is extensive, that for his works is vast. The quality of both varies widely and much of the latter is of interest primarily to specialists. What follows is a composite list of the principal works I have used and of suggestions for further reading. My greatest bibliographical debt, like that of any modern biographer of Cervantes, is to those Spanish scholars who have undertaken the main burden of archival investigation in tracking down and publishing the documents relating to Cervantes's life: Cristóbal Pérez Pastor, Francisco Rodríguez Marín, and Luis Astrana Marín. Their discoveries have proved invaluable additions to the first scholarly basic biography produced in 1819 by Martín Fernández de Navarrete. Astrana Marín merits a special mention, perhaps. Between 1948 and 1958 he produced a seven-volume work called *The Exemplary and Heroic Life of Miguel de Cervantes Saavedra*. It is an extraordinary achievement. Its title accurately reflects the work's undoubted bias in favor of its subject and its method is at times the very opposite of scholarly — hypothesis has an alarming tendency to become fact within the space of a few pages, and this while the author is himself denouncing the unscholarly procedures of others. Its defects, however, must not blind us to its strengths. Vast and rambling as it is, it contains not only the thousand hitherto unpublished documents — many of them significant ones — that Astrana Marín lays claim to, but an astonishing wealth of fascinating material relating to almost every conceivable aspect of Spanish life during Cervantes's time and to a host of individuals both famous and unknown. Every scrap of information Astrana Marín uncovered in the course of his often brilliant detective work is included, whether relevant to Cervantes or not, and it is little short of a calamity that the monumental work has — incredibly — no index. My use of Astrana's material has at times been quite extensive but it has always, I hope, been judicious, and the conclusions I have come to on the basis of it are often very different from his own. His "life" is not in any sense a readable biography and the only two twentieth-century biographies proper I would refer the reader to with any confidence are James Fitzmaurice-Kelly's memoir, which scrupulously records all the authenticated facts about Cervantes's life known in 1913, and, more recently, Richard Predmore's illustrated brief life, which is admirably well balanced.

For the sake of the reader without any Spanish, I have included in the bibliography a list of translations of Cervantes's works. The translations that appear in my text are, for good or ill, all my own.

Astrana Marín, Luis. *Vida ejemplar y heroica de Miguel de Cervantes Saavedra.* 7 Vols., Madrid, 1948–1958.

Alonso Cortés, Narciso. *Cervantes en Valladolid.* Valladolid, 1918.

Avalle-Arce, J. B., and Riley, E. C. (eds.). *Suma Cervantina.* London, 1973. Includes valuable biographical and bibliographical notes.

Braudel, Fernand. *The Mediterranean and the Mediterranean World in the Age of Philip II.* 2 Vols., London, 1972–1973.

Castro, Américo. *Cervantes y los casticismos españoles.* Madrid, 1966.

———. *Hacia Cervantes.* Second, rev. ed. Madrid, 1960.

———. *El pensamiento de Cervantes.* Enlarged ed. Barcelona, 1972.

Cervantes Saavedra, Miguel de. *Obras completas.* Ed. R. Schevill and A. Bonilla, 18 Vols., Madrid, 1914–1941.

———. *Obras completas.* Ed. A. Valbuena Prat, 2 Vols., Madrid, 1975.

———. *La Galatea.* Ed. J. B. Avalle-Arce, 2 Vols., Madrid, 1961.

———. *El ingenioso hidalgo don Quijote de la Mancha.* Ed. F. Rodríguez Marín, 8 Vols., 1922–1935.

———. *Novelas ejemplares.* Ed. R. Schevill and A. Bonilla, 3 Vols., Madrid, 1922–1925.

———. *Los trabajos de Persiles y Sigismunda.* Ed. J. B. Avalle-Arce, 2 Vols., Madrid, 1969.

———. *The Ingenious Gentleman Don Quixote de la Mancha.* Trans. Samuel Putnam, 2 Vols., New York, 1949.

———. *The Adventures of Don Quixote.* Trans. J. M. Cohen, Harmondsworth, 1950.

———. *Journey to Parnassus.* Trans. J. Y. Gibson, London, 1883.

———. *Three Exemplary Novels.* Trans. Samuel Putnam, New York, 1950.

———. *Exemplary Stories.* Trans. C. A. Jones, Harmondsworth, 1972.

———. *The Wanderings of Persiles and Sigismunda: a Northern Story.* Trans. Louisa Dorothea Stanley, London, 1854.

Chaytor, Henry J. *Dramatic Theory in Spain.* Cambridge, 1925.

Close, Anthony. *The Romantic Approach to Don Quixote.* Cambridge, 1978.

Domínguez Ortiz, Antonio. *La sociedad española en el siglo XVII.* Madrid, 1963.

Drake, Dana B. *Cervantes: A Critical Bibliography.* Vol. I, Blacksburg, 1968.

Elliott, John H. *Imperial Spain 1496–1716.* London, 1963.

Entwistle, William J. *Cervantes.* Oxford, 1940.

Fernández de Navarrete, M. *Vida de Miguel de Cervantes Saavedra.* Madrid, 1819.

Fernández y Fernández de Retana, P. Luis. *España en tiempo de Felipe II 1556–1598* (Vol. 19 of R. Menéndez Pidal's *Historia de España).* Madrid, 1958.

Fisher, Godfrey. *Barbary Legend. War, Trade and Piracy in North Africa, 1415–1830.* Oxford, 1957.

Fitzmaurice-Kelly, James. *Miguel de Cervantes Saavedra. A Memoir.* Oxford, 1913.

Forcione, Alban K. *Cervantes, Aristotle and the 'Persiles.'* Princeton, 1970.

González de Amezúa y Mayo, A. *Cervantes, creador de la novela corta española.* 2 Vols., Madrid, 1956–1968.

Guilmartin, J. F. *Gunpowder and Galleys: Changing Technology and Mediterranean Warfare at Sea in the Sixteenth Century.* Cambridge, 1974.

Haedo, P. Diego de. *Topographia e historia general de Argel.* Valladolid, 1612.

Hamilton, Earl J. *American Treasure and the Price Revolution in Spain 1501–1650.* Cambridge, Mass., 1934.

Lynch, John. *Spain under the Hapsburgs.* 2 Vols., Oxford, 1964–1969.

Madariaga, Salvador de. *Don Quixote: An Introductory Essay in Psychology.* Oxford, 1935.

Mattingly, Garrett. *The Defeat of the Spanish Armada.* London, 1959.

Nelson, Lowry (ed.). *Cervantes. A Collection of Critical Essays.* New Jersey, 1969.

Ortega y Gasset, José. *Meditaciones del Quijote.* 1914.

Parker, Geoffrey. *The Army of Flanders and the Spanish Road.* Cambridge, 1972.

Pérez Pastor, Cristóbal. *Documentos cervantinos.* 2 Vols., Madrid, 1897–1902.

Predmore, Richard L. *Cervantes.* London, 1973.

———. *The World of Don Quixote.* Cambridge, Mass., 1967.

Rennert, H. A. (with additions by Américo Castro and F. Carreter). *Vida de Lope Vega.* Salamanca, 1969.

Riley, E. C. *Cervantes's Theory of the Novel.* Oxford, 1962.

Rodríguez Marín, Francisco. *Estudios cervantinos.* Madrid, 1947.

———. *Nuevos documentos cervantinos.* Madrid, 1914.

Russell, Peter E. *"Don Quixote as a Funny Book," Modern Language Review,* LXIX (1969), pp. 312–326.

Index

Acquaviva, Cardinal, 53–56
Alarcón, Jerónima de, 139
Alba, Duke of, 44–45
Albert, Archduke of Austria, 191
Alcalá de Henares, 16–17
Alcega. *See* Perez de Alcega, Juan
Alemán, Mateo, 182, 189–190
Algiers, 62–63
Ali Pasha, 47
Ambrosio, Sante, 92
Anne of Austria, Infanta, 288
Arcadia (Sannazaro), 100, 103
Arcadia (Lope de Vega), 178, 196, 198, 199
Arganda, 13
Argensola. *See* Leonardo de Argensola, Lupercio
Avellaneda, *See* Fernández de Avellaneda, Alonso
Ayala, Isabel de, 236, 240, 241, 243

Bacon, Francis, 259
Beaumont, Francis, 271
Beauty of Angélica, The (Lope de Vega), 195–196
Becerro, Domingo, 82
Béjar, Duke of, 207
Bella, Antonio de la, 84, 85
Benávides, Diego de, 148
Benito, Nicolás, 150, 154, 177
Blanco de Paz, Juan, 82, 83, 86–87, 163–164

Boccaccio, 274
Byron, Lord, 211–212

Calderón de la Barca, Pedro, 38, 182, 257, 262
Carlos of Austria, Don (son of Philip II), 29–30
Castellano, Diego, 82, 83
Castro, Américo, 124–125
Castro y Bellvís, Guillén de, 267
Catherine, Duchess of Savoy, 179–180
Cayban (Florentine renegade), 82
Cecial, Tomé, 225
Celestina, The, 208
Cervantes, Catalina de (wife), 96–98, 110, 124, 132–133, 156, 168–169, 173, 186, 189, 191, 194, 235, 247, 249, 250, 251, 252, 260, 261, 263, 271, 291, 298
Cervantes, Juan de (grandfather), 13–15, 22
Cervantes, Juan de (cousin), 23, 26, 186
Cervantes, Leonor de (grandmother), 20, 22
Cervantes, Leonor de (mother), 16, 18–19, 27, 72–73, 79–80, 84, 94–95, 110, 158
Cervantes Saavedra, Andrea de (sister), 16, 21, 23, 26–27, 69, 70–71, 80, 92, 129, 165, 166, 187, 205,

Cervantes Saavedra, Andrea de
(*cont.*)
235, 239, 241, 245, 249, 250, 261,
262
Cervantes Saavedra, Andrés de
(uncle), 15, 19, 22, 23, 57, 159
Cervantes Saavedra, Andrés de
(brother), 16
Cervantes Saavedra, Isabel de
(daughter). See Saavedra, Isabel
de
Cervantes Saavedra, Luisa de (sister), 16, 26
Cervantes Saavedra, Magdalena de
(sister), 15, 20, 21, 26, 27, 69–71,
79, 92–93, 95, 158, 167, 173, 185,
186–187, 207, 235, 240–241, 245,
249, 250, 261, 263–264, 266
Cervantes Saavedra, María de
(aunt), 14–15, 18, 19–20
Cervantes Saavedra, Miguel de
LIFE, self-description, 277; ancestors, 13–16; birth (1547), 16,
17; childhood and education,
18–23, 28–29, 30–31; early career
as poet, 27–30; enlisted as soldier (1568?), 40–43; in Rome
(1569), 36, 38, 42; chamberlain to
Cardinal Acquaviva (1569?), 53–
56; ordered arrested for wounding a man in Madrid (?) (1569),
37–41; battle of Lepanto (1571),
43, 46–49; in Naples (1572–75),
50, 51–53, 56–59; sired an illegitimate son (1574), 52; captivity
in Algiers (1575–80), 60–89; in
Lisbon (1581), 94; affair with
Ana de Villafranca, birth of Isabel de Saavedra (1584?), 95–96;
marriage to Catalina de Salazar
y Palacios (1584), 96–98; *The
Galatea* published (1585), 98–
103; early plays and poems (c.
1585), 103–112; commissary to
the Armada (1587–94), 115–159;
collector of taxes (1594–95), 161–
168; writing and imprisonment
in Seville (1596–1602), 169–194;
in Esquivias and Madrid, writing short stories (1602–03), 195–
205; relationship with Lope de
Vega, 195–201, 246–247, 251; in
Valladolid (1604–05), *Don Quixote, Part I*, published, 207–209;
Ezpeleta affair (1605), 236–243;
writing plays and short stories in
Madrid (1606–12), 249–259; joins
religious brotherhood (1609),
261–262; publishes *Exemplary
Tales* (1613), 271, 272–276; writes
Journey to Parnassus (1614),
279–281; finds a patron, joins
Franciscan Tertiaries (1613),
281–282, 295; writes *Postscript
to Parnassus* (1614), 283–284;
completes *Don Quixote, Part II*
(1614–15), 285–289; publishes
Eight Plays and Eight Interludes
(1615), 289–291; completes *Trials
of Persiles and Sigismunda*
(published 1617), 292–297; death
(1616), 297
WORKS, sonnet to Elizabeth of
Valois (mid-1560s), 28; *The
Feigned Aunt* (attributed), 28,
272, 275; four poems in López de
Hoyos' *History of Elizabeth of
Valois* (1569), 30; *The Naval
Battle* (lost), 49; verse epistle to
Mateo Vázquez (c. 1579), 62, 74;
The Siege of Numancia (1580s),
105, 108, 110; *The Traffic of Algiers* (1580s), 80, 105, 109–110;
"Jealousy" (c. 1585), 52, 112, 147;
"Disdain" (c. 1585), 112, 152;
The Comedy of Confusion (lost),
104, 105, 290; *The Treaty of
Constantinople and Death of
Selim* (lost), 104; "Elicio" (c.
1585), 112; *The Galatea* (1585),
4, 52, 53, 56, 60–61, 94, 98–103,
112, 121, 172, 196, 271, 291, 296;
two patriotic odes (1588), 116,
135–136; poem to St. Hyacinth
(1595), 166; sonnet on the Marquis of Santa Cruz (1596), 169;
sonnet on the Duke of Medina
Sidonia (1596), 169–170; *On
Philip II's Catafalque in Seville*
(1598), 185; sonnet for Lope de

Vega's *Beauty of Angélica* (1602), 196; three satirical sonnets against Lope de Vega (attributed), 197–198; *Don Quixote*, 3–7, 57–58, 89, 123, 131, 140, 142–143, 168, 171, 175, 204, 210–230, 233–234, 263; *Part I* (1605), 47–48, 50–51, 106–107, 192–194, 198–199, 206, 207–209, 214, 217, 221–222, 229, 231, 244, 276, 282; *Exemplary Tales* (1613), 201–205, 230, 245, 251–252, 271, 272–276; prologue, 48–49, 277–278, 281; *The Little Gypsy Girl*, 38, 41, 202, 234, 243, 250, 282; *The Generous Lover*, 43, 89, 171; *Rinconete and Cortadillo*, 175, 179, 190, 201, 232, 257, 272–273, 290; *The English Spanishwoman*, 61, 116, 275; *The Licentiate of Glass*, 28, 41–42, 43, 53, 202, 204, 205, 252, 257; *The Force of Blood*, 158, 245, 282; *The Jealous Extremuduran*, 201, 202–203, 232, 243, 245, 257, 272, 273; *The Illustrious Kitchen Maid*, 202, 242, 243, 250; *The Two Damsels*, 275; *The Lady Cornelia*, 275; *The Deceitful Marriage*, 202, 203–205; *The Dogs' Colloquy*, 19, 21–22, 100, 123, 148, 172, 178, 202, 203–205, 257, 263; poem to Teresa of Ávila (1614), 284–285; *Journey to Parnassus* (1614), 40, 111, 185, 200, 217, 266–267, 277, 279–281, 283, 284; *Postscript to Parnassus* (1614), 247, 251, 283–284, 285, 289; *Eight Plays and Eight Interludes* (1615), 250–251, 268–269, 289–291; prologue, 24–25, 112, 200, 290–291; *The Gallant Spaniard*, 38, 243–244; *The House of Jealousy and Woods of Ardenia*, 289; *The Bagnios of Algiers*, 140; *The Fortunate Ruffian*, 268–269; *The Grand Sultana*, 250; *The Labyrinth of Love*, 243–244, 290; *The Comedy of Entertainment*, 246, 258–259;

Pedro de Urdemalas, 255–256; 257, 258, 269; *The Divorce-Court Judge*, 160; *The Widowed Ruffian*, 290; *The Anxious Guard*, 199, 269; *The Sham Biscayan*, 268; *The Cave of Salamanca*, 290; *The Jealous Old Man*, 257–258, 274; *Don Quixote, Part II* (1615), 200, 214–215, 219, 220, 224–225, 227, 229, 232, 252–253, 263, 267, 275, 276–277, 281, 284, 285, 287–289, 292; *The Trials of Persiles and Sigismunda* (1617), 4–5, 42, 94, 172, 174, 227–228, 263, 275, 277, 284, 289, 291, 292–297, 298; *Weeks in a Garden* (not written?), 277, 291, 296; *The Famous Bernardo* (not written?), 296

Cervantes Saavedra, Rodrigo de (father), 14, 15–16, 18, 19–21, 22–23, 25, 26, 27, 72, 90, 110

Cervantes Saavedra, Rodrigo de (brother), 16, 19, 26, 50, 53, 59, 60, 73, 74–75, 92, 93, 95, 122, 191–192, 264

Cervantes Saavedra, Rodrigo de (cousin), 127, 132

Cetina, Agustín de, 161, 189

Cisneros, Francisco Jiménez de (Cardinal), 16

Colonna, Ascanio (Cardinal), 56, 99

Concentaina, Count of, 239

Córdoba, Martín de, 78

Cortinas, Leonor de. *See* Cervantes, Leonor de (mother)

Cuesta, Juan de la, 207, 276

Cyprus, 43, 44

Diana, The (Montemayer), 101, 208

Diana in Love (Polo), 101

Don Juan (Byron), 211–212

Don Policisne de Boecia (Silva y Toledo), 206

Don Quixote (Avellaneda), 199, 200, 219, 220, 229, 232, 247, 253, 285–288

Don Quixote, The Knight of the Burning Pestle (Beaumont), 271

"Dorador, El," 75, 76
Drake, Francis, 116

Elizabeth I of England, 33, 116
Elizabeth (Isabel) of Valois, 28, 29
Elizabeth Stuart, 282
England, 33, 35
Espinosa, Cardinal (Inquisitor General), 30
Ethiopian History of the Loves of Teagenes and Cariclea (Heliodorus), 294–295
Eujd Ali, 63
Exarque, Onofré, 81, 82, 83
Ezpeleta, Gaspar de, 236–241, 243

Falces, Marquis of, 236
Fernández de Avellaneda, Alonso, 199, 200, 219, 220, 229, 232, 247, 253, 285–288
Figueroa, Costanza de (Cervantes's niece), 26, 165–166, 235, 241, 250, 260, 263, 264
Figueroa. *See* Mosquera de Figueroa, Cristóbal
Figueroa, Francisco de, 95
Figueroa, Lope de, 50, 52, 53
Fletcher, John, 282
Fortuny, Juan de, 95, 150–151
France, 35
Freire de Lima, Simón, 165, 166–167, 173
Fuentes, Alonso de, 176

Gaitán, Juana (wife of poet Pedro Laínez), 98, 235, 239, 240, 241, 242, 247
Gálvez de Montalvo, Luis, 99
Garcilaso de la Vega, 41
Gaván, Melchor, 237, 238
Gil, Juan, 84, 85, 86, 87
Girón, The Licentiate, 81, 83
Gómez de Quevedo y Villegas, Francisco, 182, 261, 284
Góngora y Argote, Luis de, 198, 236, 262, 265
Gracián, Baltasar, 262

Granero, Sebastián, 253
Guevara, Antonio de, 115, 122, 129, 134, 135, 136–137, 144, 153
Gutiérrez, Tomás, 118, 121, 129, 139, 147, 151, 156–157, 176
Guzmán de Alfarache (Alemán), 189–190, 208

Haëdo, Diego de, 87–88, 279
Hamete (Mahamet Bey), 50
Hassan Pasha, 76–79, 82, 83, 84, 85, 86
Heliodorus, 294–295
Hernández, Inés, 237
Higares, Count of, 239
History of Cardenio, The (Shakespeare and Fletcher), 282
Howard, Charles, Earl of Nottingham, 234, 235
Hurtado de Mendoza, Diego, 103

Infantado, Duke of, 14
Isabella of Bourbon, 288
Isunza, Pedro de, 149, 150, 153, 154, 155, 156, 157, 177
Italy, 33, 35–36

Jáurequi, Juan de, 277–278
John of Austria, Don, natural son of Charles V, 45–46, 47, 50, 51, 53, 57, 80
Journey to Parnassus (Perusino), 280
Juan (a gardener), 75, 77

Laínez, Pedro, 95, 98, 235
Lanuza y de Perellós, Pedro de, 165–166
Laurel of Apollo (Lope de Vega), 201
Lemos, Count of, 265, 281, 284, 288, 289, 292, 296
Leonardo de Argensola, Lupercio, 265
Lepanto, battle of (1571), 43, 45–49
Lerma, Duke of, 191, 248, 261, 265
Life of a Rogue, The (Quevedo), 284
Locadelo, Giovanni Francesco, 27

López de Hoyos, Juan, 30–31
Louis XIII of France, 288
Luján, Micaela de, 191, 235

Maltrapillo (a renegade captain), 83
Mami, Arnaute, 60, 61
Mami, Dali, 60, 62, 75, 77
Margaret of Austria, Archduchess, 181, 187, 248
María of Austria, Empress, 191, 248
Marquesa (ship), 46–48
Márquez Torres, Licentiate, 288, 298
Mary Tudor, Queen of Scots, 33, 113
Maurice of Nassau, 191
Maximilian II of Austria, Emperor, 44, 191
Medina Sidonia, Duke of, 113, 130–131, 169–170
Méndez, Simón, 234, 239, 241, 242, 243
Mendoza, Martín de, 14–15
Middleton, Thomas, 282
Miranda, Diego de, 236, 239, 241, 242
Molina, Isabel de. See Saavedra, Isabel de
Molina, Luis de, 254, 260, 264, 269–270
Montalvo. See Gálvez de Montalvo, Luis
Montemayor, Jorge de, 101
Montoya, Luisa de, 235, 236, 237, 240, 247
Moriscos, 34, 44, 262–263
Moscoso, Francisco, 152–153, 154–155
Mosquera de Figueroa, Cristóbal, 121–122, 169
Muley, Xeque, Prince, 140

Netherlands, 33–34, 44–45

Olivar, Jorge del, 77–78
Olmedilla, Bernardo de, 167
Orlando Furioso (Ariosto), 231
Osorio, Rodrigo, 152
Ottoman Empire, 34, 44, 51

Oudin, César, 276
Ovando, Nicolás de, 26–27
Oviedo, Miguel de, 157, 159

Pacheco Portocarrero, Alonso, 69–71, 79, 80
Pacheco Portocarrero, Pedro (father), 69
Pacheco Portocarrero, Pedro (son), 70
Padilla, Pedro de, 103
Palacios, Catalina de, 110, 132–133
Palacios, Fernando de, 169, 191
Palacios, Francisco de, 124, 166, 168–169, 194–195, 260–261, 271
Palacios, Juan de, 97, 168, 194
Palafox, Enrique de, 264
Palatine, Elector of, 282
Papacy, 35
Pastrana, Duke of, 239
Pérez de Alcega, Juan, 92–93
Perusino, César Caporal, 280
Philip II, 28, 29–30, 33–34, 44, 51, 94, 116, 181, 184
Philip III, 181–182, 191, 234, 248, 261
Philip IV, 182, 234, 288
Poetics (Aristotle), 5
Polo, Gil, 101
Ponce de León, Manuel, 50
Porras, Gaspar de, 104, 105, 110
Porras de la Cámara, Francisco de, 232, 272
Portocarrero, Alonso. See Pacheco Portocarrero, Alonso
Portocarrero, Pedro (father). See Pacheco Portocarrero, Pedro (father)
Portocarrero, Pedro (son). See Pacheco Portocarrero, Pedro (son)

Quevedo. See Gómez de Quevedo y Villegas, Francisco

Ramírez, Mariana, 235–236, 239, 240, 241, 242, 247
Rey de Artieda, Andrés, 57
Ribadeneyra, Pedro de, 135
Ríos, Nicolás de los, 257

Rivera, Pedro de, 87
Robles, Blas, 99
Robles, Francisco de, 206, 208, 250, 251, 252, 275, 289, 291
Rodríguez, Alonso, 95
Rodríguez, Ana, 186
Rodríguez, Gabriel, 166
Rojas, Luisa de, 186
Rowley, William, 282
Rueda, Lope de, 23–25
Ruffino, Bartolomeo, 68
Rufo, Juan, 95
Ruskin, John, 212
Ruy Saenz, Diego de, 149

Saavedra, Isabel de, 95–96, 185–186, 187, 235, 240, 241, 242–243, 246, 247, 249, 253–255, 260, 261, 263, 264–265, 269–270
Salazar y Palacios, Catalina de. *See* Cervantes, Catalina de
Salazar y Palacios, María de, 169
Sandoval y Rojas, Bernardo de, Archbishop of Toledo, 288–289, 292, 295
Santa Cruz, Marquis de, 50, 113, 130
Santisteban, Mateo de, 42–43
Sanz, Isabel, 253, 254, 264
Sanz del Águila, Diego, 249
Selim II, 44
Sessa, Duke of, 57, 80, 200
Sevilla, Fernando de, 131
Shakespeare, William, 282, 297
Shelton, Thomas, 276, 282
Sigura, Antonio de, 37, 41
Silva y Toledo, Juan de, 206
Slaves of Algiers, The (Lope de Vega), 109
Spanish Armada (1588), 112–117, 135–136
Spanish Gypsy, The (Middleton and Rowley), 282
Spiritual Garden (Padilla), 103
Suárez de Figueroa, Cristóbal, 279

Suárez Gasco, Francisco, 162, 173, 174, 255
Sun (ship), 59, 60

Tamayo, Juan de, 147
Tapia, Rodrigo de, 284
Téllez, Fray Gabriel (Tirso de Molina), 182, 257, 262
Tirso de Molina. *See* Téllez, Fray Gabriel
To Love Without Knowing Whom (Lope de Vega), 201
Toledo, Antonio de, 74
Toledo, Archbishop of. *See* Sandoval y Rojas, Bernardo de
Topography and General History of Algiers (Haëdo), 87, 279
Toro, Salvador de, 150, 154
Torres, Hernando de, 80
Traveller, The (Suárez de Figueroa), 279

Urbina, Diego de, 43, 49
Urbina, Juan de, 249, 253–254, 264–265, 269–270

Valdivia, Diego de, 115, 122, 125, 126
Valdivielso, José de, 283
Valencia, Francisco de, 74
Vázquez, Mateo, 62, 74, 277
Vega Carpio, Lope Félix de, 106, 107, 108, 109, 117, 178, 182, 191, 195–201, 235, 246–247, 250, 251, 257, 261, 262, 265, 272, 279, 285, 286–287, 291, 298
Velázquez, Diego, 182
Velázquez, Jerónimo, 105
Veneziani, Antonio, 84
Venice, 45, 51
Vigny, Alfred de, 219–220
Villafranca, Ana de (Ana Franca de Rojas), 95–96, 185
Villarroel, Cristóbal, 236, 237–239, 240–241
Villarroel, Juan de, 290, 291, 298